Application of Artificial Intelligence in Early Detection of Lung Cancer

Application of Artificial Intelligence in Early Detection of Lung Cancer

Jhilam Mukherjee

Department of CSE, Adamas University, West Bengal, India

Madhuchanda Kar

Department of Oncology, Peerless Hospital,
Kolkata, West Bengal, India

Amlan Chakrabarti

A.K. Choudhury School of Information Technology,
University of Calcutta, Kolkata, West Bengal, India

Sayan Das

Department of Interventional Radiology and Imaging,
Peerless Hospital, Kolkata, West Bengal, India

ELSEVIER

ACADEMIC PRESS
An imprint of Elsevier

Academic Press is an imprint of Elsevier
125 London Wall, London EC2Y 5AS, United Kingdom
525 B Street, Suite 1650, San Diego, CA 92101, United States
50 Hampshire Street, 5th Floor, Cambridge, MA 02139, United States

Notices

Knowledge and best practice in this field are constantly changing. As new research and experience broaden our understanding, changes in research methods, professional practices, or medical treatment may become necessary.

Practitioners and researchers must always rely on their own experience and knowledge in evaluating and using any information, methods, compounds, or experiments described herein. In using such information or methods they should be mindful of their own safety and the safety of others, including parties for whom they have a professional responsibility.

To the fullest extent of the law, neither the Publisher nor the authors, contributors, or editors, assume any liability for any injury and/or damage to persons or property as a matter of products liability, negligence or otherwise, or from any use or operation of any methods, products, instructions, or ideas contained in the material herein.

ISBN: 978-0-323-95245-3

For information on all Academic Press publications visit our website at
https://www.elsevier.com/books-and-journals

Publisher: Stacy Masucci
Acquisitions Editor: Linda Buschman
Editorial Project Manager: Samantha Allard
Production Project Manager: Selvaraj Raviraj
Cover Designer: Christian Bilbow

Typeset by TNQ Technologies

Working together
to grow libraries in
developing countries

www.elsevier.com • www.bookaid.org

Contents

Overview of computer-aided detection model

Artificial intelligence (AI)-based models play a critical role in the early detection of lung cancer. Their ability to achieve high accuracy and sensitivity in analyzing medical imaging data, such as computed tomography (CT) scans, surpasses human capabilities. By identifying subtle patterns and abnormalities, these models can detect lung cancer at its early stages when it is most treatable. Early detection enables timely intervention and treatment, leading to improved patient outcomes and survival rates. Moreover, AI models can efficiently handle the complexity of large and complex datasets, extracting relevant features and patterns that may be missed by human observers. This reduces the potential for human error and variability, ensuring consistent and objective assessments. By streamlining the detection process, AI models enhance the efficiency and workflow of healthcare providers, enabling faster diagnosis and reducing waiting times for patients. Additionally, AI models can assist in risk stratification, predicting the likelihood of malignancy or disease progression based on imaging data and clinical parameters. This personalized approach enables healthcare providers to tailor treatment plans and surveillance strategies to individual patients. Furthermore, AI contributes to knowledge discovery and research in lung cancer by analyzing large datasets and identifying new insights and correlations. Overall, AI-based models are indispensable in the early detection of lung cancer, offering improved accuracy, personalized care and advancements in research and understanding of the disease.

1.1 Computer-aided detection and diagnosis

In the present era, medical images play an important role in the diagnosis of the disease. However, due to the presence of an extensive workload, the manual visualization of the signs of the disease may be prone to error. In this regard, various computer algorithms can be applied to these medical images to assist doctors in deciding the appropriate diagnostics protocol for the patient. These methodologies are termed computer-aided detection (CADx) and computer-aided diagnosis (CADe) or in short CAD. The primary objective of the CADx methodologies is to confirm the presence of abnormalities in medical images. On the other hand, a CADe method either explores the disease's characteristics or provides useful information that can assist doctors in the diagnosis of the disease. In reference, we know that CT scan images are widely used in the diagnosis of lung cancer. Detection of the abnormalities on CT images is considered CADx and quantification of the probability of malignancy of the abnormalities is known as CADe.

Application of Artificial Intelligence in Early Detection of Lung Cancer. https://doi.org/10.1016/B978-0-323-95245-3.00001-9

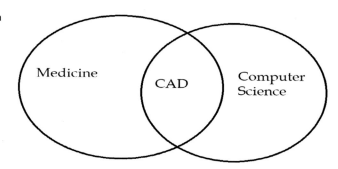

Fig. 1.1 represents the CAD interface. According to the published literature, there exist four types of CAD systems, that is, Type I, Type II, Type III and Type IV. The Type I CAD systems aim to improve the visual verification of the lesions, whereas the Type II CAD systems extract different valuable pieces of information from the lesions which will help to decide the actual status of the disease. Type III CAD systems interpret the disease conditions. Type IV reveals the anatomical and functional tissue characteristics of the disease. However, Type IV CAD systems can't be implemented through medical images. Table 1.1 exhibits the challenges of CAD system that the researchers of both domain faces.

Discussion of Type IV CAD systems is out of the scope of this book. This book will discuss Type I, II, and III CAD systems. For example, the CAD system for lung cancer detection can be represented as a combination of these three types of CAD. The pulmonary nodule detection methodology is considered the Type I CAD model, analysis of morphological features is the representation of the Type II model, and risk prediction is the Type III model.

Table 1.1   Grouping the seven challenges in terms of the two constituent fields.

Challenges	CAD constituent field	
	Medicine	Computer science
Data collection and quality assessment	Yes	No
Developing advanced segmentation approaches for medical imaging	No	Yes
Developing advanced feature extraction/selection approaches	No	Yes
Developing better classification and other data mining approaches	No	Yes
Dealing with bigdata	No	Yes
Developing standard performance assessment approaches for CAD systems	No	Yes
Adopting CAD systems for clinical practice	Yes	No

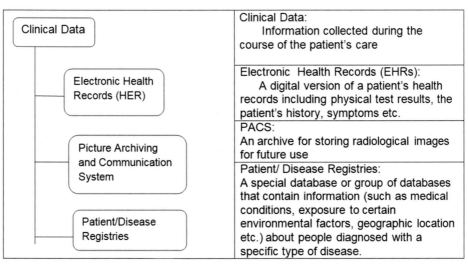

FIGURE 1.2 Data description for CAD implementation.

1.1.1   Objectives of the CAD system

1. **Managing large volumes of clinical data:** In order to establish CAD methodologies for clinical use, researchers require a variety of clinical data like laboratory test results, medication doses, disease symptoms, family history of the disease, genetic aspects, etc. In the present clinical context, most hospitals and clinics keep these data in a digital format using an electronic health record (EHR) format. On the other hand, the radiology information system keeps follow-up scans of a particular patient. This generates an extensive and complicated volume of clinical data for designing a CAD model.

   In this present big data era, CAD models can access and analyze this huge data to implement the model. Fig. 1.2 depicts the clinical data.

2. **Objective and quantitative judgements:** The traditional diagnostics system solely depends on the opinion of the clinicians, that is, the diagnosis procedures vary depending upon their experiences. As a consequence, there exists inter-observer variability in manual interpretation. Moreover, in the present clinical context, the volumetric scan of an individual patient poses an extensive workload to clinicians. Furthermore, due to extensive fatigue, depression and stress, clinicians may overlook the early signs of the disease. In response to this context, a CAD methodology can assist doctors by identifying the early signs of the disease.

3. **Effectiveness and efficacy:** In daily clinical practice, it has been observed that there exist a couple of diseases that can't exhibit early symptoms of the disease. However,

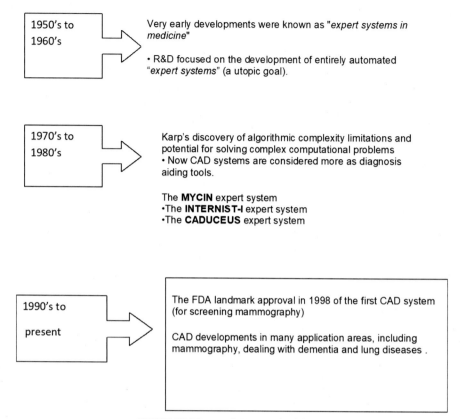

FIGURE 1.3 History of CAD methodology.

these signs are often visualized through some radiological images. If these diseases are overlooked in the early stages, they can pose different invasive procedures like surgery, biopsy, etc., as well as a financial burden to the patients. In this context, a CAD tool can analyze these routine imaging tests and confirm the status of the disease. As a consequence, the diagnostics overflow of the disease can improve which directly influences the efficacy and efficiency of the diagnostics procedures.

1.1.2   History of CAD methodology

In late 1950, researchers started integrating computer algorithms with medicine. These systems were termed expert systems in medicine. These methodologies interpret results based on symptoms of the disease along with test results. Fig. 1.3 depicts different expert systems in medicine.

In 1975, the MYCIN expert system was developed. In the early 1980s, INTERNIST-1 expert system was developed. In 1984, CADUCEUS expert system was implemented. The limitations of these systems are that these models have been considering flowcharts, statistical pattern matching or probability theories. Realizing these limitations, in the 1990s, researchers began to implement automated CADe tools by incorporating AI in health care. Fig. 1.2 represents the history of CAD implementation and Fig. 1.3 represents different AI-based CAD methodologies.

1.1.3   How does AI influence the CAD?

Machine learning, as a subset of AI, also called traditional AI, was applied to diagnostic imaging in started 1980s. Users first predefine explicit parameters and features of the imaging based on expert knowledge. For instance, the shapes, areas and histograms of image pixels of the regions of interest (i.e. tumour regions) can be extracted. Usually, for a given number of available data entries, part of them is used as training and the rest is for testing. Certain machine learning algorithm is selected for the training to understand the features. Some examples of the algorithms are principal component analysis (PCA), support vector machines (SVMs), convolutional neural networks (CNNs), etc. Then, for a given testing image, the trained algorithm is supposed to recognize the features and classify the image.

One of the problems of machine learning is that users need to select the features that define the class of the image it belongs to. However, this might miss some contributing factors. For instance, lung tumour diagnosis requires the user to segment the tumour region as structure features. Due to the patient and user variation, the consistency of the manual feature selection has always been a challenge. Deep learning, however, does not require explicit user input of the features. As its name suggests, deep learning learns from significantly more amount of data. It uses models of deep artificial neural networks. Deep learning uses multiple layers to progressively extract higher-level features from raw image input. It helps to disentangle the abstractions and picks out the features that can improve performance. The concept of deep learning was proposed decades ago. Only in recent decades, has the application of deep learning become feasible due to an enormous number of medical images being produced and advancements in the development of hardware, like graphics processing units (GPUs). However, with machine learning gaining its relevance and importance every day, even GPU became somewhat lacking. To combat this situation, Google developed an AI accelerator integrated circuit which would be used by its TensorFlow AI framework − tensor processing unit (TPU). TPU is designed specifically for neural network machine learning and would have the potential to be applied to medical imaging research as well.

The main research area in diagnostic imaging is detection. Researchers started developing computer-aided detection (CAD) systems in the 1980s. Traditional machine learning algorithms were applied to image modalities like CT, MRI, and mammography. Despite a lot of effort made in the research area, the real clinical applications were not promising. Several large trials came to the conclusion that CAD has at best delivered no benefit and at worst has reduced radiology accuracy, resulting in higher recall and biopsy rates.

The new era of AI — deep learning has so far demonstrated promising improvements in the research area over traditional machine learning. As an example, Ardila et al. proposed a deep learning algorithm that uses a patient's current and prior CT volumes to predict the risk of lung cancer. The model achieved a state-of-the-art performance (94.4% area under the curve (AUC)) on 6716 national lung cancer screening trial cases and performed similarly on an independent clinical validation set of 1139 cases. As a comparison of conventional screening by low-dose CT, per cancer.gov, there are several associated harms: false-positive exams, overdiagnosis, complications of diagnostic evaluation, increase in lung cancer mortality and radiation exposure. One false-positive exam example provided on the website was 60%. Overdiagnosis was estimated at 67%. There is also the radiation-induced risk of developing lung cancer or other types of cancer later in life. AI-based diagnosis reduced these risks.

Deep learning algorithms have become a methodology of choice for radiology imaging analysis. This includes different image modalities like CT, MRI, PET, ultrasonography, etc., and different tasks like tumour detection, segmentation, disease prediction, etc. Research has shown that AI/deep learning-based methods have substantial performance improvements over conventional machine learning algorithms. Similar to human learning, deep learning learns from the enormous amount of image examples. However, it might take much less time, as it solely depends on curated data and the corresponding metadata rather than domain expertise, which usually takes years to develop. As traditional AI requires predefined features and has shown plateauing performance over recent years, and with the current success of AI/deep learning in image research, it is expected that AI will further dominate image research in radiology.

1.1.4   Stages involved in CAD methodologies

Each of the CAD methodologies consists of four stages namely pre-processing, image segmentation, CADx and CADe. Fig. 1.4 provides the outlines of the different stages of CAD methodology. Later this section elaborately describes these aforementioned stages.

1.1.4.1   Preparation of test data sets

The basic requirements in implementing the CAD methodologies are the digital image data and supporting pathological information. This image data can be obtained either by

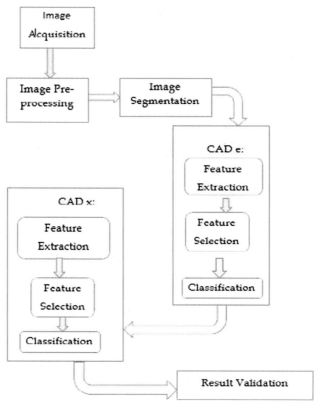

FIGURE 1.4 Stages of CAD methodology.

converting the image films or by collecting them from the scanner machines of different hospitals. When these digital image data have been collected from the hospitals, we have to abide by Helsinki guidelines for human research. The collection procedure of these data is known as the study design. A good study design will help us to implement an efficient CAD model. In the study design, we have to consider the following aspects:

1. Sample size of the CAD model
2. Ethical considerations
3. What activities will be performed and with what frequency and intensity?

1.1.5   Sample size of the CAD model

About modern statistics, it has been observed that an accurate sample size of a study can help the prediction model to provide useful information about the study. A study with too small a sample may produce an inconclusive result. On the other hand, a study with a larger sample may be considered a waste of resources. Moreover, it could be considered as unethical as a needless risk has been exposed to human subjects or lab animals. In response to this context, most of the researchers have considered the precision-based sample size technique as it provides more information than other sample size calculation algorithms.

Sample size can be calculated as:

$$N = \frac{z^2 p(1-p)}{d^2}$$

where N = number of samples

z = confidence level
p = prevalence of the disease
d = marginal error

1.1.6   Ethical consideration

In order to use Computer-Aided Diagnosis (CAD), a radiological imaging collection must be carefully prepared while adhering to strict ethical guidelines. Ensuring patient privacy and confidentiality involves adhering to privacy standards such as HIPAA and anonymizing identifying information. It is essential to have patients' informed consent before using their datasets. To prevent unwanted access, strong data security procedures must be put in place. In order to guarantee justice and representativeness, biases in dataset curation must be addressed. It is crucial to maintain ownership, share, and transparency about the features and constraints. Prioritising patient welfare in the development and implementation of CAD systems can help to maximise benefit while maximising diagnostic accuracy. Research involving human subjects must adhere to legal restrictions and obtain clearance from ethical committees or IRBs. Together, these factors encourage the ethical and appropriate use of radiological datasets for CAD development, building healthcare-related confidence in AI applications. of the dataset.

1.1.7   Image pre-processing

Image pre-processing is a step of computer vision whose aim is to reduce unwanted distortions from the images and enhance some features of the digital images that could take important roles in the implementation of CAD methodologies.

In medical image analysis, these pre-processing steps are applied to the following fields.

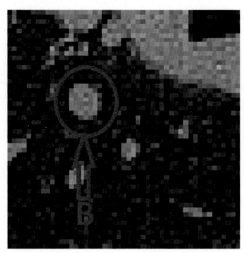

FIGURE 1.5 Region of interest or volume of interest.

1. Volume of interest: Here, the pre-processing steps reduce the redundant data to increase the execution times of the CAD steps.
2. Region of interest: Here, the pre-processing steps help retain the targeted objects' different properties.
3. Intensity of interest: Here, the pre-processing steps improve the intensity characteristics of the lesions.

In CAD methodologies, the prime objective of the pre-processing step is to enhance some features of the digital image. The medical images can be distorted due to the presence of noise incorporated at the time of image acquisition. It often doesn't provide the actual soft tissue values of the organs. Inappropriate selection of pre-processing steps may reduce the minute details of the abnormalities and can produce different image artefacts.

1.1.8 Image segmentation

Image segmentation is a classification process where different types of objects are subdivided by considering similar intensity and region properties. Fig. 1.5 overviews the region of interest or volume of interest. In lung nodule CAD methodology, all the abnormalities present in lung parenchyma are separated from the background. In Chapter 4, we discussed the working principles of different segmentation methodologies (Fig. 1.6).

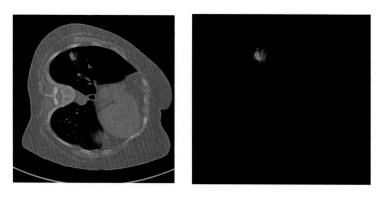

Input Image   Segmented Image

FIGURE 1.6 Image segmentation.

1.1.9   ROI selection/detection

This stage aims to confirm the presence of abnormalities in the images. According to computer science, several supervised learning methodologies are implemented to verify the presence of abnormalities in this stage. This stage consists of three sub-stages, namely feature extraction, feature selection and classification. The feature extraction step has been extracted, and the requisite amount of features has been extracted from the segmented objects. It has been observed that all the extracted features do not have equal contributions in classification. The feature selection methodologies select the most important features from the extracted features. In the final stage, different supervised learning methodologies confirm the presence of abnormalities in the images.

1.1.9.1   CADx

The CADe step confirms the presence of pulmonary nodules. As per the statistics of the American Cancer Society, 60% of these pulmonary nodules are benign, that is, it has no probability of becoming cancerous in the near future. In the CADx step, researchers have confirmed the conditions of the disease, that is, the pulmonary nodules are benign or malignant. Like CADe, this stage also consisted of the same three stages. The only difference is that here the class labels are different in each of the cases.

Selection of appropriate criteria for determining the ground truth or reference standard data for designing the model:

The CAD problem is either a binary class problem or a multi-class problem. Depending upon the problem definition, researchers have to annotate the entire data for model implementation.

A ground-truth dataset is **a regular dataset but with annotations added to it**. Annotations can be boxes drawn over images, written text indicating samples, a new column of a spreadsheet or anything else the machine learning algorithm should learn to output. The ground truth data have been prepared in two ways.

1. The pathological test reports will label the data.
2. A group of observers marked the lesions and based on the majority voting, the dataset was labelled.

When the researchers want to implement the cancer CAD like lung nodule risk prediction model, the state of malignancy is obtained from the histopathology of fine needle aspiration cytology (FNAC) report. However, there exist some diseases like pulmonary emphysema whose confirmation is not performed by any pathological tests, then a group of radiologists have annotated the emphysema in a blind and unblind manner. In a blind read phase, a set of radiologists separately annotated different types of abnormalities of a particular organ. On the other hand in an unblind read phase, they annotated the abnormalities by a joint discussion. Fig. 1.7 depicts some annotated data.

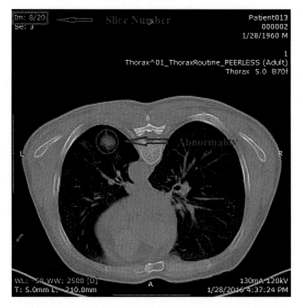

FIGURE 1.7 Ground truth data visible on CT image slice.

```xml
<?xml version="1.0" encoding="UTF-8"?>
- <Patient263>
  - <Characteristics>
      <PatientID/>
      <Age>55</Age>
      <Gender> Male</Gender>
      <PreviousHistory> No</PreviousHistory>
      <Size>16.500000</Size>
      <Shape> Oval</Shape>
      <Margin> Lobulation</Margin>
      <Enhance> Homogeneous</Enhance>
      <CALCIFICATION> No</CALCIFICATION>
      <TypeOfNodule> solid</TypeOfNodule>
      <Position> Right Upper</Position>
      <Necrosis> no</Necrosis>
      <State> Malignant</State>
    - <ROI>
      - <UnblindReview>
        - <Reviewer1>
          - <SliceNumber>
              62
              <object>Nodule</object>
              <Xcoordinate>124.000000</Xcoordinate>
              <Ycoordinate>209.000000</Ycoordinate>
              <Xcoordinate>125.000000</Xcoordinate>
              <Ycoordinate>217.000000</Ycoordinate>
              <Xcoordinate>129.000000</Xcoordinate>
              <Ycoordinate>225.000000</Ycoordinate>
              <Xcoordinate>127.000000</Xcoordinate>
              <Ycoordinate>238.000000</Ycoordinate>
              <Xcoordinate>116.000000</Xcoordinate>
              <Ycoordinate>251.000000</Ycoordinate>
              <Xcoordinate>116.000000</Xcoordinate>
              <Ycoordinate>251.000000</Ycoordinate>
            </SliceNumber>
          - <SliceNumber>
              63
              <object>Nodule</object>
              <Xcoordinate>120.000000</Xcoordinate>
              <Ycoordinate>206.000000</Ycoordinate>
              <Xcoordinate>123.000000</Xcoordinate>
              <Ycoordinate>211.000000</Ycoordinate>
              <Xcoordinate>126.000000</Xcoordinate>
```

1.1.10   Evaluation of computer-aided detection and diagnosis systems

According to the opinions of AAPM CADSC members, the evaluation of CAD method-ologies is necessary for estimating algorithms' performance and effectiveness of use. In this section, we will discuss the performance evaluation of both standalone CAD systems, that is, a CAD system without an end-user and a CAD system with the user.

The assessment process depends on several factors:

Proper selection of training and testing data sets at the time of development and validation of the model.

Accurate detection and localization of true-positive, true-negative, false-positive, and false-negative cases.

Metrics and methodologies are considered for the assessment of the performance of standalone CAD systems.

Selection of appropriate criteria for determining the ground truth or reference standard data for designing the model.

Methodologies and metrics for assessing the acceptance of the model by clinicians.

1.1.11   Proper selection of training and testing data sets at the time of development and validation of the model

Methodologies and metrics for assessing the acceptance of the model by clinicians.

Metric	Formula	Description
Sensitivity	$\frac{TP}{TP + FN}(\times 100)$	Percentage of abnormalities correctly detected/classified.
Specificity	$\frac{TN}{TN + FP}(\times 100)$	Percentage of normal structures not incorrectly detected/classified as possible abnormalities.
Accuracy	$\frac{TN + TP}{TN + TP + FN + FP}(\times 100)$	Percentage of abnormalities and normal structures correctly classified/detected.
Precision	$\frac{TP}{TP + FP}(\times 100)$	Percentage of detected structures that are abnormalities.
F-measure	$\frac{TP}{TP + \frac{1}{2}(FP + FN)}$	Weighted harmonic means of precision and sensitivity
Similarity	$\frac{2 \times TP}{2 \times TP + FP + FN}(\times 100)$	Representation of the level of matching between the obtained results and the expected results (taken as true).
Negative predictive value	$\frac{TP}{TP + FN}(\times 100)$	Percentage of normal structures detected/classified that do not represent abnormalities.

Relative area difference: This metric quantifies the amount of under-segmentation and over-segmentation occurred by the segmentation algorithm.

$$Relative\ Area\ Difference = \frac{|A_{seg}| - |A_{manual}|}{|A_{manual}|}$$

Overlap: Like relative area difference, this metric also quantifies how much over-segmentation and/or under-segmentation have taken place.

$$Ovarlap = \frac{|A_{seg} \cap A_{manual}|}{|A_{seg} \cup A_{manual}|}$$

where A_{seg} denotes the segmented area of the objects.

A_{manual} denotes the actual area marked by the clinicians.

Dice coefficient: Like relative area difference, this metric also quantifies how much over-segmentation and/or under-segmentation have taken place.

$$Dice\ Coefficient = \frac{2TP}{2TP + FN + FP}$$

True positive (TP): True-positive detection reveals that both the classification algorithm and the ground truth data marked the object as a positive detection.

True negative (TN): True-negative detection reveals that both the classification algorithm and the ground truth data marked the object as a negative detection.

False positive (FP): It is a positive detection by the model; however, the ground truth data are marked as negative findings.

False negative (FN): False-negative detection is a negative finding by the algorithm, but in ground truth data, it is denoted as a positive finding.

Peak signal to noise ratio (PSNR): It is the ratio between the maximum possible power of a signal and the power of corrupting noise that affects the fidelity of its representation.

$$PSNR = 10\frac{MAX}{MSE}$$

where MAX = maximum intensity

MSE = mean square error

1.1.12   Root mean suare error

$$RMSE = \frac{1}{c \times r} \sum_{i=1}^{c} \sum_{j=1}^{r} I_1(i,j) - I_2(i,j)$$

where c = number of columns of the matrix

r = number of rows of the matrix

DSSIM:

$$DSSIM = 1 - \frac{SSIM}{2}$$

Jaccard coefficient (*JC*):

$$JC = \frac{I_1 \widehat{I_2}}{I_1 I_2^\smile}$$

where, I_1 = input image, I_2 = segmented image.

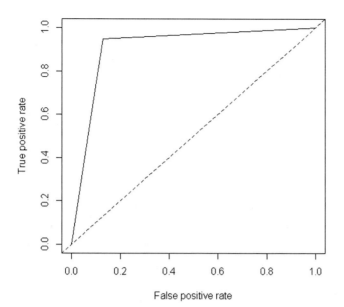

FIGURE 1.8 Sample ROC curve.

Dice coefficient:

$$DC = \frac{2TP}{2TP + FN + FP}$$

where, TP = true positive, FN=false negative, FP=false positive.

Receiver operating characteristics (ROC) curve: Receiver operating characteristic (ROC) curve is the plot that depicts the trade-off between the sensitivity and specificity across a series of cut-off points when the diagnostic test is continuous or on an ordinal scale (minimum five categories). This is an effective method for assessing the performance of a diagnostic test. The area under the curve (often referred to as simply the AUC) is equal to the probability that a classifier will rank a randomly chosen positive instance higher than a randomly chosen negative one (assuming 'positive' ranks higher than 'negative'). This can be seen as follows: the area under the curve is given by (the integral boundaries are reversed as large T has a lower value on the x-axis). Fig. 1.8 represents an ROC curve.

1.1.13   Cross-validation

A statistical technique called cross-validation is used to gauge the expertise of machine learning models.

Because it is simple to comprehend, simple to implement and produces skill estimates that often have a smaller bias than other methods, it is frequently used in applied machine learning to compare and select a model for a specific predictive modelling problem.

1.1.14   K-fold cross-validation

The process contains a single parameter, k, that designates how many groups should be created from a given data sample. As a result, the process is frequently referred to as k-fold cross-validation. When a particular number for k is selected, it may be substituted for k in the model's reference, such as when k = 10 is used to refer to cross-validation by a 10-fold factor.

The k value must be selected carefully for a given data sample because an inappropriate consideration of the k value may result in a high bias or high variance in the dataset which affects the performance of the model.

k-fold repeated cross-validation: Single k-fold cross-validation often provides noisy estimation. Repeated k-fold cross-validation offers a means to raise an estimated machine learning model's performance. This just entails carrying out the cross-validation process repeatedly and providing the average result over all folds and runs. This average result, which was determined using the standard error, is anticipated to provide a more accurate representation of the model's actual, unmeasured mean performance on the dataset. In order to overcome the noisy estimation of the single k-fold repeated cross-validation, a k-fold cross-validation is executed multiple times. The same dataset that has been divided into various folds must be used for each repetition of the k-fold cross-validation procedure.

Repeated k-fold cross-validation improves the estimate of the mean model performance at the expense of fitting and assessing a large number of additional models. Similar to k-fold cross-validation itself, repeated k-fold cross-validation is simple to parallelize, allowing for the execution of each fold or repeated cross-validation process on several cores or machines.

Leave-One-Out Cross-Validation: Leave-One-Out Cross-Validation (LOOCV) is a cross-validation approach commonly employed in machine learning to evaluate the performance of predictive models. In LOOCV, the model is trained on all data points except one, which is set aside for validation. This process is repeated for each data point in the dataset, and performance metrics, such as accuracy or mean squared error, are computed for each iteration. The final performance assessment is obtained by averaging these metrics. While LOOCV provides an unbiased evaluation since each data point serves as both training and validation, it can be computationally intensive, especially for larger datasets. Despite this drawback, LOOCV is particularly useful in scenarios with limited data, offering a thorough assessment of model performance.

1.1.15   Challenges in CAD

1. **Data collection and quality assessment:** The primary challenge of CAD methodologies is the collection of sufficient and quality data for the implementation and evaluation of the system. In this regard, EHRs and picture archiving and communication systems (PACSs) play an important role. EHR is a web-based tool that can

store and update patients' health records, that is, patient's previous disease conditions, family history of the disease, patient demographic details, pathological test reports and medication history in a digitized and secure format. On the other hand, PACS is also an archiving tool that stores radiological images like X-rays, computer tomography, MRI, etc., so that it can be used for future diagnosis and research. According to the survey of the National Health Mission, United States of America, in 2020, 86% of the World's Hospitals have adopted EHR systems; however, the basic problem of EHR systems is that there exist no standard guidelines. Hence, a poorly designed EHR system doesn't provide quality data to the researchers. Moreover, the data records are often missed from the health records, users may mistype the disease history while inserting the records. As a consequence, the overall performance of the CAD models is degraded.

Another interesting aspect of collecting these data is to avoid data biases in the training data. Bias data often affects the efficacy of the proposed CAD model. Another noteworthy fact is that in clinical practice, there exist some rare diseases, that is, clinicians often find normal cases rather than abnormal ones. For example, we can tell that the prediction of cancer of any organ is considered a rare disease in CAD modelling. Inadequate distributions of the clinical data often affect the performance of the model.

Implementation of easily accessible PACS, well-designed EHR systems and imbalance class modelling is the present challenge in the implementation of a good quality CAD model.

2. **Developing advanced segmentation approaches for medical imaging:** Image segmentation or object segmentation is the initial step in designing a CAD system. Segmentation of a procedure where the image pixels are sub-divided among various clusters based on several uniform conditions.

   Published literature reveals that there exist numerous segmentation algorithms that are capable of segmenting the ROIs from two-dimensional images. Despite having several well-suited segmentation algorithms in computer vision, implementation of advanced segmentation algorithms is required as these algorithms are incapable of segmenting the region of interest from three-dimensional images. Moreover, due to the presence of high-volume data of a single patient, the segmentation of the region of interest becomes time-consuming. Consequently, designing multi-dimensional segmentation algorithms with low execution time poses a great challenge to CAD researchers.

3. **Developing advanced feature extraction/selection approaches**: The success of traditional machine learning algorithms, as well as deep learning methodologies, are solely dependent on the set of appropriate features. These features may be the intensity distribution of the pixels or some shape, texture and statistical features of the segmented objects. The literature reveals that the existing feature extraction methodologies can extract numerous aforementioned features from the segmented objects, though all these features have not equal contributions to the decision of

the model. Undoubtedly, these irrelevant features often include noise in the test data. Moreover, due to the presence of these large data, more storage space and computational time are required while accessing the data. This consequently decreases the performance of the prediction model. In this regard, most of the researchers either opted for several feature selection algorithms or considered the dimension reduction algorithms that can easily quantify the important features of that particular problem. In this context, the selection of an appropriate feature selection algorithm is a challenging problem for researchers.

4. **Developing better classification and other data mining approaches:** The most important step in the CAD model is the detection/delineation of the lesions and also confirmation of the state of the disease. As per the public literature, this purpose is solved by implementing several supervised learning methodologies. However, there exist several unsupervised learning methodologies that can also achieve the aim of a CAD model. The selection of this classification algorithm is entirely dependent on the nature of the selected features, that is, a strong classifier of a particular problem may behave as a weak classifier in another classification problem. Another noteworthy aspect of the lower efficiency of the model is the presence of imbalanced test data. This often generates an over-fitted prediction model, that is, the accuracy of the model is quite high, but it often fails to correctly classify the minority class samples. This leads to an unstable CAD model.

   Apart from the aforementioned challenges, conventional AI-based methodologies worked as a black box model, that is, it can decide whether the lesion is present or the status of the disease but can't interpret which features are responsible for this decision.

   Hence, the selection of appropriate classification algorithms or the implementation of advanced algorithms incorporating explain ability in the model can be considered the future research scope of this domain.

5. **Dealing with big data:** Another challenge in the implementation of CAD methodologies is managing big data. Big data represents 3 V aspects, that is, volume, velocity and variety. These 3V's are explained as follows:

   Volume: This represents the size of the patient data. In the present clinical scenario, when researchers have considered a thoracic CT scan of a patient and the Institute has a 64 slice CT scanner. Then, he has to analyze more than 400 image slices of an individual patient.

   Variety: Apart from these digital image data, most of the data are in an unstructured form. Often unstructured data require human interpretation to read and understand them correctly.

   Velocity: Huge volumes of patient data are often required to store and analyze in real-time or nearly real-time. Processing and analyzing large-scale data in a timely manner is one of the significant challenges of CAD systems today and it is known as the data velocity problem.

The big data solutions can assist in taking CAD systems to the next level, which can bring a revolutionary impact on the fields of medicine and computer science. The field of computer science is required to provide solution approaches capable of dealing with this fast-growing challenge category

6. **Developing standard performance assessment approaches for CAD systems:** There exist no standard performance assessment metrics that can evaluate the CAD tools. The existing methodologies like ROC curve, the AUC, the precision-recall (PR) curve and the positive and negative predictive values serve fewer purposes, but can't predict the overall performance of the CAD. Therefore, in order to secure patient safety, more assessment techniques like the unit misclassification costs for false-positive and false-negative errors need to be assessed more accurately. The American Association of Physicists in Medicine (AAPM) has formed the Computer Aided Detection in Diagnostic Imaging Subcommittee (CADSC) whose aim was to establish a standardized protocol for assessing the overall performance of the CAD. In order to be able to evaluate the performance of CAD systems more objectively, the unit misclassification costs for false-positive and false-negative errors need to be assessed more accurately. Furthermore, methods need to be established for assessing CAD performance in a standardized manner.

7. **Adopting CAD systems for clinical practice:** In 1998, US government approved the use of CAD tools in clinical care. The basic problem of incorporating CAD in AI is the inadequate knowledge of the medical practitioner on these methodologies. Instead of this aforementioned challenge, integration of the model with clinical workstations, that is, PACS and imaging workstation poses challenges in the adaptation of CAD tools in clinical practice.

Computer-aided detection and diagnosis (CAD) represents a transformative approach at the intersection of medicine and computer science. This interdisciplinary methodology harnesses advanced technologies to augment medical professionals' abilities in detecting and diagnosing diseases. By merging medical expertise with computational power, CAD systems provide invaluable support across various medical fields.

The introduction to CAD emphasizes its role as a collaborative tool that enhances diagnostic accuracy. Medical imaging, such as X-rays, MRIs and CT scans, generates vast amounts of data that can be overwhelming to interpret manually. CAD algorithms analyze these images, pinpointing subtle anomalies that might escape the human eye. This process empowers healthcare practitioners with an additional layer of insight, enabling early detection and accurate diagnosis.

The interdisciplinary nature of CAD transcends traditional boundaries. Radiologists, clinicians and computer scientists collaborate to develop and refine CAD systems. Radiologists provide domain knowledge, clinicians offer real-world insights and computer scientists contribute technical expertise to create algorithms that improve accuracy and efficiency.

This synergistic approach yields remarkable benefits across specialties. For instance, in radiology, CAD assists in detecting abnormalities like tumours and nodules. In cardiology, it aids in identifying cardiovascular diseases from medical images. Additionally, CAD is pivotal in pathology by automating the analysis of tissue samples.

In summary, computer-aided detection and diagnosis heralds a new era of interdisciplinary collaboration. By merging medical expertise with cutting-edge technology, CAD empowers medical professionals to provide more accurate and timely diagnoses, thereby enhancing patient care and outcomes. This collaborative fusion underscores the transformative potential of interdisciplinary approaches in the advancement of healthcare.

Further reading

[1] Doi K. Computer-aided diagnosis in medical imaging: historical review, current status and future potential. Computerized Medical Imaging and Graphics June 1, 2007;31(4–5):198–211.

[2] Halalli B, Makandar A. Computer aided diagnosis-medical image analysis techniques. Breast Imaging January 17, 2018;85:85–109.

[3] Mayo RC, Leung J. Artificial intelligence and deep learning—Radiology's next frontier? Clinical Imaging May 1, 2018;49:87–8.

[4] Eves K, Salmon J, Olsen J, Fagergren F. A comparative analysis of computer-aided design team performance with collaboration software. Computer-Aided Design and Applications July 4, 2018; 15(4):476–87.

[5] Mittal H, Pandey AC, Saraswat M, Kumar S, Pal R, Modwel G. A comprehensive survey of image segmentation: clustering methods, performance parameters, and benchmark datasets. Multimedia Tools and Applications February 9, 2021:1–26.

[6] Hand DJ. Assessing the performance of classification methods. International Statistical Review December 2012;80(3):400–14.

[7] Nahm FS. Receiver operating characteristic curve: overview and practical use for clinicians. Korean Journal of Anesthesiology February 1, 2022;75(1):25–36.

[8] Park B, Park H, Lee SM, Seo JB, Kim N. Lung segmentation on HRCT and volumetric CT for diffuse interstitial lung disease using deep convolutional neural networks. Journal of Digital Imaging December 2019;32:1019–26.

[9] El-Baz A, Beache GM, Gimel'farb G, Suzuki K, Okada K, Elnakib A, et al. Computer-aided diagnosis systems for lung cancer: challenges and methodologies. International Journal of Biomedical Imaging 2013;2013.

[10] Pourhoseingholi MA, Vahedi M, Rahimzadeh M. Sample size calculation in medical studies. Gastroenterology and Hepatology from bed to bench 2013;6(1):14.

[11] Breslow NE. Statistics in epidemiology: the case-control study. Journal of the American Statistical Association March 1, 1996;91(433):14–28.

[12] Fitzner K, Heckinger E. Sample size calculation and power analysis: a quick review. The Diabetes Educator September 2010;36(5):701–7.

[13] Stark M, Zapf A. Sample size calculation and re-estimation based on the prevalence in a single-arm confirmatory diagnostic accuracy study. Statistical Methods in Medical Research 2020;29(10): 2958–71.

[14] Thompson BW. HIPAA guidelines for using PDAs. Nursing November 1, 2005;35(11):24.

[15] Krleža-Jerić K, Lemmens T. 7th revision of the Declaration of Helsinki: good news for the transparency of clinical trials. Croatian Medical Journal April 2009;50(2):105.

Basic terminologies of computed tomography scan

2.1 Introduction

Computed tomography (CT) is a sophisticated imaging technique that has revolutionized the field of diagnostic medicine, providing detailed cross-sectional images of the body's internal structures. The fundamental ideas and terminology needed to comprehend and use CT technology effectively are introduced in this chapter. Our goal as we explore the topic of computed tomography is to give readers a firm foundation in its fundamental ideas, operational mechanics, and the important terminology employed by experts in the field.

2.2 Basic terminologies

2.2.1 Computed tomography (CT)

CT is a computerized X-ray imaging method that uses an X-ray beam to create a volume scan of an organ on a patient's body. This volume scan is then reconstructed into several two-dimensional cross-sectional pictures of varying thicknesses (0.6, 1, 5 mm, etc.) and planes (axial, coronal, sagittal) (Fig. 2.1).

2.2.2 Thin slice vs thick slice CT

Thin slice CT scans with slice thicknesses ranging from 0.5 to 1.25 mm are critical in detecting lung nodules. These high-resolution scans provide extraordinary clarity, allowing radiologists to precisely visualize microscopic nodules and subtle abnormalities. The comprehensive images aid in precisely characterizing nodules, identifying benign from malignant ones and assisting in appropriate patient care. Although thin slice CT exposes patients to more radiation and creates more data, the increased sensitivity and diagnostic accuracy it provides make it invaluable for the early detection and accurate diagnosis of lung nodules.

CT scan with a thin slice: Thick slice CT scans, on the other hand, with slice thicknesses ranging from 5 to 10 mm, provide coarser pictures with lower spatial resolution. These scans are advantageous in terms of scanning speed and radiation dose, making them appropriate for regular screening or follow-up examinations where the primary focus is not on a comprehensive evaluation of lung nodules. Thick slice CT scans can

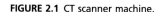

FIGURE 2.1 CT scanner machine.

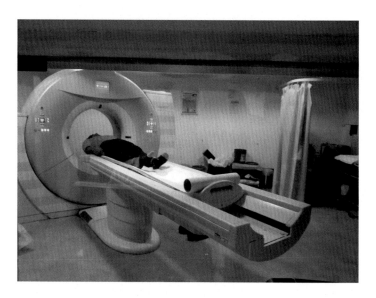

provide an overview of the lungs as well as reveal larger, more visible nodules, making them useful for general lung examinations. The coarser spatial resolution, on the other hand, restricts its sensitivity for detecting minute or faint nodules, and it may not provide enough data for correct categorization, especially in circumstances where exact evaluation is essential.

The decision between thin slice and thick slice CT in pulmonary nodule detection is determined by the clinical aims and specific examination requirements. Thin slice CT provides greater spatial resolution, which is critical for spotting small or subtle nodules and allowing for early discovery and accurate characterization. Thick slice CT, on the other hand, is appropriate for routine screening and follow-up evaluations where the focus is on bigger lesions and broader lung assessments. To optimize pulmonary nodule identification and diagnosis, radiologists must carefully examine the clinical context and trade-offs between spatial resolution, radiation dose, and image processing needs.

2.2.3   HRCT (high-resolution computed tomography)

HRCT is a specialized imaging technology that produces high-resolution cross-sectional pictures of the lungs and other thoracic tissues. To capture delicate anatomical details, it employs a narrow collimation and tiny slice thickness (about 0.5−1 mm). HRCT is especially helpful in identifying lung parenchyma, bronchial structures and tiny pulmonary nodules. It is a useful tool for detecting and monitoring a variety of lung illnesses such as interstitial lung disease, pulmonary fibrosis, emphysema and pulmonary nodules.

2.2.4   Contrast enhanced computed tomography (CECT)

CECT is a type of CT that uses contrast chemicals given intravenously to improve the visualization of blood arteries and other structures. The contrast material highlights vascular structures and improves tissue differentiation, assisting in the detection and characterization of anomalies. CECT is widely employed in a variety of therapeutic settings, including the evaluation of pulmonary embolisms, vascular abnormalities and tumours.

2.2.5   Importance of HRCT and CECT in the context of pulmonary nodule detection

CECT is particularly important when there is suspicion of vascular involvement or when assessing certain types of pulmonary nodules, especially those suspected to be malignant or with potential vascular abnormalities. The contrast agent injected intravenously enhances the visualization of blood vessels and highlights vascular structures, providing valuable information about nodule vascularity and its relationship with adjacent vessels. This can aid in the identification of enhancing nodules, which are more likely to be malignant. CECT is also valuable in diagnosing pulmonary embolism and other vascular pathologies, which may present with nodules as a secondary manifestation.

On the other hand, HRCT is crucial for the accurate characterization and early diagnosis of pulmonary nodules. Due to its great spatial resolution, it is possible to see microscopic nodules, bronchial structures and other fine anatomical details with outstanding clarity. Based on their form, density and other characteristics, benign and malignant nodules can often be distinguished by HRCT. It is essential in the detection and monitoring of lung cancer as well as the diagnosis of interstitial lung disorders and other lung pathologies that may present as nodules (Fig. 2.2).

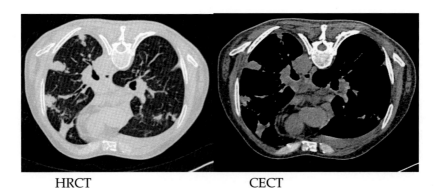

HRCT   CECT

FIGURE 2.2 HRCT and CECT.

2.2.5.1   Visualization

CECT improves blood vessel visibility and can be used to spot vascular involvement or vascular anomalies linked to lung nodules.

The lung parenchyma and tiny pulmonary nodules can be seen in great detail in HRCT pictures, which are excellent at displaying fine anatomical structures.

2.2.5.2   Contrast agent

To improve the imaging of vascular structures with CECT, a contrast agent must be given intravenously.

HRCT uses only X-ray data and specialized image reconstruction algorithms; contrast agents are not needed for imaging.

2.2.5.2.1   Clinical indications

When there is a possibility of vascular involvement, cancer or to assess pulmonary embolism, CECT is frequently employed.

The diagnosis of interstitial lung illness, the screening for lung cancer and the overall evaluation of pulmonary nodules all use HRCT.

In conclusion, lung nodule detection with CECT and HRCT is critical, although their respective roles and clinical applications are distinct. While HRCT excels in providing high-resolution images for early diagnosis and detailed characterization of pulmonary nodules, CECT is useful for determining vascular involvement and improving the visualization of some types of nodules. The decision between CECT and HRCT is based on the specific clinical indications and pathology that is suspected; they can work in tandem to provide a thorough evaluation of lung nodules.

2.3 Generations of CT scanner machines

Every generation of CT scanners has improved on the previous one in terms of technology, picture quality, speed and patient safety. Here are a few brief observations regarding the various CT scanner generations.

2.3.1   First-generation CT scanners (1971)

Principle: Single-detector fan-beam CT.

Characteristics: Early in the 1970s, Sir Godfrey Hounsfield unveiled the first CT scanner. A rotating X-ray tube and a single X-ray detector were used to gather data. The scanning process was slow and time-consuming because the scanner only captured one slice of data every rotation. These scanners provided largely low-resolution images used for brain imaging.

New Features: A single detector and a rotating X-ray tube is utilized to obtain a single-slice of image per rotation.

Advantages: Pioneering technology, provided the first-ever cross-sectional images of the brain, laid the foundation for future CT scanner development.

Disadvantages: Slow scanning times, limited image resolution, and only suitable for brain imaging, not practical for whole-body applications.

2.3.2   Second-generation CT scanners (1974)

Principle: Multiple-detector fan-beam CT.

Characteristics: By employing numerous detectors lined up in a row across from the X-ray source, second-generation CT scanners increased speed. A fan-shaped beam that revolved around the patient was created by the detectors and the X-ray tube. Due to the simultaneous data capture from numerous detectors during each rotation made possible by this design, scan times were shortened and image quality was enhanced. The first scanners to be widely employed for a variety of body imaging applications were those from the second generation.

New Features: In each of the rotations, multiple detectors are arranged in a row to obtain acquired data. This process occurs simultaneously.

Advantage: Body imaging is made possible by improved image quality and quicker scan times compared to first-generation scanners.

Disadvantage: The amount of slices that may be acquired every rotation is constrained, and the scanner is still comparatively slow in comparison to current scanners.

2.3.3   Third-generation CT scanners (1976)

Principle: Curved-array detectors.

Characteristics: By deploying curved arrays of detectors opposing the X-ray source, third-generation CT scanners considerably enhanced image quality. With this approach, fewer artefacts occurred and more precise diagnostic data was obtained. Up until the release of the fourth generation of scanners, the third generation remained common.

2.3.4   Fourth-generation CT scanners (1989)

Principle: Slip-ring technology.

Characteristics: Slip-ring technology was introduced in fourth-generation CT scanners, allowing the X-ray tube and detectors to rotate continuously around the patient without having to halt and reverse direction. Through a significant reduction in scanning time, imaging has become quicker and more effective. With the advent of these scanners, dynamic imaging became feasible.

Fresh features curved-array detectors were installed in front of the X-ray source to enhance image quality and minimize artefacts.

Advantages: Improved diagnostic information and image accuracy, especially in complicated anatomical regions.

Cons: A little bit more expensive and sophisticated than second-generation scanners.

2.3.5   Spiral or helical CT scanners (1990s)

Principle: Continuous volume scanning.

Characteristics: Helical or spiral CT scanners were a major advance in CT imaging. They made it possible to continuously collect data while the patient table was being moved across the gantry. Through the elimination of pause-and-shoot scanning, continuous volume scanning sped up image acquisition and made three-dimensional (3D) imaging possible. The development of helical CT scanners expanded the field of cardiac and vascular imaging.

Fresh features introduced continuous volume scanning, which made it possible to acquire data while moving the patient table.

Faster image capture, easier 3D imaging and better imaging of dynamic structures are all benefits.

Cons: The constant rotation results in a higher radiation exposure than standard step-and-shoot scanning.

2.3.6   Multislice or multi-detector CT scanners (late 1990s)

Principle: Multiple detector rows.

Characteristics: The presence of many detector rows—typically 4, 16, 64, or more—in multislice CT scanners was a significant improvement. With the ability to simultaneously acquire numerous data slices during a single rotation, these scanners greatly increased scan speed and volume coverage. The temporal resolution of multislice CT scanners was enhanced, making them suited for imaging dynamic structures and organs like the heart.

Numerous detector rows (4, 16, 64, or more) were included as new features, enabling the acquisition of numerous slices simultaneously during one rotation.

Benefits: Significantly faster scan times, better volume coverage and higher temporal resolution for dynamic imaging.

A higher initial cost and greater need for data storage to manage the vast number of data created are disadvantages.

2.3.7   Dual-source CT scanners (2006)

Principle: Dual X-ray sources and detectors.

Two X-ray tubes and accompanying detector arrays operating at various energies were used in dual-source CT scanners. This innovation enhanced temporal resolution and made dual-energy CT and other cutting-edge imaging techniques possible. In cardiac imaging, dual-source scanners excelled at minimizing motion artefacts and producing sharper images of rapidly moving structures.

Improved temporal resolution was achieved by using dual X-ray sources and detectors that operated at various energies.

Excellent temporal resolution, fewer motion artefacts and cutting-edge imaging tools like dual-energy CT are benefits.

Advantages: Limited to specialized applications, such as heart imaging; higher equipment cost and complexity.

2.4 CT scanning technology

This section briefs the entire procedure of the CT imaging technology.

2.4.1 Acquisition systems

CT scanning technology aims to provide a precise cross sectional images of the entire body. In order to achieve this the X-ray data is recorded by the acquisition system, which is subsequently processed to rebuild specific and instructive images utilized by medical experts for diagnosis, treatment planning and tracking patient progress. The main elements and purposes of the CT scanner acquisition system are examined in this article along with the role it plays in medical imaging and the technological developments that have revolutionized the field of radiology.

The CT scanner acquisition system is made up of a number of crucial parts that work together to gather the information required for image reconstruction. The X-ray tube, detector array, gantry, patient table, data acquisition system and computer for data processing are the acquisition system's main parts. A narrow X-ray beam that travels through the patient's body is produced while the X-ray tube spins around them during a CT scan. The detector array, which is placed across from the X-ray tube, measures the transmitted X-ray intensity and records the information needed to produce the images.

The multislice or multidetector technology is one of the most important developments in CT scanner acquisition systems. Per rotation, traditional single-slice CT scanners collected data from a single detector row. A multislice CT scanner, on the other hand, may record multiple slices of data concurrently during a single rotation, significantly speeding up imaging and expanding the area covered. Comprehensive imaging of huge body areas can be done in a matter of seconds thanks to the availability of 16, 64 or even more detector rows. Emergency care, trauma treatment and standard diagnostic procedures have all been revolutionized by multislice CT scanners, which offer quick and precise imagery to support crucial judgements.

The adoption of helical or spiral CT scanning is a further important development. The patient table and X-ray tube can both move at the same time throughout the scan, thanks to this continuous volume scanning approach. The table moves as the X-ray tube revolves around the patient, which causes continuous data to be collected along the Z-axis (patient's body). Helical CT scanning is helpful for reconstructing the anatomy in three dimensions (3D) and is perfect for imaging dynamic structures and organs, such as the heart and blood vessels.

The capacity to produce accurate cross-sectional images of the human anatomy makes the CT scanner acquisition system significant. A variety of medical diseases, including cancer detection, cardiovascular disease assessment, trauma evaluation and neurological disorders, can be diagnosed and monitored with the help of CT imaging. For emergency situations, where prompt diagnosis and treatment choices are crucial, the acquisition system's speed and accuracy are crucial.

The CT scanner acquisition system has drawbacks in addition to its strengths. The possible risk of exposing patients to ionizing radiation is one of the main worries. The radiation dose is continuously being reduced while retaining image quality. In addition, the expense of purchasing and maintaining modern CT scanning equipment can be high, necessitating careful evaluation of the imaging requirements and budget of the healthcare facility (Fig. 2.3).

The process of capturing and collecting X-ray data while the X-ray tube spins around the patient during a CT scan provides the basis for the operation of the CT scanner acquisition system. The data required to rebuild precise cross-sectional pictures of the patient's anatomy must be collected by the acquisition system. Here is a more thorough explanation of how the CT scanner acquisition system operates:

Source and Detectors for X-rays: The CT scanner acquisition system comprises of an X-ray tube and a collection of detectors placed across from it. The X-ray tube acts as the radiation's source, emitting a focussed beam of radiation that travels through the patient's body.

Attenuation of X-rays: The X-ray beam interacts with the tissues it encounters as it travels through the body. Different tissues exhibit varying degrees of attenuation (decrease in X-ray intensity) as the X-rays pass through them due to their different densities and atomic compositions. Soft tissues attenuate X-rays less than dense solids like bones.

FIGURE 2.3 CT imaging procedures.

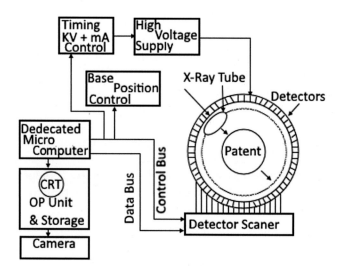

2.4.2   Data acquisition

During the CT scan, the X-ray tube and detector array rotate around the patient. The detectors measure the intensity of the X-rays that pass through the body at various angles. The acquisition system collects data from multiple detectors simultaneously to capture information from different parts of the patient's anatomy.

2.4.2.1   Continuous rotation (spiral CT)

In modern CT scanners, particularly in spiral or helical CT scans, the X-ray tube and detectors rotate continuously around the patient as the patient table moves through the gantry. This continuous rotation allows for the acquisition of volumetric data in a helical fashion, covering the entire length of the patient's body.

2.4.2.2   Step-and-shoot rotation (conventional CT)

In conventional CT scanners, the X-ray tube and detectors rotate in discrete steps (typically 360°) around the patient. At each step, data is acquired, and the system pauses momentarily before moving to the next position. This process is repeated until data is collected from all desired angles.

2.4.2.3   Digital conversion

The measured X-ray intensity data from the detectors are converted into digital signals. Analog-to-digital converters convert the analog signal (X-ray intensity) into a digital format that can be processed and stored in a computer.

2.4.3   Data processing and storage

After the digital data from the detectors is acquired, it is transferred to a computer for processing and image reconstruction. Preprocessing can be used to adjust the data for things like detector response, patient movements, and beam-hardening artefacts.

2.4.4   Image reconstruction

From the collected data, the computer reconstructs cross-sectional images (slices) of the patient's anatomy using complex mathematical procedures, such as filtered back-projection. The obtained projection data are translated into two-dimensional images throughout the reconstruction phase.

Image Display and Analysis: Radiologists and other healthcare professionals can analyze the reconstructed images by seeing them on a computer screen or printing them on film. The diagnosis and planning of treatments for numerous medical disorders are made easier by the detailed information these images provide about the body's internal components.

2.4.5 X-ray generators and tube

High-frequency X-ray generators are required to produce potent X-ray beams quickly enough for high-speed scanning. The range of a typical operating frequency is 20–50 kHz (kHz). Generator power ratings of 80–120 kW are normal, according to manufacturer specification tables for commercial systems accessible in the United States. A wide range of exposure techniques can be used with most generators employing voltages between 80 and 140 kV and currents between 30 and 500 mA (mA). Some generators include a lower tube potential option (70 kVp) to reduce radiation exposure. Generators are located on the revolving scan frame inside the CT gantry and are powered by a low-voltage power source that is delivered via the slip ring, along with the X-ray tube and detector assembly.

Modern generators come with a wide range of features that enable them to adjust and enhance radiation output and image quality while scanning in real time. The use of computer-controlled X-ray techniques generated by the scanner's master control computer is made possible by the generator's computerized and adjustable architecture. The change of tube current based on patient thickness is a frequent feature. The tube current of a patient's tube may be altered by scanners along the patient's z-axis, in the x–y plane, or in both directions. Several technologies allow for the dynamic or automated selection of kVp depending on the research kind or patient size. One technique for dual-energy (spectral) imaging that makes advantage of a high-performance generator is fast kV switching. Generators in these systems are capable of rapid switching between two operational voltages (often within 150 milliseconds).

In order to maintain a high X-ray output, modern CT scanner X-ray tubes use cutting-edge cooling methods and revolving anodes. Many tubes employ focal spot modulation technology or 'flying focal spot' technology. These tubes not only provide large and small focal spots but also have the ability to instantly adjust the chosen focal spot's location throughout the scan. The resolution of the picture data is improved as a result of changing the scanner's sampling behaviour. A typical modern CT scanner has tubes with a heat storage capacity of 30 million heat units (30 MHU) and a continuous output power capability of 120 kW.

2.4.6 Filters

In CT scanners, X-ray filters are employed to alter the beam's shape and spectrum. The typical filter is made of aluminium, just like a radiographic tube filter, but it has a very different shape. CT filters are usually thicker than radiographic filters and frequently combine copper and other materials (like Teflon) with aluminium. The CT beam has a higher average energy and fewer low-energy photons than a radiography beam at the same kVp (Figs. 2.4–2.7), making it much 'harder' than radiography. Because low-energy photons are more likely to deliver a dose to the patient without contributing to the image, this is done to reduce the patient's radiation exposure. Although the lower-energy

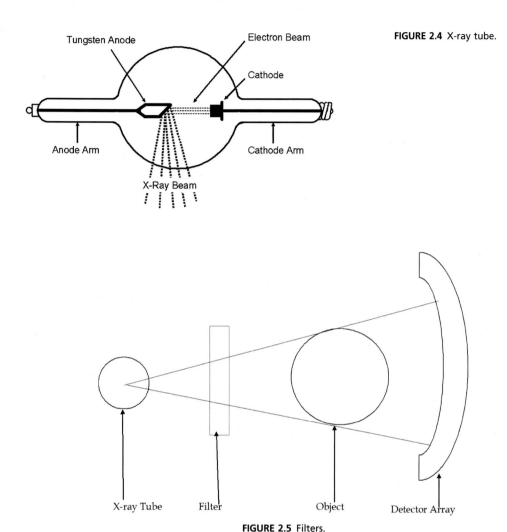

FIGURE 2.4 X-ray tube.

FIGURE 2.5 Filters.

photons employed in radiography help to create contrast in the image, CT has a much higher natural sensitivity to contrast.

The compensating filters used in CT are usually referred to as bowtie filters due to their design. The filter is thinner in the fan beam's centre and thicker near its azimuthal edges. As a result, the thinner portion of the filter lines with the patient's body's thickest path length as the gantry rotates, while the thicker portion of the filter aligns with the patient's peripheral anatomy. The filter slightly shifts the contour of the patient's body thickness. In contrast to what would happen if the beam simply passed through the patient for any line across the FOV, the overall attenuation and beam hardening along the X-ray path are substantially more uniform. The dynamic range at the detectors can be reduced by adjusting for attenuation variations, and the quantitative accuracy of the

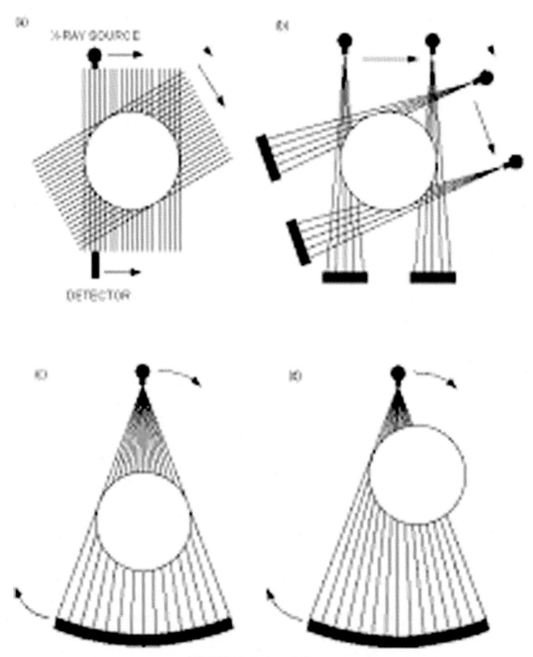

FIGURE 2.6 Detectors of CT scanner.

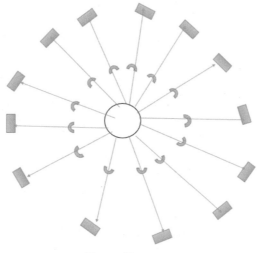

Fan Beam

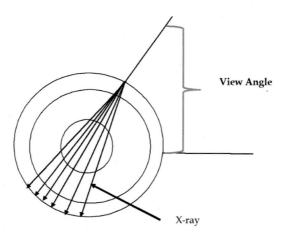

View Angle

X-ray

Cone Beam

FIGURE 2.7 Fan beam and cone beam.

scanner's representation of tissue attenuation as CT number values (HUs) is increased by adjusting for beam hardening. To compensate for head and body scans, a scanner will include at least two distinct bowtie filters, and some scanners have as many as five or six to accommodate a range of patient body sizes. Based on the scan setting selected by the operator, the scanner automatically selects and switches the bowtie filter into the beam path.

2.4.7 Detector

Scintillation crystals are used in CT scanners to transform X-rays into pulses of visible light that can be detected and counted by electronic circuits. Traditional detectors generate voltage and light pulses, which yield a straightforward count of detected X-ray photons. The development of photon counting instruments that can count X-ray photons and determine the energy of each photon is currently being researched.

CT detectors use crystals constructed of fast scintillator ceramics like gadolinium oxysulfide and cadmium telluride. Research is being done to produce new crystal materials to further improve scanner performance, and each CT company has newer unique crystal types that are either already available or being developed. The crystals convert X-rays into light pulses whose intensities are inversely correlated to the total energy of photons impacting the crystal. The light is converted into current, which creates a voltage across a resistance after the conversion. The voltage is then recognized as digital data by the detection system for use by the reconstruction system. This multistep process of transforming analogue signals to digital data results in flaws and inefficiencies such as electrical noise, sampling and recovery speed, and quantization error. Despite these drawbacks, even the most basic CT scanners can reliably image a variety of extreme densities, such as bone, air and water, by properly measuring low-level signals over a wide dynamic range with great precision.

Detector arrays are growing, enabling small pixel sizes with increased anatomic coverage, even though individual detector elements are still quite small. Common detector arrays provide scanning of 80–160 mm of coverage in a single tube rotation with the resolution of 0.5–0.6 mm, allowing for the acquisition of entire portions of the patient's anatomy in a single revolution of the rotating frame of the CT scanner, which takes less than 1 second.

Due to the tube/detector pair's fixed position, the associated detectors and electronics system must be stable, homogeneous and able to track through a wide dynamic range. Noncompensation for errors are as little as a few thousandths of 1% and can lead to visible (ring) artefacts. Additionally, the data sample may have issues with spatial resolution, a vital indicator of the quality of a CT picture (more on that later). In this geometric link, the spatial resolution depends on how closely spaced the rays are in each view, while the number of detectors in the arc or array affects data sampling.

Typically, the array has between 600 and 900 detectors. These values result in a maximum spatial resolution of between 5 and 10 line pairs per centimetre (lp/cm), depending on the reconstruction type (filter), reconstruction matrix size and scan FOV. According to sampling theory, in order to visualize an item, the sample frequency must be at least twice as high as the spatial frequency associated with it. Higher sample rates are actually preferable. The axial resolution of more than 5–10 lp/cm (0.5–1.0 mm) may be limiting for some therapeutic applications.

2.4.8   Scanner operation and geometry

Throughout the development of CT, a variety of X-ray tube and detector movement combinations were used to collect data. The most practical design for high-speed scanning in multidetector-row systems developed as the rotate/rotate geometry, which is still used in modern multidetector CT systems.

Figs. 2.4−2.5 depicts the rotate/rotate configuration of the revolving scan frame with the X-ray tube and detector array placed across from one another. In a wide-angle fan-beam geometry (50−55°), an arc of detectors and the X-ray tube continuously rotate 360° around the subject. The projection data (or data samples) that were obtained at different angles are used to generate a view for each angular sample that is acquired at a position of the tube and detector.

The detectors in rotate/rotate geometry are fixed radially and occasionally look at the scan zone. Only the array's centre detectors can 'see' the pixels in the FOV's centre. Due to this reliable connection, the detectors may be extensively collimated, greatly reducing the quantity of diffused radiation that may be detected. By maintaining contrast, the observer can see details against a background with greater background noise (or mottle, or grainy background).

The scanner geometry has been exploited by manufacturers in a number of ways to overcome the spatial resolution limitations imposed by detector size. By moving the detector array's offset from the rotational centre by a quarter-ray or an eighth-ray, for instance, it is possible to increase spatial sampling (and spatial resolution). By allowing data obtained during the second half of a 360-degree rotation to be blended with that of the first half, this effectively doubles the sampling and resolution. Patient mobility may reduce its benefits. Additionally, this method is only appropriate for specific spiral CT scanning types where it is possible to interleave data from 360-degree projections.

Another effective method to boost data sampling is to oscillate the X-ray tube focal spot a few millimetres throughout a scan. This results in interleaved data samples. The revolving frame's rotational speed and location are both accurately controlled and synchronized with the placement of the focal point. Data gathered during the use of each focal point position is first captured independently and then interleaved to provide a more complete spatial sampling of the tissue. This method can be used to increase scanning plane sampling. Focussed spot modulation along the z-axis enables the creation of sagittal and coronal reformatted images with smaller pixel sizes than would be possible with simply the physical detector elements. For example, a scanner with 32 detector rows may be advertised as '64 slice', and a scanner with 128 detector rows may be advertised as '256 slice'. Systems with this capability are frequently advertised as having more 'slices' than the actual number of detector rows that are present on the scanner.

Proper view sampling is necessary for spatial resolution to prevent aliasing problems. Views (angular projections) are constrained by the scanner's electronic measurement capabilities, which are frequently not the gating element for maximum resolution. These factors are unique to each CT maker and have a big impact on how well a scanner works all around.

2.5 Reconstruction

2.5.1   Filtered backpropagation

It is clear how CT imaging projection data is acquired, thanks to the forward-projection method, which is used in iterative reconstruction. The forward-projection process, as seen in this Figure, is an addition operation where we are adding up data in each pixel along the ray path.

From this single viewpoint of parallel beam projections, you can observe that each detector value is the same in this case. Therefore, if we just have one perspective of the projection data, it won't be sufficient to recreate the image. The way that CT imaging differs from X-ray radiography in this regard is by providing more images that better distinguish structural details.

Projection data from 180° is required to faithfully reconstruct the object in parallel beam acquisitions. Here we illustrate a forward projection rotated by 90° concerning the initial forward projection.

The back-projection process essentially aims to carry out the forward-projection operation backward. Since the forward-projection operation mapped from the image into the detector space, the back-projection operation maps from the detector to the image in reverse.

After we begin with data in the detector, the back-projection technique paints the values back into the picture matrix in the direction of measurement.

Sinogram: Using the object in the last demonstration, we talked about the mathematical technique of forward projection. When we turn on our X-ray tube and acquire one view of the detector, the X-ray system conducts the forward projection for us.

Since its projections are parallel to one another (achieved by translating the source and detector), the first-generation CT scanner has the simplest geometry.

For each perspective, you get one projection, one line, or one row in the sinogram. In a sinogram, the x direction is frequently used to represent the detector channel direction and the y direction to represent the view direction (i.e., to indicate the gantry rotation angle).

Normally, one detector row's worth of the sinogram is displayed, as it is in this case. In our fictitious example, we assume that our parallel beam system only has one detector row, therefore this is all the projection data.

The ability of the sinogram to help pinpoint the source of various visual artefacts is just one of its interesting qualities. For instance, a damaged detector cell in the sinogram will look like a vertical line because the same detector is out for all views.

Like this, if you look at a sinogram and see that one row is wholly different from the others, it means that something—like a tube arc—happened within that view (i.e., tube spit).

The next procedure we want to discuss is the conversion of the sinogram into an image. That method is known as picture reconstruction.

Using the back-projection technique to construct the image would be the logical first step as we are aware that it operates in reverse to the forward-projection procedure. So, let's look into what happens when we simply use back projection to create a picture.

As we previously demonstrated, the back-projection process will distribute the information back into the image for each view. One example you can utilize is the back-projection technique, which is similar to painting the image data back from each perspective, one view at a time.

Therefore, if the back-projection technique is only used for one perspective, the image will appear smeared. This is due to the artist's limited ability to make multiple passes across the canvas. As we just established, each back projection has information that is unique to that view only. That explains why, when only one projection's worth of information is used, the image looks so foggy.

This back projection, which began at the top, spread the information throughout the image. The advantage of computed tomography is its capacity to combine data from all viewpoints to produce an image.

As we add more views, you can see how the back-projection image fills in with the new data. For each perspective, we fill in the specifics that were noted along those ray paths.

We arrive at a picture that resembles the one we expected but is hazy after completing the back projection for each viewpoint.

Considering that iterative reconstruction and filtered back projection are the only two methods currently used in clinical settings to create CT images. Interpolation is a vital step that radiologic professionals frequently find difficult due to the mathematical concepts involved.

In this video, the back-projection method is explained in depth, as well as the fact that linear interpolation is just drawing a line and shifting it slightly in the direction determined by the slope of the line. In our final section, we cover interpolation in CT and why it is crucial to have a small display field of view (DFOV) for high-resolution imaging so that interpolation mostly takes place on the CT detector and not in the picture space.

2.5.2   Interactive reconstruction

Interactive reconstruction is a different possible technique to lessen the amount of noise present in the CT images. These techniques require significantly more processing than back projection since they aim to adjust for noise and other distortions. The method starts with an estimate and improves after several tries because iteration is used. Iterative reconstruction frequently starts with a regular filtered back-projection image. Then, a CT reconstruction is simulated using this basic premise. By looking at the difference (or 'error') in the reconstruction, you can obtain a better sense. Following that, this process is repeated for a certain number of cycles.

Approaches to iterative reconstruction replicate the noise and attenuation processes that take place in the real world. Thus, it usually performs better in high-noise situations (like scans with low radiation doses) and in highly high attenuation situations (like metal implants). As a trade-off, as was already established, the images also have a different subjective quality from filtered back projection.

Acquisition in Multi-slice CT scanner: The z-volume coverage speed, z-axis resolution and slice thickness of a single-slice CT are all influenced by the X-ray beam collimation or the thickness of the X-ray beam. Excellent z-axis resolution requires a thin X-ray collimation, whereas quick large volume coverage calls for a thick collimation. Users of single-slice CT are faced with competing needs when both high z-axis resolution and rapid volume coverage are needed. In a single-slice CT, the detector row collimation is either not used or included in the post-patient collimation of the X-ray beam.

One of the essential components of a multi-slice CT system is the multi-row detector array. The overall X-ray beam, which is still defined by the X-ray beam collimation, can be further divided into several subdivided beams that are decided by the detector row collimation, also known as the detector row aperture. Although the total X-ray collimation still reflects the volume coverage speed, the detector row collimation determines the z-axis resolution, or the thickness of the slice, in the multi-slice CT system. According to tradition, D and d are both determined at the rotational axis. If the gaps, or dead region, between nearby detector rows, are small and can be disregarded, the detector row spacing is equal to the detector row collimation, also known as d. The detector row collimation or spacing, d, and the X-ray beam collimation have the following relationship:

$$d(\text{mm}) = \frac{D(\text{mm})}{N}$$

where N is the number of detector row.

In a single-slice CT, the collimation of the detector row and the collimation of the X-ray beam are identical and interchangeable. Only $1/N$ of the X-ray beam collimation is applied to the detector row collimation in a multi-slice CT scan. This greatly improved relaxed connection allows for large volume coverage speed and good z-axis resolution at the same time. The volume coverage speed performance frequently improves as detector row N increases.

2.6 Cone-beam geometry versus parallel fan-beams geometry

Cone-beam geometry and parallel fan-beam geometry are two distinct configurations used in computed tomography (CT) imaging. Each geometry has its advantages and limitations, making them suitable for different applications.

2.6.1   Cone-beam geometry

In cone-beam CT, also known as 3D CT or cone-beam computed tomography (CBCT), the X-ray source emits a cone-shaped beam that encompasses a larger volume of the patient or object being imaged. The detector array, positioned opposite the X-ray source, captures the transmitted radiation from various angles as both the X-ray source and detector rotate around the object. This configuration allows for the acquisition of a complete 3D dataset in a single rotation.

2.6.1.1   Advantages of cone-beam geometry
Efficiency: Cone-beam CT captures a 3D volume in a single rotation, reducing scanning time and patient exposure compared to traditional step-and-shoot fan-beam methods.

3D Visualization: The captured volumetric data enables detailed 3D visualization and reconstructions, making it particularly useful in applications such as dental and orthopaedic imaging, where spatial relationships are crucial.

2.6.1.2   Limitations of cone-beam geometry
Image Artefacts: Cone-beam geometry is prone to cone-beam artefacts, which can distort images due to incomplete data sampling and scatter.

Dose Distribution: The wider X-ray beam used in cone-beam CT can result in uneven dose distribution within the patient, potentially leading to dose variations.

2.6.2   Parallel beam geometry

In parallel fan-beam CT, the X-ray source emits a fan-shaped beam that is parallel to the object being imaged. The detector array, positioned on the opposite side, captures the X-rays after they pass through the object. The source and detector array can be rotated around the object or moved linearly to capture projections from multiple angles.

2.6.2.1   Advantages of parallel fan-beam geometry
Reduced Artefacts: Parallel fan-beam geometry is less prone to cone-beam artefacts, leading to clearer and more accurate images.

Dose Distribution: The parallel X-ray beam provides more uniform dose distribution, minimizing variations in patient dose.

2.6.2.2   Limitations of parallel fan-beam geometry
Scanning Time: Parallel fan-beam CT requires multiple rotations or translations to acquire a complete 3D dataset, leading to longer scanning times compared to cone-beam CT.

2D Imaging: While it can be extended to 3D imaging through multiple rotations, parallel fan-beam geometry is inherently better suited for 2D imaging applications.

In summary, cone-beam geometry and parallel fan-beam geometry each have their strengths and weaknesses. Cone-beam CT is well-suited for applications requiring rapid

3D volumetric imaging, such as dental and interventional radiology. On the other hand, parallel fan-beam CT is often preferred for applications where image quality and reduced artefacts are essential, such as medical diagnostic CT scans. The choice between these geometries depends on the specific clinical or research requirements and the trade-offs between imaging speed, image quality, and dose considerations (Fig. 2.8).

2.6.3   Parallel fan-beam procedure

2.6.3.1   Acquisition

This section details out the entire procedures of the acquisitions of parallel fan-beam geometry.

2.6.3.1.1   Scan projection radiographs

It analyze projections when doing diagnostic imaging, radiographs, sometimes referred to as radiographic projections or X-ray projections, use X-rays to create two-dimensional images of the patient's body. These radiographs give important insight into the patient's interior anatomy, which helps with the diagnosis and assessment of a variety of medical disorders. An explanation of scan projection radiography is provided below.

2.6.3.1.2   Generation of X-rays

X-ray machines, which emit X-ray beams, are used to create scan projection radiographs. An X-ray tube, which emits high-energy photons, produces the X-ray beam. On one side of the patient's body is the X-ray tube, and on the other is an X-ray detector (such as a film cassette or digital detector).

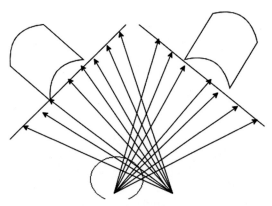

FIGURE 2.8 Filter back propagation.

2.6.3.1.3   X-ray beam interaction

The X-ray beam interacts with many tissues and structures as it travels through the body of the patient. The density and makeup of the tissues they encounter determine the degree to which the X-ray photons are attenuated or absorbed. Less dense structures, like air or soft tissues, allow more X-ray photons to pass through and appear as darker areas on the radiograph. Dense structures, like bones, absorb more X-ray photons and appear as bright white areas on the radiograph.

Patient Positioning: The patient is positioned appropriately to take radiographs of particular bodily regions or structures. Depending on the area of interest, several projections, including anteroposterior (AP), posteroanterior (PA), lateral, oblique or specialized projections, may be utilized. In order to avoid distortion or superimposition of features and to provide a correct portrayal of the anatomy, proper patient posture is crucial.

2.6.3.1.4   Image acquisition

The X-ray machine is turned on after the patient is in place, and X-ray beams are pointed in its direction. An X-ray image is captured on the detector as the X-ray photons interact with the tissues as they move through the body. In conventional radiography, the picture is recorded on a film cassette, developed, and then viewed as a physical radiograph. An electronic detector is used to capture the X-ray image in digital radiography, which is subsequently processed and shown on a computer screen.

2.6.3.1.5   Interpretation and diagnosis

Clinicians and radiologists review the radiographs produced by scan projections to understand the results and establish a diagnosis. In order to find anomalies, fractures, tumours, infections or other disorders, they evaluate the structures, densities and interactions between anatomical components. To acquire more detailed information, the radiographs may be compared to earlier research or other imaging modalities.

2.6.3.1.6   Advantages and limitations

Scan projection radiographs are advantageous for diagnostic imaging in several ways. They are accessible, reasonably quick and reasonably priced. They can identify anomalies in the chest, abdomen, extremities and other parts of the body and provide useful information regarding bone structures. The two-dimensional character of radiographs, which can lead to overlapping structures and a restricted ability to examine soft tissues, is one of their drawbacks. Additionally, as radiographs expose the user to ionizing radiation, radiation safety measures must be taken.

Detection, diagnosis and monitoring of a variety of medical disorders are all made possible by scan projection radiographs, which are a crucial imaging modality in healthcare. They are an important first step in the diagnostic process and frequently work in conjunction with more sophisticated imaging techniques to provide a thorough assessment of the patient's health.

2.7 Single-slice CT

One slice of the patient's body is photographed at a time during single-slice computed tomography, which is also referred to as conventional or axial CT. A single X-ray source and detector pair rotate around the patient in this method, collecting a sequence of two-dimensional images or slices that are then layered to provide a three-dimensional depiction of the scanned region. Here's an explanation of single-slice CT.

2.7.1   X-ray generation and detection

A detector assembly and an X-ray tube make up single-slice CT scanners. A focussed beam of X-ray photons is emitted by the X-ray tube and travels through the body of the patient. The X-rays that are emitted from the patient are captured by the detector assembly, which is placed across from the X-ray tube. It measures the transmitted X-ray intensity, which is inversely proportional to the X-ray attenuation caused by the various tissues encountered.

Patient Positioning: The gantry, a sizeable ring-shaped structure housing the X-ray tube and detector assembly, is entered after the patient has been placed on a mobile table. To reduce motion artefacts, the patient is typically instructed to lie still and hold their breath throughout the scan.

2.7.2   X-ray beam rotation

The X-ray tube and detector assembly spin encircling the subject during a single-slice CT scan. A variety of X-ray projections are taken while they spin at various angles. These projections are gathered at regular intervals, usually in 1-degree increments, and the result is a collection of X-ray images captured from various angles.

2.7.3   Image reconstruction

A procedure known as image reconstruction is used to transform the collection of two-dimensional X-ray images into a three-dimensional representation of the scanned area once the X-ray projections are recorded. The reconstruction methodology determines the attenuation values of the tissues at each voxel within the scanned volume using mathematical methods like filtered back projection or iterative reconstruction.

2.7.4   Slice thickness and interval

The thickness of each reconstructed slice in single-slice CT can vary, often falling between 1 mm and several millimetres. The table increment, which is the distance the patient is shifted longitudinally between two succeeding X-ray projections, determines the distance or interval between neighbouring slices. The spatial resolution of the reconstructed volume is determined by this spacing, which also influences how much neighbouring slices overlap.

2.7.5 Clinical applications

In several medical disciplines, single-slice CT has been extensively employed for diagnostic purposes. It is especially helpful for visualizing the abdomen and pelvis, diagnosing fractures, imaging bony structures and assessing lung illnesses. However, single-slice CT scanners are constrained in terms of scan speed, coverage and the capacity to record minute details or dynamic processes in comparison to more sophisticated multi-slice CT scanners.

Multi-slice CT technology has largely superseded single-slice CT in recent years since it provides quicker scans, better picture quality and volumetric imaging capabilities. Single-slice CT is still a possibility, nevertheless, in some circumstances where the restricted imaging capabilities are adequate or when multi-slice CT is not easily accessible.

2.7.6 Windowing

By choosing a certain range of pixel values and allocating them to a specific range of grey levels or colours, windowing is a technique used to modify the display of computed tomography (CT) images. Adjusting the image's brightness and contrast, it enables radiologists and doctors to more effectively visualize certain tissues or structures of interest. An explanation of windowing in CT scans is provided below.

2.7.6.1 Pixel intensity range
A CT image is made up of a matrix of pixels, each of which corresponds to a volume element (or 'voxel') inside the scanned anatomy and has an associated X-ray attenuation value. Hounsfield Units (HU) are the standard unit of measurement for these attenuation levels. The HU scale gives solid substances like bone positive values and air a value of -1000 HU. Water is given a value of 0.

2.7.6.2 Window level
The midway of the range of pixel values that will be displayed with the best brightness is determined by the window level, also known as the centre or the brightness. It relates to the shade of grey or colour allocated to the window's centre-positioned pixel value. Typically, the window level is selected based on the tissue or structure that the radiologist wants to see.

2.7.6.3 Window width
The span of pixel values that will be translated to various shades of grey or colours is determined by the window width, commonly referred to as the range or contrast. It establishes the size of the visible range of pixel values around the window level. The amount of contrast that is seen in the image depends on the window's width.

2.7.6.4   Effect of windowing

Different anatomical components or disorders can be emphasized or muted by modifying the window's level and width.

Narrow Window Width: Tissues with various attenuation values will be more contrasted since a narrow window width emphasizes a small range of pixel values. Structures with minute density variations, including soft tissue or contrast-enhanced vessels, can be seen with this technique.

Wide Window Width: Because a wide window width shows a wider range of pixel values, the contrast is reduced. This can be used to visualize structures having a large range of attenuation values, such as the lungs or bones, where the attenuation values of various tissues vary considerably.

Bone Window: This option draws attention to high-density features, such as bones. It often has a high window level and a broad window width, which improves the visibility of the bone structures and reduces the visibility of the nearby soft tissues.

Lung Window: The setup for the lung window is ideal for viewing the lung parenchyma. While decreasing the visibility of bones and other high-density structures, it often has a low window level and a broad window width, which improves the visualization of lung tissue.

Radiologists and clinicians choose the best window settings based on the clinical query, the target anatomical structure and the intended diagnostic outcome. Within the same CT scan, multiple window settings may be used to evaluate various regions or diseases.

Radiologists can increase the visibility of particular tissues or structures, boost diagnostic precision and promote improved CT picture interpretation by using windowing techniques. The anatomy may be visualized more precisely and specifically, allowing doctors to gather crucial data for diagnosis and therapy planning.

2.8 Image quality

CT image quality refers to the clarity, resolution, and diagnostic value of the images produced by a CT scanner. Accurate diagnosis, therapy planning, and patient monitoring are dependent on high-quality CT images across a variety of medical disciplines. Image quality is influenced by a number of variables, including as noise levels, artefact suppression, contrast resolution, and spatial resolution. While contrast resolution describes the ability to discriminate between tissues with various densities, spatial resolution controls the CT scanner's capacity to identify minute structures and details within the scanned anatomy. Later of this section provides a detail description of Noise and other image artefacts.

2.8.1   Noise

The quality of thoracic CT scans can be impacted by a variety of noises, which can reduce diagnostic precision. Here are the various noises that can be heard during thoracic CT imaging:

Shot noise, or quantum noise: The nature of X-ray photon detection includes quantum noise. There is a stochastic variance in the quantity of X-ray photons discovered, which causes intensity changes from pixel to pixel. Particularly in regions with low X-ray photon counts, quantum noise manifests as a grainy or speckled pattern in the image. It can compromise the detection of fine objects like lung nodules and reduce picture clarity.

Electronic noise: The CT system's electronic parts, such as the detectors and amplifiers, are the source of electronic noise. It causes pixel-level differences by introducing random fluctuations into the signal during capture. Electronic noise can appear in an image as a consistent background noise, lowering contrast overall and possibly hiding minute features.

Through the use of numerous methods, including the optimization of acquisition parameters, sophisticated reconstruction algorithms, and noise reduction filters, these noises and artefacts can be reduced in thoracic CT imaging. Additionally, motion artefacts can be reduced with the aid of patient preparation techniques like breath-holding or respiratory gating. Thoracic imaging specialists in radiologists can use their visual interpretation abilities to distinguish real abnormalities from noise and artefacts, resulting in appropriate diagnosis and treatment.

2.8.2   Image artefact

In radiography, it has been noted that a few chemicals that cannot exist on both normal and diseased tissues may emerge on the images. This distortion could result from the patient moving during the scanning process, from the presence of a metallic body, or from the presence of any barrier. There are various forms of artefacts that might appear in CT images, including noise, ring artefacts, partial volume effects and motion artefacts.

2.8.2.1   *Partial volume effect*

An imaging phenomenon known as the partial volume effect can be seen in computed tomography (CT) images, especially when thoracic imaging is being discussed. It develops as a result of the CT scanner's low spatial resolution and the mixing of several tissue types inside a single voxel.

A CT scanner measures the attenuation of X-rays as they go through the body to produce an image. The scanner's resolution is constrained, so rather than a single point, each voxel in the generated image represents a volume of tissue. The boundaries between entities in thoracic CT imaging that have different densities, such as lung tissue, blood arteries and solid organs, may not be precisely caught by the scanner.

As a result, voxels at the interfaces between different tissues can contain a mixture of attenuations, causing blurring or inaccuracies in the image. This blurring effect is known as the partial volume effect. It occurs because the scanner assigns a single attenuation value to the entire voxel, even though different tissues may be present within that voxel.

The partial volume effect can lead to several challenges in thoracic CT image analysis, including

1. Segmentation: Due to the partial volume effect's blurring, it might be difficult to precisely segment lung tissue, blood veins and other structures. Structure boundaries may appear less defined, making it challenging to precisely distinguish and identify them.
2. Quantification: When estimating the size or volume of certain structures, such as blood arteries or lung nodules, the partial volume effect may introduce errors. Measurement errors may result from mixed attenuations within voxels.
3. Visualization: Thoracic CT images' aesthetic appeal may be impacted by the partial volume effect's blurring. Fine features and borders could not be as clearly defined, which could affect how well the photos can be understood.

To mitigate the partial volume effect, various techniques can be employed, such as

1. Smoothing and Filtering: By employing the appropriate smoothing and filtering techniques, it is feasible to reduce noise and enhance the visibility of structures that are impacted by the partial volume effect.
2. Multi-Slice Reconstruction: To improve spatial resolution and eliminate the partial volume effect, multi-slice reconstruction techniques are used.
3. Advanced Reconstruction Algorithms: Iterative reconstruction techniques, for example, are advanced reconstruction algorithms that can be used to enhance image quality and lessen the blurring effect.
4. The partial volume effect and its effects on image interpretation and analysis should be understood by radiologists and academics working with thoracic CT images. Selecting the best approaches for precise segmentation, quantification and visualization of thoracic structures is aided by an understanding of this phenomenon.
How partial volume effects creates problem in pulmonary nodule detection
5. In computed tomography (CT) images, lung nodule diagnosis might be difficult due to partial volume effects. Partial volume effects may have the following effects on the precision and dependability of pulmonary nodule detection:
6. Smoothing and Blurring The distinctions between pulmonary nodules and the surrounding lung parenchyma can become muddled and smoothed as a result of partial volume effects. It may become more challenging to distinguish and characterize the nodules because of this blurring effect, which can lessen the visibility and sharpness of nodule edges.

7. Nodule Size Estimation: The size of pulmonary nodules may not be accurately estimated due to partial volume effects. A nodule may span numerous voxels, therefore the average attenuation inside the voxel might be a combination of attenuations in the nodule and the lung tissue around it. The nodule size may be underestimated or overestimated as a result of this mixing effect, which may influence size-based diagnostic criteria and longitudinal surveillance.

8. Nodule Density Assessment: It is crucial to accurately quantify nodule density to differentiate between benign and malignant nodules. Density measurements may be off due to partial volume effects that combine nodule attenuation with surrounding lung tissue attenuation. This may affect how pulmonary nodules are described and categorized.

9. False-Positive and False-Negative Results: The lung parenchyma surrounding nodules may exhibit erroneous densities and attenuation fluctuations due to partial volume effects. These changes can cause false-positive and false-negative results in the detection of nodules because they can be mistaken for nodules or disguise the appearance of real nodules.

To address the challenges posed by partial volume effects in pulmonary nodule detection, several strategies can be employed

10. Thin-Slice Imaging: By lowering the volume averaging within each voxel and enhancing spatial resolution, acquiring CT images with thinner slice thickness can help alleviate partial volume effects. This makes it possible to more clearly see and define the boundaries of nodules.

11. Advanced Reconstruction Techniques: Iterative or model-based reconstructions are examples of advanced reconstruction methods that can be used to improve image quality and lessen the impacts of partial volume effects. These methods try to maintain small details and increase spatial resolution.

12. Multi-Planar Assessment: The constraints brought on by partial volume effects can be solved by analyzing CT images in various planes (axial, coronal and sagittal), as well as by using 3D visualization. Considering nodules from various angles allows for a more thorough knowledge of their properties.

13. Segmentation and Region-Growing Techniques: Employing sophisticated segmentation algorithms or region growing techniques that account for partial volume effects can aid in accurate delineation and characterization of pulmonary nodules.

2.8.2.2 Motion artefact

The constraints brought on by partial volume effects can be solved by using 3D visualization and evaluating CT scans in various planes (axial, coronal and sagittal). A more thorough grasp of the properties of nodules can be obtained by evaluating them from various angles.

1. Blurring: Structures in an image may get blurred as a result of rapid movement during the acquisition of the image. This fuzziness can hide minute details and make it challenging to tell between nearby structures.
2. Streaking: In the CT picture, sudden movement or motion in a particular direction can produce streak-like artefacts. These streaks, which commonly come from high-density structures like bones or thick organs, can appear as lines or bands across the image.
3. Misalignment: Misalignment artefacts might appear if the patient's position significantly changes between slices or scans. This may lead to uneven anatomical registration between slices, which makes it difficult to analyze the pictures coherently.
4. Ghosting: Ghosting artefacts appear in future photos when there is lingering signal from earlier acquisitions or movements. This may result in overlapping or blurry views of the structures, which could be confusing or interpreted incorrectly.

The presence of motion artefacts can impact various aspects of thoracic CT image analysis, including

1. Image quality: Motion artefacts reduce the sharpness and clarity of structures by degrading the overall image quality. This may make it harder to provide an accurate diagnosis and identify anomalies.
2. Measurement and segmentation mistakes can be caused by motion artefacts, which can also affect quantitative assessments of features like blood arteries or lung nodules. The precision of a structure's delineation and measurement can be impacted by its distorted appearance.
3. Motion artefacts can make it more challenging for radiologists to interpret thoracic CT images. It might be tough to distinguish between normal and pathological structures or to spot mild diseases because of the blurring, streaking and misalignment.

In order to minimize motion artefacts in thoracic CT imaging, several strategies can be employed:

1. Breathing Holding: Asking the patient to hold their breath during image capture can assist lessen the motion artefacts brought on by breathing motion. It is possible to use breath-hold techniques or synchronized imaging with particular respiratory cycle stages.
2. Monitoring and Gating: To reduce motion artefacts, real-time monitoring of patient movements during the scan and gating techniques, in which images are taken only at certain points in the cardiac or respiratory cycles, can be utilized.
3. Patients who are unable to comply or hold their breath long enough during the scan may in some circumstances be given sedation or anaesthesia.
4. Techniques for Post-Processing: Advanced post-processing techniques, including image registration or motion correction algorithms, can be employed to correct motion artefacts and improve image quality.

5. Working with thoracic CT images requires radiologists and researchers to be aware of motion artefacts and their potential effects. Using post-processing techniques and taking the right precautions to reduce these artefacts can improve image quality and make it easier to interpret and analyze thoracic anatomy accurately.

   How motion artefact creates problems in pulmonary nodule detection:

The diagnosis of pulmonary nodules in computed tomography (CT) images might be complicated by motion artefacts. Motion artefacts can influence the precision and dependability of lung nodule identification in the following ways:

6. Motion during image capture might cause lung structures, particularly nodules, to become blurred or smudged. The sharpness and clarity of nodule boundaries may be diminished as a result of this blurring effect, making nodule detection and delineation more difficult.

7. Nodule Distortion: Pulmonary nodules can become distorted in size and shape due to rapid or erratic patient movement. Due to this distortion, it may be challenging to determine the nodules' exact size, shape and margins—all crucial factors in the characterization and classification of nodules.

8. Misalignment: Motion artefacts can cause separate image slices or scans to be out of alignment, which makes it difficult to connect and compare nodules across various pictures. Accurate nodule monitoring, measurement, and follow-up assessment may be hampered by this misalignment.

9. False-Positive and False-Negative Results: Motion artefacts can cause erroneous densities, streaks or blurring in the lung parenchyma surrounding nodules, which can produce false positive or false negative results in the detection of nodules. These artefacts may look like nodules or obscure them, leading to misinterpretations.

   To address the challenges posed by motion artefacts in pulmonary nodule detection, several strategies can be employed:

10. Breath-Hold Technique: Asking the patient to hold their breath while the image is being taken helps lessen the number of motion artefacts brought on by breathing motion. It is possible to use breath-hold techniques or synchronized imaging with particular respiratory cycle stages.

11. Monitoring and Gating: To reduce motion artefacts, real-time monitoring of patient movements throughout the scan and gating techniques, in which images are taken only at certain points in the respiratory or cardiac cycles, can be utilized.

12. Post-processing Techniques: To correct for motion artefacts and enhance image quality, advanced post-processing techniques can be used, such as image registration or motion correction algorithms. By aligning and combining pictures, these methods can lessen the effect of motion on nodule detection.

13. Multi-Planar Assessment: In order to get over motion artefacts' restrictions, it is sometimes helpful to evaluate CT images in different planes (axial, coronal and

sagittal). It might be more accurate and give a more thorough insight of nodules' characteristics to evaluate them from several angles.

Awareness of the potential impact of motion artefacts on pulmonary nodule detection is crucial for radiologists and researchers. Implementing techniques to minimize motion artefacts, utilizing advanced imaging protocols and post-processing methods, and incorporating multi-planar assessment can help improve the accuracy and reliability of pulmonary nodule detection in CT images.

2.8.2.3 Beam hardening

Beam hardening artefacts in thoracic CT images are a type of image distortion that occurs due to the interaction of X-rays with different densities of tissues within the thorax. These artefacts are particularly prominent in CT scans of the chest region, where the presence of various structures with different attenuations can lead to beam hardening effects. Here's a further explanation of beam hardening artefacts in thoracic CT images.

2.8.2.3.1 Principle of beam hardening

The X-ray beam used in CT imaging travels through soft tissues, bones and lungs, among other densities of tissue. As the X-rays pass through these objects, they are attenuated to variable degrees. The amount of X-rays absorbed increases with the tissue's density. The amount of X-ray energy that reaches the detector is diminished as a result of this absorption.

But compared to higher-energy X-rays, lower-energy X-rays are often absorbed more. The lower-energy X-rays are gradually filtered out as the X-ray beam travels through the body, leaving behind a harder or higher-energy beam. Beam hardening artefacts result from the mismatch between the assumed energy spectrum utilized for picture reconstruction and the actual spectrum caused by this spectral change.

2.8.2.3.2 Appearance of beam hardening artefacts

In the CT scans, beam hardening artefacts often take the form of dark bands or streaks. These streaks can spread into surrounding tissues, such as the lungs and soft tissues, after starting in dense structures like the mediastinum, ribs, or the spinal column. Streaks might make it difficult to adequately analyze structures in the thoracic region and hide anatomical details.

2.8.2.3.3 Causes and factors influencing beam hardening artefacts

Several factors can contribute to the severity and extent of beam hardening artefacts in thoracic CT images.

1. High-density structures: Bones and calcifications in the chest, such as ribs or vascular calcifications, can significantly influence beam hardening artefacts.
2. Large patient size: Patients with larger body sizes tend to exhibit more pronounced beam hardening effects due to the increased thickness of tissues the X-ray beam must pass through.

3. Low-kilovoltage imaging: Because different tissues attenuate X-rays differently, using lower kilovoltage settings during picture capture can worsen beam hardening artefacts.
4. Metal artefacts: The presence of metal implants or other devices in the chest might have a beam hardening effect and leave streaked artefacts in the tissues around it.

2.8.2.3.4 Minimizing and managing beam hardening artefacts

To minimize the impact of beam hardening artefacts in thoracic CT imaging, several techniques can be employed:

1. Choosing the right tube voltage can help to lessen the occurrence of beam hardening artefacts.
2. Iterative reconstruction algorithms: To lessen the impacts of beam hardening and enhance image quality, advanced reconstruction techniques can be used.
3. Techniques for reducing metal artefacts: When metal implants or devices are present, specialized algorithms and protocols can be used to reduce metal artefacts.
4. Beam hardening correction: Post-acquisition beam hardening artefacts may be corrected using particular software or techniques. These techniques try to gauge and account for spectrum shifts in the X-ray beam.

    Radiologists and researchers must be aware of beam hardening artefacts in thoracic CT scans to recognize and correctly interpret image findings. Thoracic CT pictures can be made more diagnostically accurate by using methods like altering imaging parameters, applying sophisticated reconstruction algorithms and using metal artefact reduction procedures.

    In computed tomography (CT) images, pulmonary nodule detection may be hindered by beam hardening artefacts. Beam hardening artefacts can have the following effects on pulmonary nodule detection's accuracy and dependability

5. Positive- and negative-false results: False-positive detections can result from beam hardening artefacts that produce fictitious densities and streaks in the lung area. These artefacts may resemble or hide pulmonary nodules, causing missed or incorrectly identified nodules as well as false negative detections.
6. Reduced Nodule Contrast: In the lung parenchyma surrounding the nodules, beam hardening artefacts can produce streaks and shading effects. As a result, it may be harder to detect and correctly identify nodules from other structures. This may reduce the contrast between the nodules and the surrounding tissue.
7. Shape Distortion: The pulmonary nodules' shape and borders may be altered by the streaks and shadows produced by beam hardening artefacts. Due to this distortion, it may be challenging to precisely determine the nodules' size, shape and margins—important factors for nodule characterization and categorization.
8. Increased Reader Uncertainty: Beam hardening artefacts might make it more difficult for radiologists and automated detection systems to make accurate diagnoses. Due to the confusing effects of beam hardening artefacts, radiologists may have trouble clearly diagnosing and characterizing lung nodules.

To mitigate the impact of beam hardening artefacts on pulmonary nodule detection, several strategies can be employed:

1. Image Reconstruction Techniques: You can lessen the effect of beam hardening artefacts on the CT images by using iterative reconstruction algorithms or precise correction techniques.
2. Dual-Energy CT: Dual-energy CT imaging, which makes use of two different X-ray energies, can give more details to help distinguish between beam hardening artefacts and real pulmonary nodules. The accuracy of nodule detection and characterization can be increased with the use of this technique.
3. Image post-processing techniques, such as noise reduction algorithms or adaptive filtering, can be used to improve the visibility of pulmonary nodules and lessen the sight of beam hardening artefacts.
4. Multi-View Assessment: Using 3D visualisation tools and reviewing CT scans in various planes (such as axial, coronal and sagittal) can help to get beyond the restrictions imposed by beam hardening artefacts. These methods lessen the reliance on potentially harmed picture slices by offering a thorough assessment of lung nodules from several angles.

Radiologists and researchers must be aware of the potential effects of beam hardening artefacts on the detection of lung nodules. The accuracy and reliability of pulmonary nodule diagnosis in CT images can be increased by putting strategies in place to reduce these artefacts and by using a multimodal strategy that takes clinical and contextual information into account.

2.8.2.4 Ring artefacts

In computed tomography (CT) imaging, notably thoracic CT scans, ring artefacts are one sort of image artefact that might appear. They appear as varying picture intensities in the form of ring- or circle-shaped patterns. Ring artefacts can be distracting to the eye and can affect how accurately the CT scans can be interpreted and diagnosed.

2.8.2.4.1 Cause of ring artefacts

1. Inconsistencies or flaws in the CT scanner's detectors or data collecting system are the main causes of ring artefacts in CT pictures. These flaws may be caused by a number of things, such as:
2. Defective or damaged detector elements can cause changes in X-ray attenuation values and ring artefacts. If one or more CT scanner detector elements are defective or have differing sensitivities, this can happen.
3. An irregularity in the X-ray beam: Ring artefacts can develop due to differences in the detected signal brought on by non-uniformities in the X-ray beam, such as changes in X-ray intensity or energy.

4. Corrupted projection data: When reconstructing an image, rings may appear due to errors or inconsistencies in the raw projection data that were captured during the scanning process, such as faulty calibration or data acquisition issues.

2.8.2.4.2 Appearance of ring artefacts

In thoracic CT scans, rings or rings-like patterns with alternating zones of greater and lower image intensity are the most common form of ring artefacts. Depending on the type and intensity of the artefact, the rings may be whole or broken. Ring artefacts can emerge in a variety of shapes, sizes and locations.

2.8.2.4.2.1 Impact of ring artefacts on the CT images of the thorax Ring artefacts can have several implications for thoracic CT imaging

1. Ring artefacts can impair the clarity and appearance of anatomical structures, such as pulmonary nodules, lung parenchyma and blood vessels. Image quality might also be affected. The capacity to identify and characterise anomalies as well as the diagnostic accuracy may be impacted by this degradation.
2. Diagnostic Accuracy: Ring artefacts can introduce erroneous imaging characteristics and alter how pulmonary structures appear. This can result in pathology being misinterpreted or misdiagnosed, such as when a ring artefact is mistaken for a real anatomical anomaly or vice versa.
3. Quantitative Analysis: Ring artefacts can affect quantitative data, including volumetric analysis, nodule size, and density. These artefacts could induce inaccuracies into the readings, which would compromise the ability to accurately identify and track pulmonary abnormalities over time.

2.8.2.4.2.2 How ring artefact create problems in pulmonary nodule detection When detecting pulmonary nodules, ring artefacts can pose a number of problems that could compromise the process's accuracy and dependability. The following are some ways that ring artefacts may affect the identification of pulmonary nodules:

1. Positive false alarms: Circular or ring-shaped markings known as ring artefacts might resemble lung nodules in appearance. These artefacts may produce fictitious circular formations or changes in density, resulting in false-positive detections. These artefacts may be falsely identified as nodules by radiologists or automated detection systems, leading to pointless follow-up exams or procedures.
2. Nodule masking: Ring artefacts can hide or partially cover pulmonary nodules from view. The nodules may be obscured by the circular patterns and intensity changes associated with ring artefacts, making them harder to see or locate. This may cause nodules to be ignored or disregarded, leading to false-negative detections.
3. The shape, size and borders of pulmonary nodules can be distorted by ring artefacts, which can also alter other nodule characteristics. It might be difficult to precisely determine the properties of nodules because of the abnormalities or changes that the presence of these artefacts can cause in their appearance. Nodule classification, staging and treatment planning may be impacted by this distortion.

4. Ring artefacts may reduce the contrast between nodules and the lung tissue surrounding them. The intensity changes brought on by these artefacts might lessen the contrast between nodules and healthy lung parenchyma, which can make nodules less visible. This may make it harder to tell nodules apart from nearby structures, making it more likely that nodules may be missed or misidentified.

To mitigate the impact of ring artefacts on pulmonary nodule detection, several strategies can be employed:

1. Quality Control: Routine quality control procedures, such as scanner upkeep, calibration and detector performance evaluations, can lessen the frequency and severity of ring artefacts.
2. Modern Reconstruction Methods: Ring artefacts can be reduced and picture quality can be improved for nodule detection by using advanced image reconstruction algorithms, such as iterative reconstruction methods or metal artefact reduction approaches.
3. Retrospective Correction: After picture acquisition, ring artefacts might be less visible by using post-processing methods like image filtering or artefact correction algorithms. These methods are intended to improve the visibility of nodules and bring them back to their previous appearance.
4. Multi-Planar Assessment: In order to get beyond the restrictions put forward by ring artefacts, CT images should be assessed in a variety of planes (axial, coronal and sagittal). It might be more accurate and give a more thorough insight of nodules' characteristics to evaluate them from several angles.
5. Radiologists and researchers must be aware of the existence and features of ring artefacts in order to detect lung nodules. Ring artefacts present a number of challenges that can be mitigated by employing methods to reduce these artefacts during image acquisition, applying advanced reconstruction algorithms, and incorporating multiplanar assessment. These methods can also increase the precision and dependability of pulmonary nodule detection in CT images.

2.8.2.4.3 Minimizing and managing ring artefacts
Efforts are made to minimize and manage ring artefacts in thoracic CT imaging.

1. Quality Control: Identifying and addressing probable sources of ring artefacts can be aided by routine CT scanner maintenance and calibration, which includes detector performance checks and system calibrations.
2. Utilizing sophisticated image reconstruction techniques, such as iterative reconstruction approaches, can lessen the effects of ring artefacts and enhance image quality.
3. After image acquisition and reconstruction, ring artefacts may be corrected or made less visible using specific image processing techniques or post-processing algorithms.

4. Retrospective methods: In some circumstances, if ring artefacts are severe or persistent, other imaging methods, such as rescanning the patient or utilizing different imaging modalities, may be taken into consideration to get higher-quality pictures for a precise diagnosis.
5. Radiologists and researchers must be aware of the existence and features of ring artefacts in thoracic CT images. The quality and diagnostic value of thoracic CT scans can be increased by using ways to reduce these artefacts during image capture, adopting advanced reconstruction algorithms, and applying artefact correction procedures.

2.8.2.5   Streak artefact

A specific kind of image artefact that can appear in thoracic computed tomography (CT) pictures is called a streak artefact. They appear as dark areas, intense streaks or bands, or bands that span the entire image. The quality and diagnostic value of the CT scans can be negatively impacted by streak artefacts, which can happen for a number of reasons. A description of streak artefacts in thoracic CT images is given below:

2.8.2.5.1   Cause of streak artefacts

Streak artefacts in thoracic CT images can be caused by several factors, including

1. Metallic Objects: The presence of metallic objects within or close to the imaging region, such as surgical clips, pacemakers or prosthetic devices, might result in streak artefacts. These objects can result in streaks extending from the object in the image due to beam hardness, scattering or photon starvation.
2. Dense Structures: X-rays can be attenuated more by dense structures like bones or calcifications than by surrounding tissues. The X-ray beam is unevenly attenuated as a result, which might result in streak artefacts extending from these dense structures.
3. Patient Motion: During picture capture, motion from the patient—such as sneezing, breathing or unintentional movement—can produce streak artefacts. The projection data may become inconsistent due to the motion, resulting in streaks or blur in the reconstructed images.
4. Limited angular coverage or insufficient data gathering may result in insufficient projection data, which in some situations might result in streak artefacts. This could happen if the patient's breath-hold is not maintained consistently or if there are scanning process technical difficulties.

2.8.2.5.2   Appearance of streak artefacts

In thoracic CT images, streak artefacts generally show up as dark patches, high intensity streaks or bands, or both. Depending on the underlying cause of the artefact, the streaks' direction, length and intensity can change. The visibility of anatomical structures, such as pulmonary nodules, blood arteries or lung parenchyma, might be obscured or distorted by streak artefacts.

2.8.2.5.3 Impact on thoracic CT images

Streak artefacts can have several implications for thoracic CT imaging:

1. Image Quality: Streak artefacts can reduce image quality by obfuscating anatomical structures and introducing erroneous intensity changes. As a result, lung nodules and other diagnostic characteristics may become less distinct and visible.
2. Diagnostic Accuracy: Streak artefacts can imitate or conceal real anatomical structures, resulting in a condition being misinterpreted or misdiagnosed. They make it difficult to precisely determine the characteristics of pulmonary nodules since they might conceal or alter their appearance.
3. Quantitative data, such as nodule size, density or volumetric analyses, can be inaccurate due to streak artefacts. These artefacts could induce inaccuracies into the readings, which would compromise the ability to accurately identify and track pulmonary abnormalities over time.

2.8.2.5.4 Minimizing and managing streak artefacts

4. In thoracic CT imaging, efforts are made to reduce and manage streak artefacts:
5. Patient Preparation: Reducing motion-related streak artefacts can be accomplished by ensuring patient cooperation and compliance during picture acquisition, such as by maintaining breath-hold instructions or minimizing motion.
6. Methods for Artefact Reduction: The impact of streak artefacts can be reduced and image quality can be increased by using specialized image reconstruction algorithms, such as metal artefact reduction algorithms or iterative reconstruction techniques.
7. Artefact Correction: After image acquisition, streak artefacts may be less visible by using post-processing techniques, such as image filtering or artefact correction algorithms. By improving diagnostic precision and restoring anatomical features to their original appearance.

Retrospective Techniques: In some circumstances, additional imaging techniques or sequences, such as dual-energy CT or alternative imaging modalities, may be taken into consideration to produce better-quality pictures for an accurate diagnosis if streak artefacts are severe or persistent.

Radiologists and researchers must be aware of the existence and characteristics of streak artefacts in thoracic CT images. The challenges posed by streak artefacts can be lessened by implementing methods to reduce these artefacts during image acquisition, utilizing advanced reconstruction algorithms, and incorporating artefact reduction and correction techniques. This will enhance the quality and diagnostic utility of thoracic CT images.

2.9 Projections on CT imaging

Projections in CT imaging refer to the raw data collected by the detector array as X-ray beams pass through the patient's body from multiple angles during a scan. The information on the attenuation of X-rays by the various body tissues and structures is contained in these raw data projections. CT scanners create a comprehensive dataset that captures a three-dimensional image of the inside anatomy by acquiring projections around the patient from different angles. These projections form the basis for the reconstruction of cross-sectional pictures using advanced mathematical techniques like iterative reconstruction and filtered back projection. CT imaging is a useful tool in contemporary medical practice because of its capacity to gather projections from several angles, which allows it to produce precise and detailed images that help with the diagnosis and management of a variety of medical disorders.

2.9.1 Multiplanar reconstruction

A method called multiplanar reconstruction (MPR) is used in computed tomography (CT) imaging to reformat obtained CT data into pictures in several planes. In addition to the axial plane, which is the default plane of CT pictures, it enables the visualization of anatomical structures in other planes. Better evaluation of pathology and complex anatomical features is made possible by MPR.

Multiplanar reconstruction in CT is performed as follows:

Collecting CT Data: During a CT scan, the body is imaged in cross-section using X-rays and a revolving X-ray tube. The axial plane, which consists of a number of slices or parts of the body, is where these images are obtained.

Reconstruction Algorithms: To reconstruct the images, specialized computer techniques are used to process the collected CT data. These methods recreate a 3D image of the scanned region based on the analysis of the X-ray attenuation values received from various projections.

Multiplanar reconstruction algorithms are used to produce reformatted images in different projections after the 3D dataset has been rebuilt. The most often employed planes in MPR are

a. Axial Projection: The most typical sort of CT scan projection is referred to as transverse or cross-sectional pictures. Axial projections involve a circular motion of the X-ray source and detector around the subject, gathering information from various perspectives. These data are rebuilt by the computer into horizontal cross-sectional images that show the anatomy of the body in layers. Due to the wide range of data, they provide regarding the size, shape and placement of organs, tumours and other anomalies, axial projections are essential for diagnosing a number of diseases.

b. Sagittal Projections: The left and right halves of the body are divided by the sagittal plane, which is used to rebuild CT scan data to create sagittal projections. These projections give a side view of the structures, enabling medical professionals to look at the body from a different angle. Sagittal pictures are very helpful for examining midline structures like the spinal cord, blood arteries and various organs. They are helpful in identifying problems such as spinal deformities, vascular anomalies and specific disorders of the central nervous system.

c. Coronal Projections: Coronal projections entail the division of the body into the front and back halves by reconstructing the CT scan data in the coronal plane. In addition to the knowledge gained from axial and sagittal projections, coronal pictures offer a perspective of structures from an anterior to posterior orientation. These projections are useful for assessing organs like the heart, lungs and digestive system. Coronal pictures are useful in the diagnosis of abdominal pathologies, heart anomalies and lung disorders (Fig. 2.9).

2.9.2   3D volume rendering

In order to construct a 3D representation of volumetric data, volume rendering is a complex visualization technique used in medical imaging, particularly in computed tomography (CT) and magnetic resonance imaging (MRI). For the purposes of diagnosis and surgical planning, it enables a more thorough understanding of the interior structures and their spatial relationships (Fig. 2.10).

By displaying 3D volumetric data on a 2D screen during the volume rendering process, an image that accurately depicts the volume's numerous structures and tissues is created. This is accomplished by giving each voxel (or 3D pixel) a colour and opacity based on its intensity value and location. The volume rendering equation expresses how the final pixel value is determined for each pixel on the 2D screen, providing a mathematical framework for this procedure.

The basic volume rendering equation is as follows:

$$C(x,y) = \int_0^\infty T(x,y,z) \cdot \sigma(x,y,z) \cdot E(x,y,z) \cdot L(x,y,z) dz$$

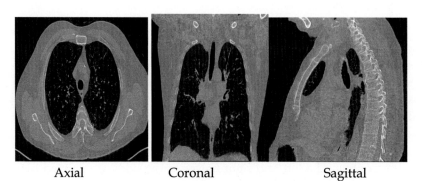

Axial   Coronal   Sagittal

FIGURE 2.9 Different projections.

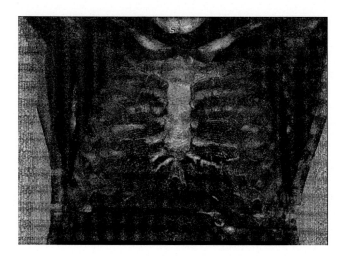

FIGURE 2.10 3D volume rendering.

where

- $C(x,y)$ is the final pixel colour at screen coordinates (x, y).
- $T(x,y,z)$ represents the transfer function, which maps the voxel intensity value to a colour and opacity value. The transfer function determines how different intensities are visualized, allowing users to emphasize specific tissues or structures in the volume.
- $\sigma(x,y,z)$ is the voxel's opacity or transparency, determining how much the voxel contributes to the final pixel colour. High opacity makes It more transparent and less visible.
- $E(x,y,z)$ is the emission coefficient, representing the amount of light emitted by the voxel. This term accounts for the intrinsic colour and brightness of the tissue or structure being visualized.
- $L(x,y,z)$ represents the light source's contribution to the final pixel colour, taking into account the direction and intensity of the light illuminating the volume.

From the observer's position through the volume to the perspective, the volume rendering equation is integrated along the ray. The final colour of each pixel on the 2D screen is represented by the resulting integral, which incorporates the contributions of all voxels along the ray.

Variations of this equation, such ray casting, are used in volume rendering techniques to quickly determine the final pixel colour for real-time or interactive visualization. With the help of these sophisticated techniques, it is made possible for the final 3D image to correctly depict the interior structures of the volume, offering crucial information for surgical planning, research, and medical diagnosis.

Image Analysis and Interpretation: For in-depth examination and interpretation of anatomical features as well as for identifying and describing anomalies or pathology, the reformatted images in various planes can be used. MPR improves the visibility of structures that may be hidden or challenging to assess using only the axial images.

Clinical decision-making is facilitated by the more thorough perspective of the scanned area that multiplanar reconstruction in CT gives clinicians. It facilitates the examination of structures from various angles and improves knowledge of the spatial relationships between structures. MPR is particularly useful for determining the degree and location of pathology or anomalies in the body, as well as complicated anatomy such as blood arteries, airways, and bony structures.

In computed tomography (CT) imaging, the Maximum Intensity Projection (MIP) technique is used to produce 2D pictures that show the maximum intensity value along a selected projection line. MIP images enable the highlighting of structures with high contrast or high attenuation values by visualizing the brightest pixels along a particular viewing direction. The maximum intensity value for each projection pixel is determined by the MIP algorithm using a mathematical equation.

The general equation for Maximum Intensity Projection is as follows:

$$\text{MIP}(x,y) = \max\left[V(x,y,z1), V(x,y,z2), \ldots, V(x,y,zn)\right]$$

where

MIP(x, y) represents the pixel value at coordinates (x, y) in the MIP image.
$V(x, y, zi)$ represents the voxel value at coordinates (x, y, zi) in the 3D CT volume.
$z1, z2, \ldots, zn$ represent the different axial planes along the projection path.

The 2D MIP image's pixel locations (x, y) are scanned by the MIP algorithm, which then calculates the highest voxel value along the projection path that corresponds to each pixel. The MIP image pixel at that point is then given the maximum value, producing a brighter pixel that represents the peak intensity seen along the viewing direction.

The angle of projection, the thickness of the slab being projected or a particular anatomical component of interest are a few examples of the characteristics that can be used to determine the projection path in MIP. The projection path can be changed depending on the intended visualization, however it is typically perpendicular to the imaging plane (often axial).

A clear portrayal of the vessel tree or regions with greater contrast uptake is possible with MIP pictures, which are frequently utilized to highlight structures like blood vessels or contrast-enhanced lesions. In difficult anatomical areas, MIP can help with abnormality detection, vascular flow assessment, and structural relationship evaluation.

It's vital to remember that MIP images contain drawbacks, like the possibility of structural overlap or the loss of depth perception. In order to provide a more thorough knowledge of the CT dataset, MIP pictures are frequently utilized in conjunction with other visualization techniques, such as multiplanar reconstruction (MPR).

Ray Casting: To create the final 3D image, the volume rendering technique uses ray casting. From the viewpoint of the viewer, rays are followed as they pass through each pixel of the image plane, sampling the appropriate voxels along the way. The colour and opacity of the ray are interpolated using the voxel properties that the transfer function defines. The final generated image is produced by repeating this process for each and every pixel.

Example: Various thoracic structures and disorders can be seen by using volume rendering for thoracic CT images:

Lungs: The lungs can be shown using the volume rendering approach, highlighting lung diseases like tumours, nodules, or areas of consolidation. To help with visualization within the surrounding healthy lung tissue, diseased lung tissue might be given particular opacities or colours by modifying the transfer function.

Mediastinum: The heart, major arteries, thymus, and lymph nodes are all depicted in three dimensions using the volume rendering approach. Volume rendering offers a thorough visualization of these structures' spatial relationships and any potential irregularities by giving them various colours and opacities.

Bones and Ribs: Volume rendering allows for the visualization of thoracic bones and ribs. By adjusting the transfer function, bones can be assigned higher opacities, enhancing their visibility. This facilitates the assessment of fractures, degenerative changes or anatomical variations.

Blood Vessels: The technique is also useful for visualizing blood vessels within the thoracic region. By assigning higher opacities to voxels with high-intensity values (representing contrast-enhanced blood), volume rendering can create a detailed and transparent representation of the vascular structures, including the pulmonary arteries and veins.

By offering a thorough 3D visualization of the full thoracic volume, the volume rendering technique improves the interpretation of thoracic CT scans. With more accurate diagnosis, treatment planning, and communication with patients and coworkers, complex structures, spatial linkages, and diseases can be evaluated.

2.10 Digital Imaging and Communications in Medicine

This picture standard, which is available in Digital Imaging and Communications in Medicine (DICOM) format, gives the medical professional information about the tissue. International medical image interchange and management using the DICOM standard. Interoperability between devices that deal with medical images is the main goal of the DICOM standard.

Data and images are saved in the same format. Because they have to exchange several image formats, imaging devices previously had trouble communicating data. Doctors acquire photos and reports via DICOM. Because of this, they can now diagnose and evaluate data from any location.

Electronic interference is one type of noise, which is variability that is not a desired signal and is present in all electronic systems. It appears in every photograph as an uneven grainy pattern that reduces image quality. It may, to a certain extent, render images invisible or incapable of making a diagnosis. Noise should not be confused with other artefacts that are less random and, in theory, should be repeatable, even if noise is an artefact in and of itself. DICOM services come in two flavours: composite and normalized. Information management functionality was created and transformed into standard services. That's unrelated to database normalization.

Noise is an undesirable signal that can arise from a variety of sources, including electronic interference. It is a component of all electronic systems. It appears as an inconsistent granular pattern throughout all images, degrading image quality. Depending on the severity, it can render photos invisible or unable to make a diagnosis. Even if noise is an artefact in and of itself, it shouldn't be confused with other artefacts that are less random and, in theory, ought to be repeatable. Composite and normalized DICOM services are the two different categories. The functionality for information management was created, and the services were standardized. Database normalization has nothing to do with that.

2.10.1   Why DICOM standard is important

In the realm of medical imaging, the DICOM standard is crucial. The importance of the DICOM standard can be seen in the following ways:

Interoperability: DICOM ensures interoperability, enabling seamless communication and data sharing across diverse medical imaging devices and software systems from various vendors. DICOM enables the sharing, accessing, and interpretation of images and related patient data between various healthcare facilities, divisions and software platforms.

Consistency and Standardization: DICOM creates a standardized format for archiving, transferring and presenting medical images and related data. In order to guarantee consistency in picture acquisition, storage and communication, it establishes specified properties and protocols. Regardless of the imaging method or apparatus, this standardization makes correct interpretation, comparison and analysis of medical images possible.

Image Quality and Integrity: Image quality and integrity are preserved throughout storage and transmission thanks to the specifications for image compression, resolution, and information that are included in DICOM. In order to preserve the diagnostic value of medical photographs and make sure that key information is not lost or damaged, this is essential.

Patient safety and privacy are taken into consideration by DICOM, which also includes methods for storing and transmitting data about patients. It has mechanisms for anonymization, patient permission, and secure data transfer, protecting patient privacy and guaranteeing adherence to privacy laws.

Process Effectiveness: Medical imaging workflows such as image acquisition, storage, retrieval, and analysis are supported by the DICOM standard.

Efficiency of Workflow: The DICOM standard covers a number of medical imaging operations, including image acquisition, storage, retrieval and analysis. DICOM supports the integration of various imaging devices and software systems by offering a common foundation, speeding workflow procedures, lowering mistakes and increasing overall image management efficiency.

Research and Collaboration: DICOM is essential for medical research and teamwork. Medical picture data can be accessed and analyzed from several sources, assuring consistency and comparability. DICOM also facilitates collaborative decision-making and consultations and supports the interchange of pictures and conclusions among healthcare professionals.

Future-proofing: To keep up with developments in medical imaging technology, the DICOM standard is always being improved. Future improvements will be compatible with it because it supports new imaging modalities, data kinds and analysis methods. This future-proofing feature of DICOM enables long-term medical picture preservation and retrieval and guarantees its usability throughout time.

In conclusion, the DICOM standard is crucial since it supports collaboration among researchers, interoperability, standardization, picture quality, patient safety, workflow efficiency and future flexibility in the field of medical imaging. It makes it easier to exchange, store, and seamlessly analyze medical image data, improving patient care, diagnostic precision and healthcare delivery overall.

2.10.2   The DICOM file format

A common format for storing, transmitting and distributing medical images and related data is called DICOM. It offers a standardized and organized method for classifying, encoding and storing many kinds of medical pictures, including those from X-rays, CT scans, MRIs, ultrasounds and other sources. An overview of the DICOM file format is given below:

File Organization: A header and an image data section make up a DICOM file. The image data segment carries the pixel data that represents the actual image, while the header contains metadata and other information about the image.

A DICOM file's header contains a number of properties that characterize the image and offer crucial details about the patient, the imaging device, the acquisition conditions, the image's features and more. Each attribute has a distinct tag that consists of a group number and an element number that makes it simple to identify and retrieve certain data.

Transfer Syntax: Different transfer syntaxes, supported by DICOM, specify the data's encoding and compression inside the file. Explicit VR Little Endian, Implicit VR Little Endian and JPEG Lossless Compression are examples of common transfer syntaxes. These syntaxes enable effective storage and transmission of DICOM files while ensuring data compatibility across various systems.

Pixel Data: The actual pixel values that make up the medical image are contained in the DICOM file's image data section. The pixel data can be saved in a variety of formats, such as raw pixel values or compressed formats like JPEG that can be lossless or lossy. The transfer syntax outlines the precise encoding and compression that will be used.

File Extensions: To identify its format, DICOM files commonly end in '.dcm' or '.dicom'. It's crucial to remember that the presence of these extensions does not ensure that the file complies with the DICOM standard to the letter. The information and internal organization of the file determine its file format.

DICOM Information Object Definitions (IODs): DICOM specifies a number of IODs that describe the properties and structure of various kinds of medical pictures. Based on the kind of image, these IODs provide the mandatory and optional properties that must be contained in a DICOM file to ensure consistency and interoperability.

DICOM files are created to be compatible and interoperable with a variety of imaging equipment, software programmes, and healthcare facilities. Different DICOM-compliant software and hardware systems can read, interpret and display DICOM files with accuracy because of the standardized format.

Medical images and associated data are frequently stored, transmitted and retrieved using DICOM files. The standardized format makes it possible for medical imaging technologies to be seamlessly integrated and interoperable, fostering efficient teamwork, precise diagnosis and enhanced patient care.

2.10.3   Hounsfield unit (HU)

The Hounsfield unit makes it easy to define what a certain observation might mean by characterizing radiation attenuation in various tissues. It is a quantitative scale that quantifies radiodensity.

The foundation of man is water, and air surrounds him. This served as the inspiration for developing the linear Hounsfield scale, which assigns a value of 0 to water (at STP) and a value of -1000 to air. Typical values for various substances and tissues, such as air against bone, range from -1000 to more than $+1000$. Fat has a value of -100, whereas muscle and blood are about $+40$. This enables the evaluation of objects without a clear structure, such as rounded tumours, which may or may not be benign or malignant. Cysts, for example, may contain water-like substances or exhibit a blood-like attenuation, which is obviously of significant concern to the doctor. In order to convert the displayed/generated pixel values, which are greyscale values, into the corresponding Hounsfield Unit (HU). The HU value of a particular pixel can be calculated as follows:

$$HU = Pixel\ value * slope\text{-}intercept$$

The intercept is found in the dicom header at 0028,1052 and the slope at 0028,1053. Plug these into the equation and you obtain the HU value which is simply a rescaling of the linear attenuation coefficient.

In summary, the CT scanner acquisition system is an important feature of modern medical imaging, allowing for the acquisition of high-quality cross-sectional pictures that may be used for accurate diagnosis and treatment planning. CT technological advancements such as multislice imaging, helical scanning, dual-source CT, and photon-counting capabilities have revolutionized radiology and had a significant impact on patient care. As research and technology evolve, the function of the acquisition system in providing safer, faster, and more precise imaging is projected to improve medical diagnoses and patient outcomes.

2.10.4   DICOM connectivity establishment

The process of DICOM connectivity establishment involves several steps to ensure reliable and secure communication:

Network Configuration: The first step involves configuring the network settings on both the sending and receiving devices. This includes defining IP addresses, ports and network protocols to be used for communication.

Association Establishment: DICOM uses a concept called 'Association' to establish a connection between devices. An Association is a logical connection between two DICOM devices, allowing them to exchange data. The establishment of an Association involves negotiation of parameters like the DICOM service roles (Service Class Provider and Service Class User) and presentation contexts, which define the types of services and data that can be exchanged.

AET Titles: AET (Application Entity Title) is a unique identifier for a DICOM device. During the connectivity establishment, each device specifies its AET title, which helps in identifying the devices involved in the communication.

Handshake and Authentication: Before data exchange begins, devices perform a handshake to confirm the capabilities and roles of each party. In addition, authentication and authorization mechanisms are often employed to ensure that only authorized devices can access and exchange sensitive patient information.

Data Transfer: Once the Association is established and the devices are authenticated, the actual medical image data transfer can take place. This can involve the transmission of various types of images (such as X-rays, MRIs, CT scans) along with associated metadata.

Error Handling and Verification: Throughout the communication process, error handling mechanisms ensure the integrity and reliability of the data being exchanged. Devices exchange acknowledgements and error reports to manage potential issues that might arise during transmission.

Association Release: After the data exchange is completed, the DICOM devices can release the established Association, freeing up resources and allowing the devices to establish connections with other partners.

Security and Encryption: Given the sensitivity of medical data, security measures such as encryption and data anonymization are often employed to protect patient privacy during data transmission.

Overall, DICOM connectivity establishment is a vital aspect of modern healthcare, facilitating the seamless exchange of medical images and associated information between different systems, and contributing to improved diagnostics, treatment planning and patient care.

Further reading

[1]   Rashid S, Lee SY, Hasan MK. An improved method for the removal of ring artifacts in high resolution CT imaging. EURASIP Journal on Advances in Signal Processing December 2012;2012(1):1–8.

[2]   Hasan MK, Sadi F, Lee SY. Removal of ring artifacts in micro-CT imaging using iterative morphological filters. Signal, Image and Video Processing March 2012;6:41–53.

[3]   Osman MM, Cohade C, Nakamoto Y, Wahl RL. Respiratory motion artifacts on PET emission images obtained using CT attenuation correction on PET-CT. European Journal of Nuclear Medicine and Molecular Imaging April 2003;30:603–6.

[4]   Ritchie CJ, Godwin JD, Crawford CR, Stanford W, Anno H, Kim YO. Minimum scan speeds for suppression of motion artifacts in CT. Radiology October 1992;185(1):37–42.

[5]   Yan CH, Whalen RT, Beaupre GS, Yen SY, Napel S. Reconstruction algorithm for polychromatic CT imaging: application to beam hardening correction. IEEE Transactions on Medical Imaging January 2000;19(1). 1–1.

[6]   Kitagawa K, George RT, Arbab-Zadeh A, Lima JA, Lardo AC. Characterization and correction of beam-hardening artifacts during dynamic volume CT assessment of myocardial perfusion. Radiology July 2010;256(1):111–8.

[7]   Pessis E, Campagna R, Sverzut JM, Bach F, Rodallec M, Guerini H, et al. Virtual monochromatic spectral imaging with fast kilovoltage switching: reduction of metal artifacts at CT. RadioGraphics March 2013;33(2):573–83.

[8]   Boas FE, Fleischmann D. Evaluation of two iterative techniques for reducing metal artifacts in computed tomography. Radiology June 2011;259(3):894–902.

[9]   Mustra M, Delac K, Grgic M. Overview of the DICOM standard. In: 2008 50th international symposium ELMAR. vol. 1. IEEE; September 10, 2008. p. 39–44.

[10] Bidgood Jr WD, Horii SC, Prior FW, Van Syckle DE. Understanding and using DICOM, the data interchange standard for biomedical imaging. Journal of the American Medical Informatics Association May 1, 1997;4(3):199–212.

[11] Pianykh OS, Pianykh OS. DICOM security. Springer Berlin Heidelberg; 2012.

3

Terminologies related to lung cancer

3.1 Introduction

One of the most important systems in the human body, the respiratory system, allows for the exchange of oxygen and carbon dioxide, which is essential for life. The lungs, amazing organs in charge of oxygenating the blood and exhaling waste gases, are at the centre of this complex system. Clinicians, radiologists and other healthcare workers need to understand lung anatomy, the wide range of pulmonary abnormalities and the distinctive features of pulmonary nodules. This information is the basis for diagnosing and treating a range of respiratory conditions, from mild to potentially fatal.

The pulmonary landscape is thoroughly explored in this chapter, which starts with a close look at lung anatomy. We explore the complex architecture of the lungs, which includes the pleura, alveoli and bronchi, to provide readers with a clear knowledge of the anatomical basis for respiratory function. Understanding lung anatomy is essential for deciphering the plethora of pictures and diagnostic procedures used to evaluate pulmonary health.

Once we have moved past anatomy, we will explore the wide range of pulmonary disorders that can affect these important organs. This chapter describes the wide range of lung problems that healthcare professionals deal with in their practice, ranging from benign ailments like pulmonary cysts and fibrosis to more serious pathologies including consolidation and masses. Each condition is broken down, including information on its aetiology, clinical manifestation, diagnostic techniques and treatment plans.

3.1.1 Lung anatomy

The lungs are vital organs involved in the process of respiration, allowing us to breathe in oxygen and exhale carbon dioxide. On either side of the heart, they are situated in the thoracic cavity and are shielded by the rib cage. Here is a summary of the lungs' anatomy:

Lung lobes: Each lung has several lobes. The upper, middle and lower lobes of the right lung are its three lobes.

Application of Artificial Intelligence in Early Detection of Lung Cancer. https://doi.org/10.1016/B978-0-323-95245-3.00003-2

3.1.2   Right lung

Upper lobe: The largest and topmost portion of the right lung is made up of the upper lobe. It reaches the horizontal fissure from the apex (top) of the lung. The middle lobe and upper lobe are separated by the horizontal fissure.

Middle lobe: The right lung's middle lobe is situated halfway between the upper and lower lobes. The oblique fissure and the horizontal fissure separate it from the lower lobe and upper lobe, respectively. In comparison to the top and lower lobes, the middle lobe is smaller.

Lower lobe: Following the top lobe, the lower lobe of the right lung is the largest. It reaches the base of the lung from the oblique fissure (which divides it from the middle lobe). The right oblique fissure further divides the lower lobe into superior and inferior parts (Fig. 3.1).

3.1.3   Left lung

Upper lobe: Of the two lobes of the left lung, the upper lobe is the larger. It reaches the oblique fissure from the apex. The main fissure that divides the upper and lower lobes is called the oblique fissure.

Lower lobe: The left lung's lower lobe, which is smaller than the upper lobe and is situated below the oblique fissure, is present. It reaches the base of the lung from the

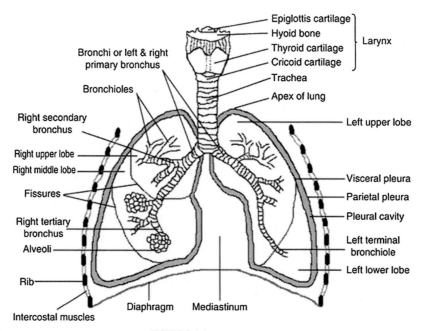

FIGURE 3.1 Lung anatomy.

oblique fissure. The left oblique fissure further divides the lower lobe into superior and inferior parts.

The split of the lungs into lobes enables effective ventilation and makes it easier for air and blood to circulate throughout the lungs. Each lobe has a separate bronchus that arises from the main bronchus and separates into smaller bronchi, bronchioles and eventually the alveoli, where gas exchange occurs.

It's important to remember that pulmonary lobe anatomical variance might occasionally occur. Some people may have extra accessory lobes, or they may not have any lobes at all. The illustration given above depicts how the pulmonary lobes are typically arranged anatomically.

3.1.4   Pulmonary fissure

Deep grooves or clefts that divide the lobes of the lungs are called pulmonary fissures, sometimes known as lung fissures or interlobar fissures. They serve as significant anatomical features that separate the lungs into various compartments. Pulmonary fissures come in two primary categories:

Oblique fissure: The main and most noticeable fissure in the lungs is called the oblique fissure. It divides the upper lobe from the lower lobe in both the right and left lungs. From the spine, the oblique fissure angles forward and downward towards the front of the chest. The right lung extends anteriorly to the sixth rib, which is located close to the mid-clavicular line, from the spine, where it begins at roughly the level of the fifth thoracic vertebra. The oblique fissure in the left lung extends from the spine, around the sixth thoracic vertebra, forward to the fifth rib, close to the mid-clavicular line (Fig. 3.2).

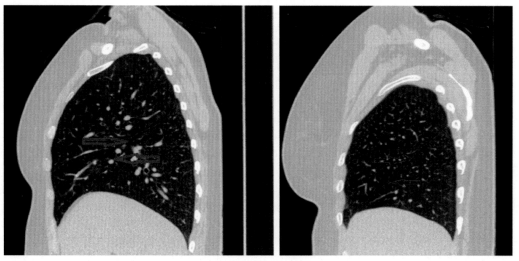

FIGURE 3.2 Pulmonary fissure.

FIGURE 3.3 Pulmonary lobes.

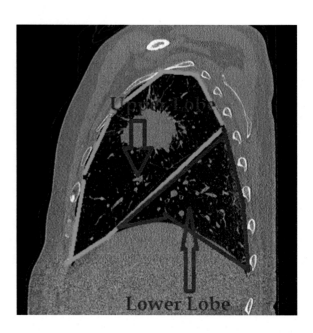

FIGURE 3.3 Pulmonary lobes.

Horizontal fissure: The right lung is the only one where the middle and upper lobes are divided by a horizontal fissure. From the oblique fissure, it extends horizontally along the anterior chest wall in a fissure that is comparatively straight. The horizontal fissure runs from the fourth rib, which is close to the mid-clavicular line, to the fifth rib, which is close to the mid-axillary line (Fig. 3.3).

The right lung is the only one where the middle and upper lobes are divided by a horizontal fissure. From the oblique fissure, it extends horizontally along the anterior chest wall in a fissure that is comparatively straight. The horizontal fissure runs from the fourth rib, which is close to the mid-clavicular line, to the fifth rib, which is close to the mid-axillary line.

Understanding pulmonary fissures is essential for clinical practice and lung imaging. Radiologists can precisely pinpoint the location and size of pulmonary abnormalities, such as nodules, masses or consolidation, using imaging techniques including chest X-rays and computed tomography (CT) scans that show the presence, integrity and appearance of fissures. Additionally, surgeons rely on their understanding of the fissures to direct their surgical strategy and, if necessary, resect particular lung lobes.

Bronchi: The trachea sometimes referred to as the windpipe divides into two main bronchi, one of which leads to each lung. In comparison to the left main bronchus, the right main bronchus is longer, wider and more vertical. The primary bronchi then further split into smaller bronchi, creating the bronchial tree, a network of branches.

Bronchioles: The bronchi divide further to form even smaller tubes known as bronchioles. The smooth muscles in the walls of these bronchioles aid in controlling airflow. They ultimately lead to little air sacs known as alveoli.

Alveoli: The lungs' alveoli serve as the principal site of gas exchange. They are tiny sacs with thin walls that are encircled by a web of capillaries. Through the alveolar walls, oxygen from the breathed air enters the bloodstream, while waste product carbon dioxide from the blood is ejected into the alveoli for exhalation.

Pleura: The pleura is a two-layered membrane that covers the lungs. The inner surface of the chest wall and the diaphragm are lined with the outer layer, also referred to as the parietal pleura. The visceral pleura, the inner layer, covers the exterior of the lungs. The pleural cavity, which is the area between the two layers, contains a small amount of pleural fluid that lubricates the lungs and permits fluid circulation while breathing.

Diaphragm: At the bottom of the thoracic cavity is a dome-shaped muscle called the diaphragm. By flattening and contracting during inhalation to make more room in the chest cavity for the lungs to expand, it plays a critical part in breathing.

Because of their extreme elasticity, the lungs can expand and contract with each breath. The complex design of the lungs and the blood veins that supply them allows for effective gas exchange, ensuring that the blood is oxygenated and that carbon dioxide is eliminated.

3.2 Pulmonary abnormalities detectable on CT scan images

An effective imaging method known as a CT scan can produce fine-grained cross-sectional images of the lungs. It is frequently used to identify and assess different pulmonary problems. On CT scan images, the following pulmonary anomalies can be seen (Fig. 3.4):

Pulmonary nodules: Small nodules, sometimes known as round or oval lesions in the lung, can be found with a CT scan. Nodules are typically identified by their size, shape, density and growth pattern and can be benign or malignant.

Pulmonary mass: Lung masses can be found with a CT scan of the lung tissue. These can be symptoms of primary lung cancer or metastatic cancer spreading from other body areas.

Ground-glass opacities: Also known as GGOs, these hazy, dense spots in the lung tissue are frequently signs of infection, inflammation or the beginning stages of lung cancer. However, these abnormalities have no structural similarities with pulmonary nodules. Hence in AI-based detection algorithms we need not to consider this abnormalities.

Consolidation: In parts of the lung, where the air-filled gaps are filled with fluid, blood or other substances, this condition is referred to as consolidation. It frequently occurs in cases of inflammation, pneumonia or lung infections.

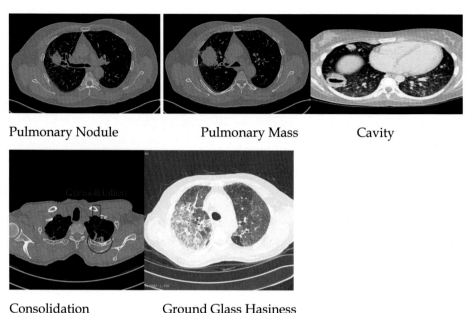

Pulmonary Nodule   Pulmonary Mass   Cavity

Consolidation   Ground Glass Hasiness

FIGURE 3.4 Pulmonary abnormalities.

Cavity: Air-filled gaps or cavities can be found within lung nodules or tumours using a CT scan. Cavities may indicate specific illnesses like tuberculosis or fungi, as well as necrotic tumour tissue.

Bronchiectasis: The abnormal dilatation and thickening of the bronchial tubes are symptoms of the illness known as bronchiectasis. Dilated bronchi and thicker bronchial walls, which are symptoms of this illness, can be seen on CT scans. However, these abnormalities have no structural similarities with pulmonary nodules. Hence in AI-based detection algorithms we need not to consider this abnormalities.

Pulmonary embolism: A specialized CT scan called a CT pulmonary angiography (CTPA) is used to assess blood flow in the pulmonary arteries in cases of pulmonary embolism. It can identify blood clots or pulmonary emboli that are obstructing the blood arteries and posing a life-threatening risk. However, these abnormalities have no structural similarities with pulmonary nodules. Hence in AI-based detection algorithms we need not to consider this abnormalities.

Pleural abnormalities: The pleura, a double-layered membrane that surrounds the lungs, can also be examined using a CT scan to look for anomalies. These could be pleural lumps, pleural thickening or pleural effusions (fluid buildup).

Various interstitial lung disorders, such as pulmonary fibrosis, sarcoidosis or hyper-sensitivity pneumonitis, can cause patterns of aberrant lung tissue, which can be detected by CT scans.

Lung collapse or atelectasis: CT scans can detect lung collapse or atelectasis, which occurs when a lung fails to properly expand in part or whole. Compression, airway occlusion and other reasons may all contribute to this. However, these abnormalities have no structural similarities with pulmonary nodules. Hence in AI-based detection algorithms we need not to consider this abnormalities.

A radiologist or other healthcare professional with competence in chest imaging should interpret CT scan images since they require special knowledge. They take into account several elements to provide an accurate diagnosis and an appropriate therapy strategy, including the location, size, form and distribution of anomalies as well as the patient's clinical history.

3.3 Pulmonary abnormalities that create accurate detection of pulmonary nodules

The aforementioned pulmonary abnormalities are easily detectable on CT scanner machines. However, all abnormalities are not responsible for lung cancer and there exist some pulmonary abnormalities which can create some hindrance in pulmonary nodule detection. This section will describe this context.

3.4 Pulmonary cyst

A fluid-filled sac or cavity within the lung tissue is referred to as a pulmonary cyst. Cysts can range in size and are usually not harmful. They may arise as a result of a variety of conditions, such as certain lung disorders or developmental anomalies. Small cysts are frequently asymptomatic and may only be found by chance during imaging tests. However, larger or symptomatic cysts may result in pain, other respiratory problems or difficulty breathing. When cysts create symptoms or issues, treatment is typically undertaken, and it may involve emptying the cyst or surgically removing it.

3.5 Pulmonary fibrosis

A lung ailment known as pulmonary fibrosis is characterized by an excessive accumulation of scar tissue (fibrosis) in the lung tissue. The lungs become stiff as a result of this fibrosis, making it challenging for them to appropriately expand and contract during breathing. Environmental exposures, autoimmune diseases and genetic predisposition are only a few of the causes. Shortness of breath, a chronic cough, exhaustion and a decline in lung function can all be symptoms of pulmonary fibrosis. Although there is no cure, available treatments try to control symptoms, halt the spread of the illness and enhance the quality of life.

3.6 Consolidation

When the air-filled spaces in the lungs, known as alveoli, fill up with fluid, pus or other substances, it is referred to as pulmonary consolidation. Infections like pneumonia or other inflammatory processes may be to blame for this. Consolidation frequently results in decreased gas exchange and can result in symptoms like coughing, fever, chest pain and breathing difficulties. Typically, imaging tests like X-rays or CT scans are used in diagnosis. Depending on the underlying reason, treatment may include supportive care, antibiotics and managing the infection or inflammation causing the consolidation.

Medical imaging images containing lung cysts, fibrosis, consolidation and pulmonary vasculature provide difficulties for artificial intelligence (AI)-based pulmonary nodule detection algorithms. Due to their ability to resemble nodules or interfere with their appearance, these factors may confuse. If not thoroughly distinguished from nodules, pulmonary cysts, which frequently have rounder forms and comparable contrast enhancement patterns, might result in misdiagnosis.

On imaging scans, nodule-like appearances can be caused by pulmonary fibrosis, which is indicated by altered lung tissue density, and consolidation, in which lung tissue solidifies. Additionally, nodules and pulmonary arteries, particularly blood vessels, may cross one another, leading to erroneous interpretations. AI algorithms must be trained thoroughly on a variety of datasets that account for these complexities to learn to distinguish between these structures based on their internal features, contextual information and distinctive qualities.

A thorough methodology is needed to develop precise AI-based nodule detection. The subtle distinctions between nodules and these confounding factors must be taught to AI algorithms. This entails putting the algorithms through extensive training in a variety of instances, such as pulmonary cysts, fibrosis, consolidation and different kinds of pulmonary arteries. Additionally, by giving a comprehensive perspective of lung anatomy, integrating contextual cues and multi-modal data (combining several forms of imaging) might improve accuracy.

The potential for AI to assist radiologists in the early and accurate detection of pulmonary nodules while navigating the complexities introduced by the surrounding lung structures and conditions will be enhanced by efforts to improve AI accuracy in the presence of these challenges.

3.7 Types of nodules based on density

The density of a pulmonary nodule, as shown on imaging tests like CT scans or chest X-rays, can also be used to classify nodules. The density of a nodule offers important details about its makeup and can help identify the root cause. Based on density, the following are some typical forms of pulmonary nodules.

3.7.1 Solid nodules

On imaging, solid nodules show up as clearly defined, homogeneous lesions with consistent density. They lack substantial calcification or cavitation and have a very homogenous composition. The possibility of benign or malignant solid nodules can be further differentiated depending on their size and other features.

3.7.2 Ground glass opacity nodule

The term 'ground glass opacity' describes a hazy, elevated density in the lung parenchyma that partially conceals the underlying structures. Although the underlying lung architecture, including blood veins, bronchi and lung markings, cannot be seen, GGO nodules emerge as areas of enhanced attenuation. Depending on the amount of solid components a nodule contains, GGO nodules can be further divided into pure GGO and part-solid nodules (Fig. 3.5).

3.7.3 Part-solid nodules

Partially solid nodules have both a solid and a ground glass component. They frequently have a solid area or nodule within a ground glass-opacity zone. Different proportions of solid and ground glass can be found in part-solid nodules, and the features of the solid component, such as size and density, are frequently crucial for predicting the possibility of malignancy.

3.8 Types of pulmonary nodules based on anatomical positions

Another way to classify pulmonary nodules is according to where they are located anatomically within the lungs. A nodule's location can reveal crucial details regarding its characteristics, origin and possible underlying causes. Based on anatomical placements, the following are some frequent forms of pulmonary nodules.

3.8.1 Solitary pulmonary nodules

A single, clearly discernible anomaly with a rounded or oval form that shows up as a discrete lesion inside the lung tissue on medical imaging scans, such as chest X-rays or CT scans, is referred to as a solitary pulmonary nodule (SPN). SPNs typically have a diameter of less than 3 cm and are frequently found by chance during regular imaging or tests unrelated to the lungs.

An SPN must be properly described to be classified as either benign or malignant. To correctly diagnose and categorize SPNs, additional imaging examinations, clinical

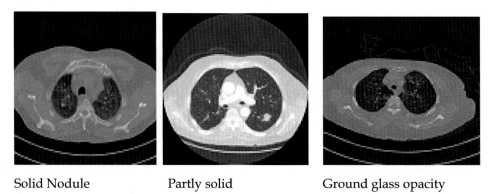

Solid Nodule   Partly solid   Ground glass opacity

FIGURE 3.5 Different types of pulmonary nodules based on density.

history, patient risk factors and occasionally other diagnostic procedures like biopsies are used. Giving patients the right kind of care and managing their disease requires being able to distinguish between benign conditions like scars or granulomas and malignant conditions like lung cancer (Fig. 3.6).

3.8.2   Juxta-pleural nodules

The term 'juxta-pleural nodule' refers to an abnormal growth or lesion that is present next to or close to the pleura, the thin membrane that lines the inner surface of the chest wall and the outer surface of the lungs. These nodules can be seen on medical imaging tests like chest X-rays or CT scans because they are located near the pleural surface.

Juxta-pleural nodules' imaging properties and appearance can vary depending on how close they are to the pleura. They may have distinctive growth, shape or density patterns as a result of their location. Juxta-pleural nodules must be evaluated to ascertain if they are benign or malignant in origin. In order to provide accurate diagnoses and direct suitable patient care and management, radiologists and other medical experts examine these nodules in conjunction with additional characteristics and clinical data.

3.8.3   Juxta-vascular nodule

A lesion or abnormal development in the lung tissue that is located next to blood arteries is referred to as a juxta-vascular nodule. These nodules can be seen on medical imaging scans like CT scans or chest X-rays because they are situated close to pulmonary blood arteries.

Juxta-vascular nodules' features and appearance on imaging may vary depending on how close they are to blood arteries. Blood arteries nearby may affect the contrast enhancement pattern of the nodule or its relationship to the lung tissue in the area. Juxta-vascular nodules must be evaluated to ascertain if they are benign or malignant in origin. In order to provide accurate diagnoses and direct suitable patient treatment and

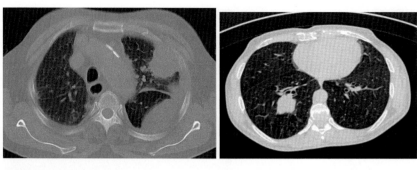

Juxta-Pleural Nodule   Solitary Pulmonary Nodule

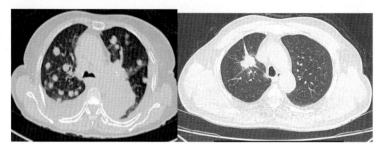

Juxta Vascular Nodule   Pleural Tail

FIGURE 3.6 Types of nodules based on radiological position.

management, radiologists and other medical professionals analyze these nodules along with additional characteristics and clinical data.

3.8.4   Pleural tail

A pleural tail nodule, also known as a 'pleural tail sign', is an imaging finding that can be seen on scans performed by doctors, often chest CT scans. The pleura, which is the thin membrane lining the outer surface of the lungs and the inner surface of the chest wall, appears as an extended, thin projection of lung tissue extending from the edge of a pulmonary nodule.

The presence of lung tissue that fills the space between a nodule and the pleural surface causes a radiological phenomenon known as the pleural tail nodule. It forms a delicate link between the nodule and the pleura that occasionally resembles a 'tail'. This characteristic, which is frequently connected to benign lesions like scars or granulomas, is thought to help distinguish benign nodules from malignant ones (Fig. 3.7).

It's important to note that the anatomical position of a pulmonary nodule is just one aspect considered in the evaluation and diagnosis. Other factors, such as nodule size, shape, density and clinical history, are also essential for determining the nature of the

FIGURE 3.7 Size of a nodule.

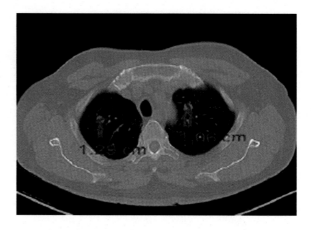

nodule and guiding appropriate management decisions. Radiologists and clinicians work together to interpret and classify pulmonary nodules accurately to ensure proper diagnosis and treatment (Fig. 3.8).

3.9 Morphologies of pulmonary nodules

The physical qualities and outward look of a lung nodule as seen on CT or X-ray images are referred to as its morphology. This contains several characteristics that collectively characterize the visual characteristics of the nodule, such as size, shape, borders, density and other aspects.

For a proper diagnosis and classification of a pulmonary nodule, it is essential to comprehend its morphology. These characteristics are used by radiologists and other medical professionals to distinguish between benign and malignant nodules, choose the best treatment option and track changes over time. Decisions about patient care and management are influenced by many morphological characteristics, which offer useful information about the probable nature of the nodule.

Size: A lung nodule's size has a significant role in determining its risk. Larger nodules (more than 30 mm) have a higher risk of cancer than smaller nodules (less than 10 mm), in general. It's crucial to remember, though, that even little nodules have the potential to develop into cancer, particularly if they show certain alarming signs.

Calcification: Calcification of pulmonary nodules refers to the deposition or accumulation of calcium within the nodules present in the lung tissue. It is a common finding in various types of nodules and can provide important diagnostic information. Here's an explanation of calcification in pulmonary nodules.

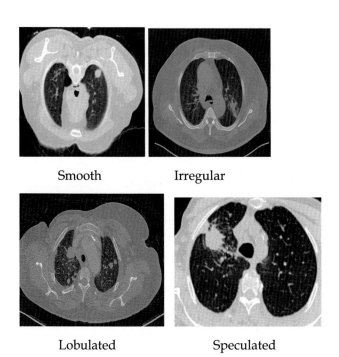

FIGURE 3.8 Margin of a nodule.

Smooth   Irregular

Lobulated   Speculated

3.10 The margin of pulmonary nodule

The term 'margin' refers to the outer boundary or edge of a pulmonary nodule, which is a small round or oval-shaped growth in the lung. The edges of these nodules are extremely important in establishing the nature, potential malignancy and necessary medical interventions of these nodules, which might vary in size, shape and appearance. Radiologists and clinicians must evaluate various lung nodule margin types as a vital part of their clinical judgement. The relevance of varied nodule edges and how they affect lung health are examined in this essay.

Smooth or well-defined margins: The presence of smooth or clearly defined edges is frequently a sign of benign pulmonary nodules. These nodules are separated from the lung tissue around them by definite boundaries. Typically, nodules with smooth borders are less likely to be malignant. Granulomas, hamartomas or inflamed regions can all be benign nodules with smooth borders. Although these nodules are often not a cause for alarm, doctors may continue to keep an eye on them over time to maintain stability and rule out any potential alterations.

Irregular margin: Nodules with irregular margins are more worrisome and give rise to concerns about cancer. The nodule's growth is likely invasive and may be penetrating the nearby lung tissue, according to irregular edges. Primary lung malignancies including adenocarcinomas and squamous cell carcinomas are frequently linked to this trait. Radiologists and other healthcare professionals pay special attention to uneven margins because they signal the need for an immediate and complete investigation, which may include biopsies and other imaging to identify the nodule's cancerousness.

Lobulated margin: Nodules having several rounded protrusions or lobes around their edges are said to have lobulated margins. They can be a sign of benign or malignant nodules, but they are more typical in some forms of lung cancer. There is a chance that nodules with lobulated margins are aggressive tumours that are actively encroaching on the lung tissue. However, not all nodules with lobulated borders are malignant; they can also signify benign illnesses like fungal infections or abscesses.

Speculated margin: Sharp, needle-like projections that extend outward from the nodule's centre define spiculated edges. These margins strongly signal cancer since they show aggressive development and invasion of the tissues around them. Adenocarcinomas and big cell carcinomas are two types of invasive lung cancer that frequently have spiculated edges. For nodules with spiculated margins, prompt evaluation, diagnosis and treatment are necessary to enable early intervention and better results.

The assessment of pulmonary nodule margins is an essential step in both the diagnosis and treatment of lung diseases. Different margin types are thoroughly studied by radiologists and doctors to ascertain the likelihood of malignancy and the best course of action. Smooth margins are often benign; however, lobulated and spiculated margins may be signs of more aggressive tumours. Irregular and spiculated margins raise concerns of malignancy. Healthcare practitioners may make well-informed judgements, offer timely interventions and give patients the best possible care for their lung health by being aware of the relevance of various margin types.

3.11 Shape of pulmonary nodule

The size, borders and most especially the shape of these nodules can vary greatly. The forms of pulmonary nodules can reveal details about the nodule's nature, the possibility that it is malignant and the best course of medical treatment, which is crucial diagnostic information. This essay explores the significance of various lung nodule shapes and their effects on pulmonary health.

Round or oval shape: Pulmonary nodules with a round or oval shape are among the most typical nodule shapes. These nodules frequently have a decreased chance of malignancy and tend to be delineated. Round or oval shapes are typically seen in benign disorders like granulomas, which are immunological reactions to infections or irritants. The shape alone cannot, however, rule out malignancy, and more testing is required to correctly identify the type of nodule (Fig. 3.9).

Irregular shape: Nodules with spiculated or irregular shapes are frequently more worrisome and give rise to cancer fears. These forms suggest that the nodule is growing in an invasive manner and may be invading the lung tissue around it. Spiculated nodules

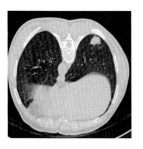 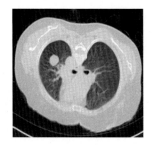 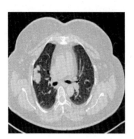

Oval Shape   Round Shape   Irregular Shape

FIGURE 3.9 Shape of pulmonary nodule.

have a strong correlation with aggressive initial lung malignancies such as squamous cell carcinomas and adenocarcinomas. For nodules with spiculated forms, a swift and thorough inspection is necessary to provide prompt diagnosis and treatment (Fig. 3.10).

3.11.1   Contrast enhancement pattern

As seen on medical imaging scans after the injection of a contrast agent, these tiny aberrant growths within the lung tissue demonstrate a change in radiodensity or brightness, which is referred to as contrast enhancement of pulmonary nodules. Contrast agents are chemicals with ingredients like iodine that absorb X-rays and show up on images as bright patches, making some structures more visible.

For instance, contrast enhancement during a CT scan entails injecting a contrast agent into the patient's bloodstream. The blood arteries in and around the pulmonary nodules are part of the blood vessels via which this substance travels. The contrast agent improves the appearance of blood vessels and other structures, including the nodules, by diffusing X-rays differently from the tissue around them.

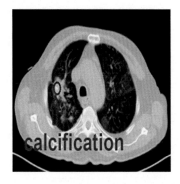 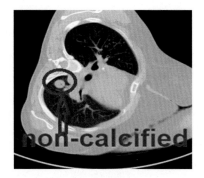

Calcified   Non-Calcified

FIGURE 3.10 Calcification.

The ensuing contrast enhancement pattern gives accurate diagnostic information about the nodule's vascularity, tissue makeup and perhaps its malignant or benign status. The possible nature of the nodule can be deduced from several enhancement patterns, such as homogeneous, heterogeneous, peripheral, central or rim enhancement. In order to make educated choices on patient care and additional diagnostic procedures, radiologists must consider these patterns in conjunction with other nodule characteristics, such as size, shape and margins.

Non-enhancement: Nodules with little to no contrast enhancement have HU values that are quite similar to the lung tissue around them. This pattern could be a sign of nodule calcification, necrosis or fibrosis. These HU values aid in separating various nodule kinds from benign, non-enhancing diseases.

Homogeneous enhancement: Homogeneous enhancement-exhibiting pulmonary nodules have constant HU values over their whole region. This consistent brightness frequently denotes well-vascularized tissue, which may indicate cancer. The elevated HU values signify the presence of dense tissue that may be malignant.

Heterogeneous enhancement: Variations in HU values are displayed as heterogeneous enhancement within a nodule. These patterns may indicate a mix of tissue types, including both benign and cancerous elements. The variety of HU values demonstrates how the nodule's cellular structures are diverse.

Based on the occurrence region of heterogeneity, it can be categorized into the following categories (Table 3.1):

3.11.2   Lung-RADS

The management and treatment of lung cancer depend heavily on the early identification and characterization of lung nodules. The Lung Imaging Reporting and Data System (Lung-RADS) was created to make consistent reporting and management decisions easier. A standardized classification system called Lung-RADS was created exclusively for lung nodules found on chest images, primarily CT scans. In the context of evaluating lung nodules, we shall examine the definition and importance of Lung-RADS in this essay.

Table 3.1   HU values in different enhancement patterns.

Enhancement pattern	HU values
Non-enhancement	Similar to surrounding tissue
Homogeneous enhancement	Higher HU values
Heterogeneous enhancement	Varied HU values

3.11.3   Defining Lung-RADS

A systematic framework called Lung-RADS seeks to standardize the reporting and management of lung nodules. It offers a systematic method to evaluate the likelihood of cancer linked to lung nodules and directs the proper follow-up methods. Lung-RADS, which was created by the American College of Radiology (ACR), classifies nodules according to their imaging characteristics and offers suggestions for further care.

3.11.4   Lung-RADS categories for solid pulmonary nodules

3.11.4.1   Lung-RADS 2: Benign appearance
Solid nodules with a Lung-RADS 2 classification are characterized by benign characteristics such as a well-defined shape, smooth borders and calcifications resembling granulomas or hamartomas. These nodules normally don't need any additional follow-up because they have a very low likelihood of being cancerous.

3.11.4.2   Lung-RADS 3: Intermediate probability
Solid nodules with a Lung-RADS 3 classification have a moderate risk of being cancerous. Nodules that do not obviously fit into the categories of benign or malignant are included in this group. It is necessary to conduct further analysis, which may entail additional imaging to help characterize the nodule, such as a follow-up CT scan or positron emission tomography (PET) scan.

3.11.5   Lung-RADS 4: Suspicious appearance

Solid nodules categorized as Lung-RADS 4 demonstrate concerning features that indicate a higher probability of malignancy. These features include irregular or spiculated margins, size growth over time or other suspicious characteristics. Additional diagnostic procedures, such as a biopsy or surgical resection, are typically recommended to confirm the presence of malignancy.

3.11.6   Lung-RADS 4X: Known malignancy

Solid nodules with a known underlying cancer elsewhere in the body fall under the Lung RADS 4X group. Based on the known underlying malignancy and its stage, these nodules are regarded as representing metastatic disease, and appropriate care methods are followed.

3.11.7   Considerations and challenges

Although Lung RADS offers a consistent method for nodule classification, it is crucial to remember that it is not a reliable diagnostic tool. It provides a framework for

management choices and helps radiologists, referring doctors and patients communi-
cate with one another.

The possibility of false-positive or false-negative results is one of the difficulties in
evaluating solid lung nodules. When evaluating the findings and selecting the best
management approach, it is important to take into account variables such as nodule
size, growth rate, patient history and clinical context.

A standardized classification system called Lung-RADS was created to make reporting
and management choices for lung nodules easier. Lung-RADS aids radiologists and
physicians in classifying nodules based on their imaging features and characteristics,
which helps them estimate the likelihood that they are malignant and choose the best
course of action. This organized framework fosters better patient care, enhances
communication and aids in the early diagnosis and treatment of lung cancer. Lung-
RADS is likely to change as science and technology develop, increasing its value in the
field of lung nodule assessment.

Solid pulmonary nodules are categorized within Lung RADS based on several
morphological characteristics, such as size, form, margin, and the presence of calcifications. These characteristics offer crucial hints about the possibility of malignancy.
Let's examine how each of these elements contributes to categorization.

3.11.8   Size

The size of the nodule has a major impact on the likelihood that it is malignant. In
comparison to bigger nodules, smaller nodules (usually less than 6 mm) typically have a
decreased risk of malignancy. Smaller nodules within Lung RADS that show no
discernible growth over time are more likely to be classified as benign (Lung-RADS 2).
On the other hand, a growth in size over time may cause concern and elevate the risk of
cancer, which would necessitate a higher classification (Lung-RADS 3 or 4).

3.11.9   Shape

The shape of the nodule should also be taken into account. The likelihood of a nodule
being classified as benign is higher when it is well-defined, round or oval-shaped (Lung-
RADS 2). A higher categorization (Lung-RADS 3 or 4) may result from irregular or
speculative nodules with an ill-defined shape, which are thought to be suspicious and
may suggest a higher likelihood of cancer.

3.11.10   Margin

The smoothness or irregularity of a nodule's margin or border is assessed. Nodules with
smooth borders are more likely to be benign and have a lower risk of cancer (Lung-RADS
2). Nodules with spiculated or irregular edges, on the other hand, are regarded as suspicious and raise the likelihood of malignancy, leading to a higher categorization (Lung-

RADS 3 or 4). It is common knowledge that aggressive tumour growth patterns are linked to spiculated margins.

3.11.11   Presence of calcification

A solid lung nodule's nature can be determined by the presence of calcifications within it. Popcorn or central calcifications are two types of calcifications that are highly suggestive of a benign aetiology. According to the Lung-RADS 2, nodules that exhibit typical benign calcifications are more likely to be classified as benign. However, malignancy is not always implied when there are no calcifications. Malignant nodules may occasionally also have calcifications, but these nodules may be classified higher (Lung-RADS 3 or 4) depending on their unique traits and distribution.

3.11.12   Contrast enhancement pattern

To assess the likelihood of malignancy and direct treatment choices, lung-RADS largely considers the morphological characteristics of the nodules found on chest imaging, such as size, shape, margin and presence of calcifications. Contrast enhancement patterns, however, may offer extra details in some circumstances and might be viewed as supporting evidence in the overall evaluation of a nodule.

Despite the lack of specific categories or criteria for Lung-RADS based on contrast enhancement patterns, some enhancement patterns may raise red flags and affect subsequent evaluation. Solid nodules with intense and uneven patterns of enhancement, indicative of enhanced vascularity, for instance, maybe more cause for concern due to their potential for malignancy. However, nodules with uniform enhancement or no discernible augmentation can be less concerning.

It's vital to remember that contrast enhancement patterns by themselves may not always indicate whether a tumour is benign or malignant. The Lung-RADS framework's overall evaluation of a lung nodule considers a variety of elements, such as morphological characteristics, patient history and clinical context. Expertise is needed to incorporate contrast enhancement patterns into the assessment, and they should be interpreted alongside other imaging and clinical results.

For nodules classified as Lung-RADS 3 (intermediate probability), contrast-enhanced imaging may occasionally be advised as part of the extra workup to further characterize the nodule and assess its likelihood of being malignant. The distinction between benign and malignant nodules can be made with the assistance of this additional imaging, which can also direct future therapeutic choices.

It is important to note that contrast-enhanced imaging is more frequently used for the assessment of uncertain lung nodules or for a more thorough study of nodule characteristics outside the purview of Lung-RADS. In certain clinical situations, advanced imaging techniques, such as dynamic contrast-enhanced CT, perfusion CT or MRI, may be used to offer additional in-depth details about the vascular and perfusion properties of the nodules.

Contrast enhancement patterns can be used as supplementary evidence in the evaluation of lung nodules even if they are not explicitly included in the Lung-RADS categorization system. To accomplish a thorough examination of lung nodules and support appropriate therapy choices, contrast-enhanced imaging should be used, together with other morphological features and clinical data. Enhancement patterns should also be interpreted in this way.

Radiologists can more accurately determine the likelihood of malignancy and direct future management decisions, such as the necessity for additional imaging or invasive procedures, by analyzing the size, shape, margin and presence of calcifications in solid lung nodules. To avoid any misdiagnosis and guarantee correct diagnoses, it is crucial to keep in mind that trained radiologists should interpret these morphological features.

Further reading

[1] Schelegle ES, Green JF. An overview of the anatomy and physiology of slowly adapting pulmonary stretch receptors. Respiration Physiology March 1, 2001;125(1−2):17−31.

[2] Horeweg N, Van Der Aalst CM, Thunnissen E, Nackaerts K, Weenink C, Groen HJ, et al. Characteristics of lung cancers detected by computer tomography screening in the randomized NELSON trial. American Journal of Respiratory and Critical Care Medicine April 15, 2013;187(8): 848−54.

[3] Martin MD, Kanne JP, Broderick LS, Kazerooni EA, Meyer CA. Lung-RADS: pushing the limits. RadioGraphics November 2017;37(7):1975−93.

[4] Erasmus JJ, Connolly JE, McAdams HP, Roggli VL. Solitary pulmonary nodules: Part I. Morphologic evaluation for differentiation of benign and malignant lesions. RadioGraphics January 2000;20(1): 43−58.

[5] Bae KT, Kim JS, Na YH, Kim KG, Kim JH. Pulmonary nodules: automated detection on CT images with morphologic matching algorithm—preliminary results. Radiology July 2005;236(1):286−93.

[6] Marchiori E, Souza Jr AS, Franquet T, Müller NL. Diffuse high-attenuation pulmonary abnormalities: a pattern-oriented diagnostic approach on high-resolution CT. American Journal of Roentgenology January 2005;184(1):273−82.

4

Feature engineering-based methodology for fully automated detection of pulmonary nodules

4.1 Introduction

We saw in Chapter 1 that the adoption of CADx methodology for automated detection of pulmonary nodules becomes a difficult research problem for the researchers to reduce the workload of the clinicians. The most important step in the implementation of the CADe approach is the appropriate segmentation of the pulmonary nodule, as this can further complicate the precise quantification of the nodule's morphological characteristics and risk classification.

In addition, there are a few fully automated methods for identifying lung nodules that take into account machine learning techniques to distinguish between pulmonary nodules and end-on-vessels. As mentioned in Chapter 2, there are a few pulmonary abnormalities on the lung parenchyma that have a similar appearance and can interfere with the proper diagnosis of pulmonary nodules. Most of the literature did not take these aberrations into account when creating their prediction model. Furthermore, the problem results in an imbalanced class problem and there is a possibility of obtaining an overfitted prediction model with greater false-positive and false-negative rates since numerous pulmonary disorders coexist in different ratios of lung parenchyma. Another interesting point is that rather than focussing on a certain slice thickness, the authors of each prediction model took into account the characteristics of the segmented ROIs from various slice thicknesses. The performance of the model is frequently diminished by the variation in slice thickness.

In order to overcome the aforementioned problem, in this chapter, a detailed description of several algorithms has been discussed which help researchers to design an efficient fully automated nodule detection methodology. Fig. 4.1 depicts different stages of a feature engineering-based fully automated nodule detection methodology.

The rest of this chapter is organized as follows: In Section 4.1, we have discussed different ideas behind multi-level thresholding. This methodology helps to retain minute intensity information of the input CT images. The next section precisely describes existing feature descriptors that will help to discriminate the pulmonary nodules from other similar looking pulmonary abnormalities and pulmonary vessels. Section 4.3 briefs some feature selection algorithms. In Section 4.4, we discussed the imbalanced learning

Application of Artificial Intelligence in Early Detection of Lung Cancer. https://doi.org/10.1016/B978-0-323-95245-3.00004-4

FIGURE 4.1 States of feature engineering-
based nodule detection.

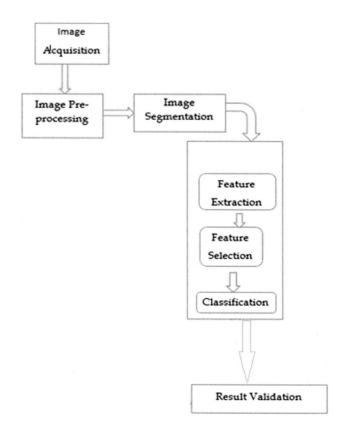

methodologies. Finally, in Section 4.5, several supervised learning methodologies have been discussed.

4.2 Pulmonary lesion segmentation

Finding an accurate segmentation methodology that is computationally less complex and can address the various difficulties of pulmonary structure segmentation. For computer vision researchers, analyzing the input image intensity value is a well-known research challenge. In several studies, the authors regarded the input images' histogram as a bimodal histogram and segmented the image using a single threshold value. However, when the various foreground objects in the image exhibit a range of intensity attributes, this technology frequently fails to preserve substantial image information. However, the process is time-consuming. On the other hand, some academics have thought about local thresholding to address the aforementioned problems.

4.2.1   Local thresholding

Local thresholding techniques for image segmentation play a crucial role in various computer vision applications. Image segmentation is the process of partitioning an image into meaningful regions or objects, enabling analysis, understanding, and extraction of relevant information. Thresholding is a fundamental technique in image processing that separates objects from the background based on pixel intensity values. While global thresholding uses a single threshold value for the entire image, local thresholding adapts the threshold value on a local neighbourhood basis, leading to more accurate and robust segmentation results.

Local thresholding techniques aim to handle images with varying illumination conditions, noise, and uneven backgrounds. By considering local characteristics, these methods can adaptively determine the threshold value for each pixel or region, improving the accuracy of object extraction. Several local thresholding techniques have been developed, each with its strengths and characteristics.

One commonly used local thresholding technique is the Niblack method. It calculates the threshold value for a pixel by considering the mean intensity and standard deviation within a local window surrounding the pixel. The threshold is computed as the mean plus a user-defined constant multiplied by the standard deviation. This method effectively handles images with non-uniform illumination and provides good results for text and document images.

The Niblack method calculates the threshold value (T) for a pixel based on the mean (μ) and standard deviation (σ) of the pixel values within a local window. The threshold is computed as the mean plus a user-defined constant (k) multiplied by the standard deviation:

$$T = \mu + k * \sigma \tag{4.1}$$

where

T: Threshold value for the pixel
μ: Mean intensity within the local window
σ: Standard deviation of intensity within the local window
k: User-defined constant (typically set to -0.2 to -0.3)

Sauvola's method is another popular local thresholding technique that considers both local mean and standard deviation but incorporates a parameter to control the sensitivity to local variations. The threshold is computed as the mean value multiplied by a factor that is determined by the standard deviation. This technique is effective for images with variable illumination conditions and produces satisfactory results for images with text or graphics.

The Sauvola method also considers the local mean (μ) and standard deviation (σ) within a window but incorporates an additional parameter (R) to control the sensitivity to local variations. The threshold is calculated as the mean multiplied by a factor (k) determined by the standard deviation:

$$T = \mu * (1 + k * ((\sigma \ / \ R) - 1)) \qquad (4.2)$$

where

  T: Threshold value for the pixel
  μ: Mean intensity within the local window
  σ: Standard deviation of intensity within the local window
  k: User-defined constant (typically set to 0.2)
  R: User-defined parameter to control sensitivity to local variations

These equations allow the Niblack and Sauvola methods to adaptively calculate threshold values for individual pixels based on the local characteristics of the image, resulting in improved segmentation performance in varying illumination conditions and complex backgrounds.

Otsu's method, originally developed for global thresholding, can also be extended to local thresholding. Otsu's method aims to find an optimal threshold that maximizes the separation between object and background classes by minimizing intra-class variance. In the case of local thresholding, the method adapts the threshold value based on local statistics, such as mean and variance, within a sliding window. This technique is widely used in various applications and can handle images with different lighting conditions and complex backgrounds.

4.2.1.1   Bradley method

The Bradley method calculates the threshold value (T) for a pixel based on the mean (μ) and standard deviation (σ) of the pixel values within a local window. It incorporates a parameter (C) to control the amount of local contrast enhancement. The threshold is computed as follows:

$$T = \mu * (1 + C * (\sigma / R - 1)) \qquad (4.3)$$

where

  T: Threshold value for the pixel
  μ: Mean intensity within the local window
  σ: Standard deviation of intensity within the local window
  C: User-defined constant to control local contrast enhancement (typically set to 0.15)
  R: User-defined parameter to normalize the standard deviation

4.2.1.2   Bernsen method

The Bernsen method uses a contrast threshold (Contrast_Threshold) to determine the threshold value (T) for a pixel. It calculates the local minimum (min) and maximum (max) pixel values within a local window and computes the threshold as follows:

$$T = (\text{max} + \text{min})/2 \qquad (4.4)$$

if (max-min) $\leq$ Contrast_Threshold,

$$T = (\max + \min) / 2$$

else,

$$T = (\max + \min) / 2 - \text{Offset} \tag{4.5}$$

where

   T: Threshold value for the pixel
   max: Maximum intensity within the local window
   min: Minimum intensity within the local window

   Contrast_Threshold: User-defined threshold for contrast variation (typically set to a small value)
   Offset: User-defined offset to adjust the threshold (typically set to a small value)

4.2.1.3 Phansalkar method
The Phansalkar method extends the Sauvola method by incorporating a noise threshold (k) to handle noisy images. It calculates the threshold value (T) as follows:

$$T = \mu * (1 + p * (\sigma / R - 1)) + q * (\mu - v) \tag{4.6}$$

where

   T: Threshold value for the pixel
   μ: Mean intensity within the local window
   σ: Standard deviation of intensity within the local window
   R: User-defined parameter to control sensitivity to local variations
   p: User-defined parameter to control sensitivity to local variations (typically set to 0.25)
   q: User-defined parameter to control the effect of intensity deviation (typically set to 10)
   v: Local mean intensity minus a correction value (typically set to a small value)

These additional local thresholding methods provide alternative approaches to adaptively determine the threshold value for each pixel based on local statistics and parameters. They can be applied in various image segmentation tasks, depending on the characteristics of the images and the desired segmentation outcomes.

In order to avoid the exclusion of peripheral nodules, the method utilizes the concept of a rolling ball algorithm described in [1]. This is a morphological closing operation with a circular structure of a specified radius. The radius of the circular structure depends on the maximum size of the lesions. If the radius is very small then the more significant peripheral nodules are discarded, whereas in the case of large structures, the algorithm yields a single region by joining the two lung areas. As a consequence, the measurement of accurate size is a challenging task for the researchers. We have considered the average size of the structures as 40 pixels after executing the algorithm over the entire images of the dataset.

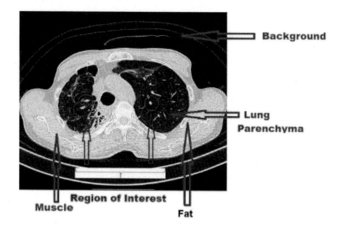

FIGURE 4.2 Anatomical figure of pulmonary nodules.

In this case, segmenting this image might be accomplished using a multi-level thresholding technique. The histogram of the input photos is displayed as multi-modal in the multilayer thresholding technique, and for each peak in intensity, the threshold value is determined by taking into account either the entropy of that specific object or the variation between classes (Otsu's method).

The histogram of Fig. 4.3 reveals that they consist of multiple peaks. The histograms also show that it has a Gaussian distribution and that a certain lesion's intensity falls inside a specific range with recurrently occurring similar intensity values. This demonstrates the multi-modal character of the image intensity values.

On the other hand, according to Fig. 4.2, an input CT scan image has four components namely, background, lung parenchyma, fat, and muscle. Moreover, due to

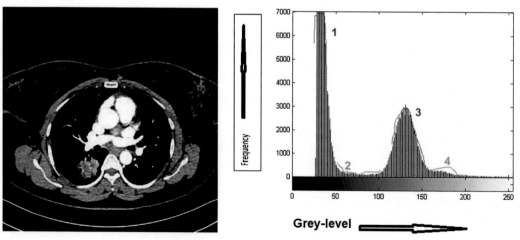

FIGURE 4.3 Input image and histogram.

the motion artefact, there may exist some traces of air on the lung parenchyma. The thresholding algorithm is capable of removing fat and muscle from the image. In order to remove the air, grayscale morphology can be applied. It is the same type of mathematical morphology operation that can only be executed on grayscale images.

Although, these methodologies are still incapable of segmenting pleural-based nodules as presented in Fig. 4.4B. In order to increase the accuracy of the pleural-based nodule, the rolling ball algorithm [2] has been applied. This is a morphological closing operation with a circular structure of a specified radius. The radius of the circular structure depends on the maximum size of the lesions. If the radius is very small, then the bigger peripheral nodules are discarded, whereas in the case of large structures, the algorithm yields a single region by joining the two lung areas. As a consequence, the measurement of accurate size is a challenging task for the researchers. The average size of the structures is considered as 40 pixels.

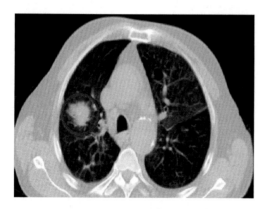

a. Solitary Pulmonary Nodule

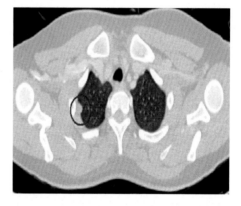

b. Pleural-based Nodule

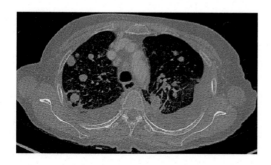

c. Juxta-vascular Nodule

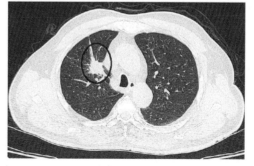

d. Pleural Tail

FIGURE 4.4 Different types of pulmonary nodules. (a) Solitary pulmonary nodule. (b) Juxta pleural nodule. (c) Juxta vascular nodule. (d) Pleural tail.

4.2.2 Entropy-based segmentation

The multi-level thresholding algorithm often calculates the optimal threshold values based on the entropy-based calculation. Among several techniques, Kapur's function and Tsallis Function are well-suited with bio-inspired meta-heuristics to obtain the threshold values. Later in this section, we will discuss the salient features of Kapur's and Tsallis's entropy.

4.2.2.1 Kapur's entropy

The Algorithm maximizes the entropy histogram of the input image. Let, th_1, th_2, th_3, ...,th_n are n number of threshold values, and if it is denoted as Th. In case of a bimodal histogram, the single threshold value can be calculated as

$$J_{max} = f_{kapur}(\text{Th}) = \sum_{j=1}^{k} H_j^C \tag{4.7}$$

Then, in case of multiple threshold calculation, the above equation is written as follows:

$$H_1^C = \sum_{j=1}^{th_1} \frac{\text{Ph}_j^C}{\omega_0^C} \ln \ln \left(\frac{\text{Ph}_j^C}{\omega_0^C} \right), \tag{4.8}$$

$$H_2^C = \sum_{j=th_1+1}^{th_2} \frac{\text{Ph}_j^C}{\omega_1^C} \ln \ln \left(\frac{\text{Ph}_j^C}{\omega_1^C} \right), \tag{4.9}$$

$$\vdots$$

$$H_n^C = \sum_{j=th_n+1}^{L} \frac{\text{Ph}_j^C}{\omega_{N-1}^C} \ln \ln \left(\frac{\text{Ph}_j^C}{\omega_{N-1}^C} \right), \tag{4.10}$$

where Ph_j^C is the probability distribution of the intensity levels, C is unity for gray level images, $\omega_0^C, \omega_1^C, ...\omega_{K-1}^C$ are the probability occurrence for n levels.

4.2.2.2 Tsallis Entropy

Tsallis Entropy can be defined as

$$S_q = \frac{1 - \sum_{j=1}^{Th} \left(p_j \right)^q}{q-1} \tag{4.11}$$

Let a grayscale image has L-1 number of gray levels with probability distributions $p_i = p_0, p_1, ...,p_{L-1}$ then the computation of multi-level thresholding values using Tsallis entropy will be as follows:

$$J_{max} = f(\text{Th}) = [\text{Th}_1, \text{Th}_2, \ldots, \text{Th}_n] = \text{argmax} \left[S_q^A(\text{Th}) + S_q^B(\text{Th}) + \ldots + S_q^N(\text{Th}) + (1-q)S_q^A(\text{Th}). \right.$$
$$\left. S_q^B(T(12)h)\cdots S_q^N(\text{Th}) \right] \tag{4.12}$$

$$\text{where } S_q^A(\text{Th}) = \frac{1 - \sum\limits_{j=0}^{t_1-1} \left(\dfrac{P_j}{P^A}\right)^q}{q-1}, P^A = \sum\limits_{j=0}^{t_1-1} P_j$$

$$S_q^B(\text{Th}) = \frac{1 - \sum\limits_{j=t_1}^{t_2-1} \left(\dfrac{P_j}{P^B}\right)^q}{q-1}, P^B = \sum\limits_{j=0}^{t_1-1} P_j$$

$$S_q^N(\text{Th}) = \frac{1 - \sum\limits_{j=t_n}^{L-1} \left(\dfrac{P_j}{P^N}\right)^q}{q-1}, P^N = \sum\limits_{j=0}^{t_1-1} P_j \tag{4.13}$$

4.2.3 Otsu's method

Between-class variance analysis is another image segmentation technique where the images are grouped into two classes namely background and foreground. It can be calculated as

$$f(t) = \sigma_0 + \sigma_1 \tag{4.13a}$$

where $\sigma_0 = \omega_0(\mu_0 - \mu_T)^2$

$$\sigma_1 = \omega_1(\mu_1 - \mu_T)^2$$

μ_T are the mean intensity values of the input image, μ_0 and μ_1 are the mean intensity values of each of the classes. The mean intensity values of each of the classes are denoted as

$$\mu_i = \sum_{i=0}^{t-1} \frac{ip_i}{\omega_i} \tag{4.14}$$

The threshold value of a binary image is calculated as

$$t^* = \text{argmax}(f(t)) \tag{4.15}$$

The calculation of the variance of multi-level thresholding are as follows:

$$f(t) = \sum_{i=1}^{n} \sigma_m \tag{4.16}$$

The variances are as follows:

$$\sigma_0 = \omega_0(\mu_0 - \mu_T)^2 \tag{4.17}$$

$$\sigma_1 = \omega_1(\mu_1 - \mu_T)^2 \tag{4.18}$$

$$\vdots$$

$$\sigma_n = \omega_n(\mu_n - \mu_T)^2 \tag{4.19}$$

The threshold values are calculated as follows:

$$t^* = \mathrm{argmax}\left(\sum_{i=1}^{n} \sigma_m \right)$$

(4.20)

4.2.4   Multi-level thresholding

Multi-level thresholding is a powerful technique used in image processing and analysis for segmenting images into multiple regions based on pixel intensities. Unlike traditional thresholding methods that separate objects from the background using a single threshold value, multi-level thresholding allows for the partitioning of an image into more than two classes or regions. This technique plays a vital role in numerous applications, including medical imaging, remote sensing, object recognition, and computer vision.

The goal of multi-level thresholding is to identify distinct regions within an image by assigning appropriate threshold values to different intensity ranges. Each threshold value determines the boundaries between adjacent regions, allowing for the extraction of meaningful information from complex images with multiple objects and varying intensities. The number of threshold values needed depends on the number of desired regions or classes in the segmented image.

There are several methods and algorithms available for multi-level thresholding, each with its own advantages and characteristics. Here, we will explore some popular techniques commonly used in practice.

4.2.4.1   Otsu's method
Otsu's method is a widely known and frequently used algorithm for multi-level thresholding. It aims to find the optimal threshold values that maximize the between-class variance while minimizing the within-class variance. This technique calculates the thresholds iteratively to achieve the desired number of regions.

4.2.4.2   Kapur's method
Kapur's method, also known as the maximum entropy thresholding, selects thresholds based on the maximum entropy of the resulting regions. It seeks to find the thresholds that maximize the information content or entropy of the segmented regions.

4.2.4.3   Huang's method
Huang's method, or the minimum cross-entropy thresholding, is based on minimizing the cross-entropy between the original image histogram and the segmented histograms. It determines the thresholds by iteratively minimizing the cross-entropy until convergence.

4.2.4.4   Kittler–Illingworth method

The Kittler–Illingworth algorithm, also known as the minimum error thresholding, estimates the thresholds by minimizing the error rate between the segmented regions and the original image. It incorporates local image statistics to adaptively assign thresholds.

4.2.4.5   Bio-inspired multi-level thresholding

Bio-inspired and swarm intelligence-based multi-level thresholding techniques leverage principles inspired by natural systems and collective behaviour to solve complex optimization problems involved in multi-level thresholding. These approaches draw inspiration from the behaviour of biological organisms or the collective intelligence of swarms to develop efficient and effective algorithms for image segmentation.

Bio-inspired multi-level thresholding methods aim to mimic the adaptive and self-organizing behaviour observed in biological systems. They typically involve population-based algorithms that simulate the evolution, interaction, or learning of individuals within a population to optimize the thresholding process.

These bio-inspired and swarm intelligence-based techniques offer advantages in terms of their ability to efficiently explore the solution space, handle complex optimization problems, and adapt to dynamic environments. They provide robustness, scalability, and the potential for parallelization in solving multi-level thresholding problems.

Multi-level thresholding brings numerous advantages to image analysis. It enables finer segmentation and classification of objects with different intensity levels, allowing for more detailed and accurate feature extraction. By dividing an image into multiple regions, it offers enhanced discrimination capabilities, making it suitable for complex scenes and images with overlapping objects.

4.2.4.5.1   Multi-level thresholding using Firefly Algorithm

Firefly algorithm is a nature-inspired metaheuristic algorithm that was inspired by the imitating patterns of fireflies. These insects generate light from their lower abdomen. This imitating behaviour is used for establishing communication between two neighbouring fireflies. The classical Firefly Algorithm was developed by considering the following considerations:

i) All the fireflies are unisex, and they are attracted to each other regardless of their sex.
ii) The luminosity is inversely correlated with the attractiveness between two fireflies. The firefly with the brighter luminance will draw the firefly with the less bright luminance for any pair of flashing fireflies. As the brightness decreases with increasing distance between fireflies, the attractiveness between two fireflies primarily depends on their Cartesian distance. If there are no fireflies with brighter brightness in a region, they will travel randomly in the 'D' dimensional search space until they locate one.

iii) The objective function is related to the brightness of the firefly.

The cost function, which tracks the optimization search, affects the FA's overall performance (exploration time, speed of convergence, and optimization accuracy). The luminance of a firefly is said to be proportional to the value of the cost function for a maximization issue.

The variations of light intensity and attractiveness between neighbouring fireflies are the key parameters in firefly optimization. These two features control the distance between two fireflies.

The variance of luminance can be calculated as

$$I(r) = I_0 \beta_0 e^{-\gamma d^2} \tag{4.21}$$

where I_0 is the original light intensity, β_0 is the absorption coefficient.

4.2.4.5.2   Multi-level thresholding using cuckoo search algorithm

Initially, the obligate brood parasitism of some cuckoo species served as the inspiration for CS. These species' female cuckoos have been known to lay their eggs in the nests of certain host birds. In the meantime, there is a chance that the horde bird will also recognize these eggs.

The horde bird then scatters the eggs from the nest or leaves the following to build a new nest.

Each host nest (containing eggs) is considered to be a candidate solution for the mathematical model. Based on this conduct, three key guidelines are drawn:

1). The population size (number of host nests available) is fixed, and the host bird has a given probability of finding a cuckoo egg. Every time they deposit an egg, cuckoos choose a different host nest.

2). To breed the following generations, the nests with the best eggs will be preserved.

The first rule is further demonstrated by the fact that new nests replace old ones with a probability of ap. The cuckoo breeding behaviour is then modelled by (Eq. 4.22) to come up with fresh ideas:

$$v_j = \begin{cases} x_{i,j+\epsilon}(x_{r1,j} - x_{r2,j}) & \text{rand} > pa \\ x_{i,j} & \text{otherwise} \end{cases} \tag{4.22}$$

The goal of the multi-level thresholding problem is to identify the best thresholds that maximise the fitness criterion $J(t)$ while remaining within the gray scale range $[0, L\ 1]$. The threshold values are determined using Otsu's between-class variance function. The number of thresholds (m) taken into account determines the search dimension of the optimization problem.

4.2.4.5.3   Flower Pollination algorithm

Flower Pollination algorithm follows two criteria namely (i) self-pollination and (ii) cross-pollination. Self-pollination means the flower of a particular plant is pollinated by another flower of the same plant. On the other hand, when different birds, bat, or flies carries pollen from another tree and the flower is pollinated.

The Flower Pollination Algorithm has the following assumptions:

1. Pollinators migrate in accordance with the Lévy flying behaviour, and biotic cross-pollination constitutes the global pollination process.
2. Global pollinations coincide with local pollination.
3. Flower constancy, which is regarded as a reproduction probability inversely correlated with the resemblance of the two flowers involved, can be developed by pollinators.
4. A switch probability influences how local and global pollination interacts with each other.

Like another meta-heuristic algorithm, FPA considered local and global search techniques. The global search technique obeys the characteristics of the cross-pollination mechanism and updates the best solution using the Lévy distribution which is expressed as

$$x_i^{g+1} = x_i^g + \gamma L(\lambda) \tag{4.23}$$

where x_g^i denotes the ith pollen in generation g; best is the current best solution;

γ is a scaling factor to control the step size;

$L(\lambda)$ is the step size randomly drawn from the Lévy distribution.

The Lévy distribution is given by

$$L \sim \frac{\lambda \Gamma(\lambda) \sin\sin\left(\frac{\pi\lambda}{2}\right)}{\pi} \frac{1}{s^{1+\lambda}} \tag{4.24}$$

where $\lambda = 1.5$, $\Gamma(\lambda)$ is the standard gamma function, and the distribution is valid for large steps s. When local pollination (rule 2) and other techniques are combined, the local search resembles the self-pollination process. The flower's persistence (rule 3). It creates a new candidate solution using two more solutions selected at random from the population and an earlier candidate solution. The new candidate solution is selected as follows:

$$x_i^{g+1} = x_i^g + \gamma L(\lambda) \tag{4.25}$$

The pollen individuals or candidate solutions are subjected to an iterative process in which their positions are updated in accordance with either (Eq. 4.7) or (Eq. 4.9) depending on whether the pollination mechanism that is probabilistically triggered is global or local. The multi-level thresholding problem has the best solution, which was found in the previous generation.

4.2.4.5.4 Genetic Algorithm

Multi-level thresholding using Genetic Algorithms (GA) is an optimization technique inspired by the process of natural selection and evolution. GA aims to find optimal threshold values for image segmentation by mimicking the principles of genetic variation, selection, and reproduction.

In multi-level thresholding, the objective is to partition an image into multiple segments based on intensity values. GA can be employed to search for the optimal threshold values that maximize the segmentation quality. The algorithm iteratively evolves a population of threshold configurations through genetic operations such as selection, crossover, and mutation.

The equation used in multi-level thresholding with GA involves fitness evaluation, selection, crossover, and mutation. Here is a high-level description of the steps involved in GA for multi-level thresholding:

Initialization: Initialize a population of threshold configurations randomly.

Fitness Evaluation: Evaluate the fitness of each threshold configuration in the population. Fitness can be measured using objective functions such as image entropy, Otsu's method, or other quality measures specific to multi-level thresholding.

Selection: Select individuals from the population based on their fitness. Higher fitness values increase the probability of selection, mimicking the principle of 'survival of the fittest'.

Crossover: Perform crossover operations between selected individuals to create new offspring. Crossover involves combining the threshold values of two parents to generate new threshold configurations. This introduces genetic diversity in the population.

Mutation: Introduce random changes in the threshold values of selected individuals through mutation. Mutation helps explore the search space beyond the influence of crossover and maintain diversity in the population.

Replace: Replace some individuals in the population with the newly generated offspring and mutated individuals.

Termination Criteria: Repeat steps 2−6 until a termination criterion is met. This criterion can be a maximum number of iterations, reaching a desired fitness threshold, or a convergence criterion indicating that the optimization process has reached a stable state.

At the end of the optimization process, the threshold configuration with the highest fitness value represents the optimal set of thresholds for segmenting the image into multiple levels.

The equations used in GA specifically depend on the fitness function used for evaluating the segmentation quality, the selection mechanism (such as roulette wheel selection or tournament selection), and the specific implementation details of the crossover and mutation operations.

By leveraging the principles of genetic variation, selection, and reproduction, multi-level thresholding using GA can effectively search for optimal threshold values for image segmentation. The iterative evolution of threshold configurations leads to improved segmentation quality and the discovery of meaningful image partitions.

4.2.4.5.5 Particle Swarm Optimization

Multi-level thresholding using Particle Swarm Optimization (PSO) is an optimization technique that combines the concept of swarm intelligence with the goal of finding optimal thresholds for image segmentation. PSO is a population-based metaheuristic algorithm inspired by the social behaviour of bird flocking or fish schooling.

In multi-level thresholding, the objective is to partition an image into multiple segments based on intensity values. PSO can be employed to search for the optimal threshold values that maximize the segmentation quality. The algorithm iteratively refines the thresholds by simulating the movement and interaction of particles within the solution space.

The equation used in multi-level thresholding with PSO involves updating the velocity and position of each particle based on its own best solution and the global best solution found by the swarm. Here is the equation for updating the velocity and position of a particle in PSO:

$$v(i,j) = w * v(i,j) + c1 * \text{rand}() * (\text{pbest}(i,j) - x(i,j)) + c2 * \text{rand}() * (\text{gbest}(j) - x(i,j)) \tag{4.26}$$

$$x(i,j) = x(i,j) + v(i,j) \tag{4.27}$$

where

$v(i,j)$ represents the velocity of the ith particle in the jth dimension.
w is the inertia weight that controls the impact of the previous velocity on the current velocity.
$c1$ and $c2$ are the acceleration coefficients that control the particle's attraction towards its personal best (pbest) and the global best (gbest) positions, respectively.
rand generates a random number between 0 and 1.
$x(i,j)$ represents the position of the ith particle in the jth dimension.

In the context of multi-level thresholding, the position of each particle represents a set of threshold values. The velocity update equation integrates the particle's historical best solution (pbest) and the swarm's global best solution (gbest) to guide the particle's movement towards better threshold configurations. The position update equation then modifies the particle's position according to the updated velocity.

During the optimization process, particles explore the solution space to find threshold values that optimize the segmentation quality. The fitness of each particle is evaluated using an objective function, such as a fitness function based on image entropy, Otsu's method, or other quality measures specific to multi-level thresholding.

The optimization continues for a predetermined number of iterations or until a termination criterion is met. At the end of the optimization process, the threshold values associated with the global best solution (gbest) are considered as the optimal thresholds for segmenting the image into multiple levels.

By leveraging the swarm intelligence of PSO, multi-level thresholding can effectively find optimal threshold values for image segmentation, enabling accurate and meaningful partitioning of images into distinct segments based on their intensity levels.

4.2.4.5.6 Ant Colony Optimization
Multi-level thresholding using Ant Colony Optimization (ACO) is an optimization algorithm inspired by the foraging behaviour of ants. ACO aims to find optimal thresholds

for image segmentation by simulating the movement and communication patterns of ants within a colony.

In multi-level thresholding, the objective is to partition an image into multiple segments based on intensity values. ACO can be employed to search for the optimal threshold values that maximize the segmentation quality. The algorithm iteratively updates the pheromone trails and selects thresholds based on the information exchanged between artificial ants.

The equation used in multi-level thresholding with ACO involves updating the pheromone trails and selecting thresholds based on a probabilistic decision-making process. Here is the equation for updating the pheromone trails and selecting thresholds in ACO:

$$\tau(i,j) = (1-\rho) * \tau(i,j) + \sum[\Delta\tau(i,j,k)] \text{ (for each threshold } j) \tag{4.28}$$

$$p(i,j) = \tau(i,j) / \sum[\tau(i,j)] \text{ (for each threshold } j) \tag{4.29}$$

$t = \text{SelectThreshold}(p(i,j))$ (threshold selection based on probability distribution $p(i,j)$)

where

$\tau(i,j)$ represents the pheromone trail value for the ith ant and the jth threshold.
ρ is the evaporation rate that controls the decay of pheromone trails over time.
$\Delta\tau(i,j,k)$ represents the pheromone update value for the ith ant and the jth threshold when considering the kth image pixel.
$p(i,j)$ is the probability distribution for the ith ant to select the jth threshold.

SelectThreshold($p(i,j)$) is the threshold selection process based on the probability distribution.

In the context of multi-level thresholding, each ant represents a potential threshold configuration. The pheromone trail represents the attractiveness of a particular threshold value based on the segmentation quality. As ants traverse the solution space, they deposit pheromone trails based on the quality of the corresponding thresholds they encounter.

During the optimization process, ants construct threshold configurations by selecting thresholds probabilistically based on the pheromone trails. The probability distribution $p(i,j)$ determines the likelihood of selecting a particular threshold based on the attractiveness represented by the pheromone trails. Ants use this information to make informed decisions about which thresholds to select.

The process continues for a predetermined number of iterations or until a termination criterion is met. At the end of the optimization process, the threshold configuration associated with the best pheromone trail is considered as the optimal set of thresholds for segmenting the image into multiple levels.

By simulating the behaviour of ants and their collective communication, multi-level thresholding using ACO can effectively find optimal threshold values for image segmentation. The exploration and exploitation capabilities of ACO enable ants to discover good threshold configurations, leading to accurate and meaningful image segmentation results.

4.2.4.5.7 Artificial Bee Colony Optimization

Multi-level thresholding using Artificial Bee Colony Optimization (ABC) is an optimization algorithm inspired by the foraging behaviour of honey bees. ABC aims to find optimal threshold values for image segmentation by simulating the foraging and communication patterns of bees within a colony.

In multi-level thresholding, the objective is to partition an image into multiple segments based on intensity values. ABC can be employed to search for the optimal threshold values that maximize the segmentation quality. The algorithm iteratively updates the solutions and employs the concept of employed bees, onlooker bees, and scout bees to explore the solution space.

The equation used in multi-level thresholding with ABC involves updating the solutions and selecting thresholds based on the quality of the solutions and the information exchanged between the bees. Here is the equation for updating the solutions and selecting thresholds in ABC:

$$vij = xij + \varphi ij * (xij - xkj) \tag{4.30}$$

where

vij represents the updated solution for the jth threshold in the ith employed bee.
xij is the current solution for the jth threshold in the ith employed bee.
φij is a random number between -1 and 1.
xkj represents the solution for the jth threshold in the kth employed bee. In the context of multi-level thresholding, each employed bee represents a potential threshold configuration. The solutions represent the thresholds for image segmentation. The equation updates the solutions by considering the current solution and a random perturbation factor φij, which allows exploration of the solution space.

During the optimization process, the employed bees search for new solutions by exploiting the information from their current solution and the solutions of other employed bees. The selection of the threshold values is based on the quality of the solutions, such as using an objective function that evaluates the segmentation quality.

The exploration and exploitation capabilities of ABC are achieved through employed bees, onlooker bees, and scout bees. The onlooker bees select thresholds probabilistically based on the quality of the solutions provided by the employed bees. The scout bees are responsible for randomly generating new solutions to introduce diversity in the search space.

The optimization continues for a predetermined number of iterations or until a termination criterion is met. At the end of the optimization process, the threshold configuration associated with the best solution is considered as the optimal set of thresholds for segmenting the image into multiple levels.

By simulating the foraging behaviour of bees and their communication patterns, multi-level thresholding using ABC can effectively find optimal threshold values for image segmentation. The exploration and exploitation capabilities of ABC enable bees to discover good threshold configurations, leading to accurate and meaningful image segmentation results.

4.3 Feature extraction

This section briefs the detailed description of several geometric and texture features from each of the segmented ROI as the study described in Ref. [3] has suggested that different types of pulmonary abnormalities can be easily distinguishable using these geometric and texture-based features.

4.3.1 Geometric features

Effective Diameter: Effective diameter illustrates the size of a lung nodule.

Eccentricity: It is a ratio between the distance of foci's and major axis. In case of an ellipse, the value of eccentricity is same as that of the second moment. The value lies between 0 and 1, 0 means the region is an ellipse and 1 denotes it's a line segment.

Circularity: It is a measurement metric for shape calculation and the value lies between 0 and 1 where 1 denotes a circle. It is defined as follows:

$$\text{Circularity} = \frac{4 \times \pi \times A}{P^2} \tag{4.31}$$

where A and P are the area and perimeters of the region, respectively.

Aspect Ratio:

$$\text{Aspect Ratio} = \frac{\min l}{\max l} \tag{4.32}$$

where $\min l$ = minimum length of the nodule candidates.
$\max l$ = maximum length of the nodule candidates.

Shape factor1 (SF1):

$$\text{Shape factor1} = \frac{\max l}{A} \tag{4.33}$$

where $\max l$ = maximum length
A = area of the nodule candidate.

Shape factor2(SF2):

$$SF2 = \frac{A}{\pi \times \frac{\max l}{2} \times \frac{\min l}{2}}$$

(4.34)

Shape factor 3(SF3):

$$SF3 = \frac{A}{\max l^3}$$

(4.35)

Roundness1:

$$Roundness1 = \left| 1 - \frac{|\max l - \min l|}{\max l} \right|$$

(4.36)

Roundness2:

$$Roundness2 = \left| 1 - \frac{\frac{\left(\frac{\max l + \min l}{2}\right)^2}{2} - A}{A} \right|$$

(4.37)

Roundness3:

$$Roundness3 = \left| 1 - \frac{\pi \times \max l - P}{P} \right|$$

(4.38)

Circularity Ratio (CR):

$$CR = \frac{\sigma_R}{\mu_R}$$

(4.39)

where σ_R is the standard deviation of radial distance from the centroid to boundary point

μ_R is mean of radial distance from the centroid to a boundary point.

Extent:

$$Extent = \frac{\text{Area of the object}}{\text{Area of the bounding box}}$$

(4.40)

Central Moment:

Central moments can be defined as

$$\mu_{pq} = \int\limits_{-\infty}^{\infty} \int\limits_{-\infty}^{\infty} \left(x - \underline{x}\right)^p \left(y - \underline{y}\right)^q f(x,y) dy dx$$

(4.41)

where $\bar{x} = \frac{M_{10}}{M_{00}}$ is the component of the centroid
$\bar{y} = \frac{M_{01}}{M_{00}}$ is the component of the centroid\\

if *f(x,y)* represents a digital image, then the central moment can be calculated as

$$\mu_{pq} = \left(x - \underline{x}\right)^p \left(y - \underline{y}\right)^q f(x,y)$$

Irregularity IndexA(IrA):

$$\text{Irregurality Index} = \frac{\text{Perimeter}}{\text{Area}} \qquad (4.42)$$

Irregularity IndexB(IrB):

$$\text{IrB} = \frac{\text{Perimeter}}{\max l} \qquad (4.43)$$

Irregularity IndexC(IrC):

$$\text{IrC} = P \times \left(\frac{1}{\min l} - \frac{1}{\max l} \right) \qquad (4.44)$$

Irregularity IndexD(IrD):

$$\text{IrD} = \max l - \min l \qquad (4.45)$$

Edge Variation (EV):

$$\text{EV} = \frac{\max l \times \min l \% 6 + 2}{100} \qquad (4.46)$$

CT Number or CT Attenuation Constant: This value is same in case of all patients for nodule and non-nodule.

Euler Number(EN):

$$\text{EN} = \frac{N_r}{N_h} \qquad (4.47)$$

where N_r = Number of objects present in the image

N_h = Number of holes present in the image

Angular Moments: Angular momentum is the rotational equivalent of linear momentum.

Boyce—Clerk Radial Function (BCRF):

$$\text{BCRF} = \sum_{i=1}^{n_p} \left| \frac{|100 \times r_1 - 100|}{\dfrac{\sum_{i=1}^{n_p} r_k}{n_p}} \right| \qquad (4.48)$$

where n_p = number of pixels in the bounding box

r_1 = distance from the centroid to bounding box
r_k = distance from the border to centroid

Spherical Disproportion (SpD):

$$\text{SpD} = \frac{P}{2\sqrt{\pi} \times A} \qquad (4.49)$$

where A = area of the object

P = Perimeter of the object

4.3.2   Texture features

Image texture refers to the visual patterns and variations observed in an image. It describes the spatial arrangement of pixel intensities and their relationships, revealing details such as smoothness, roughness, regularity, or randomness. Texture provides information about the surface properties or composition of objects or regions within the image. It is an important characteristic in image analysis, aiding in tasks such as object recognition, segmentation, and feature extraction.

4.3.2.1   GLFOS

GLFOS texture analysis measures use the image histogram or pixel occurrence probability, to calculate texture. They depend only on individual pixel values and not on the interaction or co-occurrence of neighbouring pixel values. In this study, mean, variance, energy, entropy, kurtosis, and skewness are the six GLFOS calculated.

4.3.2.2   Gray-Level Co-occurrence Matrix

The study by Haralick and Shanmugam have defined 14 different features based on the Gray-Level Co-occurrence Matrix (GLCM). The location (i,j) of a GLCM matrix defines the joint probability density of the occurrence of gray levels i and j in a specific direction θ and specified distance d from each other. Fig. 4.6 represent the properties of GLCM matrix.

1	2	3	3
1	4	3	3
2	3	3	3
4	1	4	1

A 4×4 image matrix

Run Length ⟶

Grav-Level ⟶

0 degree	1	2	3
1	4	0	0
2	2	0	0
3	0	2	1
4	3	0	0

Run Length ⟶

Grav-Level ⟶

45 degree	1	2	3	4
1	4	0	0	0
2	2	0	0	0
3	2	1	1	0
4	3	0	0	0

Run Length ⟶

Grav-Level ⟶

90 degree	1	2	3	4
1	2	1	0	0
2	2	0	0	0
3	1	0	2	0
4	3	0	0	0

Run Length ⟶

Grav-Level ⟶

135 degree	1	2	3	4
1	4	0	0	0
2	2	0	0	0
3	3	2	0	0
4	3	0	0	0

FIGURE 4.5 GLRLM matrix.

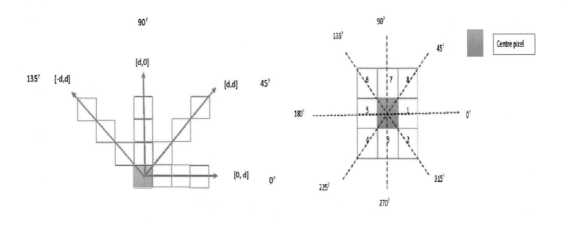

A 4×4 image

FIGURE 4.6 GLCM matrix.

A detailed description of Haralick features is as follows:
Let

ε: an arbitrarily small positive number
$P(i,j)$: the co-occurrence matrix for an arbitrary δ and θ.
$p(i,j)$: normalized co-occurrence matrix
$p_x(i)$: the marginal row probabilities
$p_y(j)$: the marginal column probabilities
N_g: the number of discrete intensity levels in the image
μ_x: mean gray level intensity of p_x
μ_y: mean gray level intensity of p_y
σ_x: standard deviation of p_x
σ_y: standard deviation of p_y

$$p_{x+y}(k) = \sum N_{gi} = \frac{1}{N_{gj}} = \frac{1}{p(i,j)}, \text{where } i+j=k \text{ and } k = 2,3,\ldots,2N_g$$

$$p_{x-y}(k) = \sum N_{gi} = \frac{1}{N_{gj}} = \frac{1}{p(i,j)}, \text{where } \|i-j=k\| \text{and } k = 0,1,\ldots,N_g-1$$

$$H_X = -\sum N_{gi} = \frac{1}{p_x(i)\log_2(p_x(i)+\epsilon)}, \text{denotes entropy of } p_x$$

$$H_Y = -\sum N_{gj} = \frac{1}{p_x(j)\log_2(p_x(j)+\epsilon)}, \text{denotes entropy of } p_y$$

$$H_{XY} = -\sum N_{gi} = \frac{1}{N_{gi}} = \frac{1}{p_x(i)\log_2(p_x(i,j)+\epsilon)}, \text{denotes entropy of } p(i,j)$$

$$H_{XY}1 = -\sum N_{gi} = \frac{1}{N_{gj}} = \frac{1}{p_x(i,j)\log_2\left(p_x(i)p_y(j)+\epsilon\right)}$$

$$H_{XY}2 = -\sum N_{gi} = \frac{1}{N_{gj}} = \frac{1}{p_x(i)p_y(j)\log_2(p_x(i,j)+\epsilon)}$$

Contrast: It measures the local intensity variation of the voxels that are away from the diagonal voxels $(i=j)$. It also correlates among neighbouring voxels if there exists a high degree of dissimilarity in intensity values.

$$\text{Contrast}_{\text{GLCM}} = \sum_{n=0}^{N_g-1} n^2 \left\{ \sum_{i=1}^{N_g} \sum_{j=1}^{N_g} p(i,j) \right\} \tag{4.50}$$

where $|i-j|=n$.

Correlation: Correlation measures the linear dependency of gray levels of neighbouring pixels.

$$\text{Correlation} = \frac{\sum_i \sum_j p(i,j) - \mu_x\mu_y}{\sigma_x\sigma_y} \tag{4.51}$$

Sum Average: The relationship between occurrences of pairs with lower intensity values and occurrences of pairs with higher intensity values has been quantified by this feature.

$$\text{Sum Average} = \sum_{i=2}^{2N_g} i p_{x+y}(i) \tag{4.52}$$

Sum Variance:
Entropy: It measures the image information and the information loss of an image.

$$\text{Entropy}_{\text{GLCM}} = -\sum_i \sum_j p(i,j)\log \log p(i,j) \tag{4.53}$$

Sum Entropy: It clustered similar gray-level intensity values in a single class.

$$\text{Sum Entropy} = -\sum_{i=2}^{2N_g} p_{x+y}(i)p_{x+y}(i) \tag{4.54}$$

Difference Entropy: It quantifies the randomness present in the difference of neighbouring intensity values.

$$\text{Difference Entropy} = \sum_{i=0}^{N_g-1} p(x,y) \tag{4.55}$$

Difference Variance: It is a measure of heterogeneity that places higher weights on differing intensity level pairs that deviate more from the mean.

$$\text{Difference Variance} = \text{variance of } p_{x-y} \tag{4.56}$$

Informational Measure of Correlation (IMC) 1: IMC1 represents the correlation between the probability distributions of i and j, using mutual information among the voxels.

$$\text{IMC1} = \frac{HXY - HXY1}{\max\{HX, HY\}} \tag{4.57}$$

Informational Measure of Correlation (IMC) 2: IMC2 also quantifies the correlation between the probability distributions of \textit{i} and \textit{j} (quantifying the complexity of the texture).

$$\text{IMC2} = \sqrt{(1 - e^{2.0}(HXY2 - HXY))} \tag{4.58}$$

Inverse Difference Moments (IDM): Inverse Difference Moment (IDM) quantifies the local homogeneity of the pixel. It is high when the gray level of the GLCM is uniform and vice-versa.

$$\text{IDM} = \sum_i \sum_j \frac{1}{1 + (i-j)^2} \tag{4.59}$$

Angular Second Moments (ASM): Angular Second Moment measures the image homogeneity. Angular Second Moment is high when image has very good homogeneity or when pixels are very similar.

$$\text{ASM} = \sum_i \sum_j \{p(i,j)\}^2 \tag{4.60}$$

Difference Average: Measures the relationship between occurrences of pairs with similar intensity values and occurrences of pairs with differing intensity values.

4.3.2.3 Gray level size zone matrix

A gray level size zone matrix (GLSZM) matrix quantifies gray level zones in an image. A gray level zone is defined as a number of connected voxels that share the same gray level intensity. A voxel is considered connected if the distance is 1 according to the infinity norm (26-connected region in a 3D, 8-connected region in 2D). In a gray level size zone matrix $P(i,j)$ the (i,j)th element equals the number of zones with gray level i and size j

appear in image. Contrary to GLCM and GLRLM, the GLSZM is rotation independent, with only one matrix calculated for all directions in the ROI.

As a two-dimensional example, consider the following 5×5 image, with five discrete gray levels:

$$\begin{vmatrix} 5 & 2 & 5 & 4 & 4 \\ 3 & 3 & 3 & 1 & 3 \\ 2 & 1 & 1 & 1 & 3 \\ 4 & 2 & 2 & 2 & 3 \\ 3 & 5 & 3 & 3 & 2 \end{vmatrix}$$

GLSZM becomes

$$\begin{bmatrix} 0 & 0 & 0 & 1 & 0 \\ 1 & 0 & 0 & 0 & 1 \\ 1 & 0 & 1 & 0 & 1 \\ 1 & 1 & 0 & 0 & 0 \\ 3 & 0 & 0 & 0 & 0 \end{bmatrix}$$

Let N_s: the number of discreet zone series in the image

N_p: the number of voxels in the image

N_z: the number of zones in the ROI and it can be calculated as follows:

$$N_z = \sum N_{gi}$$

$$= \frac{1}{\sum N_{gj}}$$

$$= \frac{1}{P_1(i,j)}$$

$P_1(i,j)$: the size zone matrix

$p_1(i,j)$: the normalized size zone matrix

N_g: the number of distance intensity levels in the image

$$p_1(i,j) = P_1(i,j)N_z$$

Small Area Emphasis (SAE): It is a measure of the distribution of small size zones, with a greater value indicative of smaller size zones and more fine textures.

$$SAE = \frac{\sum\limits_{i=1}^{N_g} \sum\limits_{j=1}^{N_s} \frac{P_1(i,j)}{j^2}}{N_z} \tag{4.61}$$

Large Area Emphasis (LAE): LAE is a measure of the distribution of large area size zones, with a greater value indicative of larger size zones and more coarse textures.

$$\text{LAE} = \frac{\sum\limits_{i=1}^{N_g} \sum\limits_{j=1}^{N_s} P_i(i,j)j^2}{N_z} \tag{4.62}$$

Gray Level Non-Uniformity (GLN): It measures the variability of gray-level intensity values in the image, with a lower value indicating more homogeneity in intensity values.

$$\text{GLN} = \frac{\sum\limits_{i=1}^{N_g} \sum\limits_{j=1}^{N_s} (P_1(i,j))^2}{N_z} \tag{4.63}$$

Gray Level Non-Uniformity Normalized (GLNN): GLNN measures the variability of gray-level intensity values in the image, with a lower value indicating a greater similarity in intensity values. This is the normalized version of the GLN formula.

$$\text{GLNN} = \frac{\sum\limits_{i=1}^{N_g} \left(\sum\limits_{j=1}^{N_s} P_1(i,j) \right)^2}{N_z^2} \tag{4.64}$$

Size-Zone Non-Uniformity (SZN): It measures the variability of size zone volumes in the image, with a lower value indicating more homogeneity in size zone volumes.

$$\text{SZN} = \frac{\sum\limits_{i=1}^{N_g} \left(\sum\limits_{j=1}^{N_s} P_1(i,j) \right)^2}{N_z} \tag{4.65}$$

Size-Zone Non-Uniformity Normalized (SZNN): It measures the variability of size zone volumes throughout the image, with a lower value indicating more homogeneity among zone size volumes in the image. This is the normalized version of the SZN formula.

$$\text{SZNN} = \frac{\sum\limits_{i=1}^{N_s} \left(\sum\limits_{j=1}^{N_g} P_1(i,j) \right)^2}{N_z^2} \tag{4.66}$$

Zone Percentage (ZP): It quantifies the coarseness of the texture by considering the ratio of number of zones and number of voxels in the ROI.

$$\text{ZP} = \frac{N_z}{N_p} \tag{4.67}$$

Gray Level Variance (GLV): It is the measurement of the variance of the gray level intensity values of each of the zones.

$$\text{GLV} = \sum\limits_{i=1}^{N_g} \sum\limits_{j=1}^{N_s} p(i,j)(i-\mu)^2 \tag{4.68}$$

Zone Variance (ZV): It is the measurement of the variance in zone size volumes for the zones.

$$ZV = \sum_{j=1}^{N_s} \sum_{i=1}^{N_g} p(i,j)(j-\mu)^2 \tag{4.69}$$

Zone Entropy (ZE): ZE measures the uncertainty/randomness in the distribution of zone sizes and gray levels. A higher value indicates more heterogeneity in the texture patterns.

$$ZE = -\sum_{i=1}^{N_g} \sum_{j=1}^{N_s} p_1(i,j)(p_1(i,j)+\epsilon) \tag{4.70}$$

Low Gray Level Zone Emphasis (LGLZE): LGLZE measures the distribution of lower gray-level size zones, with a higher value indicating a greater proportion of lower gray-level values and size zones in the image.

$$LGLZE = \frac{\sum_{i=1}^{N_g} \sum_{j=1}^{N_s} p_1(i,j)\frac{p_{1(i,j)}}{i^2}}{N_z} \tag{4.71}$$

High Gray Level Zone Emphasis (HGLZE): HGLZE measures the distribution of the higher gray-level values, with a higher value indicating a greater proportion of higher gray-level values and size zones in the image.

$$HGLZE = \frac{\sum_{i=1}^{N_g} \sum_{j=1}^{N_s} p_1(i,j)i^2}{N_z} \tag{4.72}$$

Small Area Low Gray Level Emphasis (SALGLE): SALGLE measures the proportion in the image of the joint distribution of smaller size zones with lower gray-level values.

$$SALGLE = \frac{\sum_{i=1}^{N_g} \sum_{j=1}^{N_s} p_1(i,j)\frac{p_{1(i,j)}}{i^2 j^2}}{N_z} \tag{4.73}$$

Small Area High Gray Level Emphasis (SAHGLE): SAHGLE measures the proportion in the image of the joint distribution of smaller size zones with higher gray-level values.

$$SAHGLE = \frac{\sum_{i=1}^{N_g} \sum_{j=1}^{N_s} p_1(i,j)\frac{p_{1(i,j)}}{j^2}i^2}{N_z} \tag{4.74}$$

Large Area Low Gray Level Emphasis (LALGLE): LALGLE measures the proportion in the image of the joint distribution of larger size zones with lower gray-level values.

$$LALGLE = \frac{\sum_{i=1}^{N_g} \sum_{j=1}^{N_s} p_1(i,j)\frac{p_{1(i,j)j^2}}{i^2}}{N_z} \tag{4.75}$$

Large Area High Gray Level Emphasis (LAHGLE): LAHGLE measures the proportion in the image of the joint distribution of larger size zones with higher gray-level values.

$$\text{LAHGLE} = \frac{\sum\limits_{i=1}^{N_g} \sum\limits_{j=1}^{N_s} p_1(i,j) P_1(i,j) i^2}{N_z} \tag{4.76}$$

4.3.2.4   Neighbouring Gray Tone Difference Matrix (NGTDM)

A Neighbouring Gray Tone Difference Matrix quantifies the difference between a gray value and the average gray value of its neighbours within distance δ. The sum of absolute differences for gray level i is stored in the matrix.

Let

$N_{g,p}$ represents number of gray level
p_i represents the gray level probability

$$s_i = \begin{cases} \sum\limits^{n_i} |i - \overline{A}|, \text{ for } n_i \neq 0 \\ 0 \text{ for } n_i = 0 \end{cases}$$

N_g = the number of discreet gray levels
$N_{g,p}$ = the number of gray levels where $p_i \neq 0$

Then,

Contrast: It is a measure of the spatial intensity change and is also dependent on the overall gray level dynamic range. Contrast is high when both the dynamic range and the spatial change rate are high, i.e., an image with a large range of gray levels, with large changes between voxels and their neighbourhood.

$$\text{Contrast} = \left(\frac{1}{N_{g,p}(N_{g,p}-1)} \sum_{i=1}^{N_g} \sum_{j=1}^{N_g} p_i p_j (i-j)^2 \right) \tag{4.77}$$

Coarseness: It is a measure of the average difference between the centre voxel and its neighbourhood and is an indication of the spatial rate of change. A higher value indicates a lower spatial change rate and a locally more uniform texture.

$$\text{Coarseness} = \frac{1}{\sum\limits_{i=1}^{N_g} p_i s_i} \tag{4.78}$$

Busyness: A measure of the change from a pixel to its neighbour. A high value for busyness indicates a 'busy' image, with rapid changes of intensity between pixels and its neighbourhood.

$$\text{Busyness} = \frac{\sum\limits_{i=1}^{N_g} p_i s_i}{\sum\limits_{i=1}^{N_g} \sum\limits_{j=1}^{N_g} |ip_i - jp_j|} \quad (4.79)$$

Complexity: An image is considered complex when there are many primitive components in the image, i.e., the image is non-uniform and there are many rapid changes in gray level intensity.

$$\text{Complexity} = \frac{1}{N_{v,p} \sum\limits_{i=1}^{N_g} \sum\limits_{j=1}^{N_g} |i - j| \frac{p_i s_i + p_j s_j}{p_i + p_j}} \quad (4.80)$$

Strength: Strength is a measure of the primitives in an image. Its value is high when the primitives are easily defined and visible, i.e., an image with slow change in intensity but more large coarse differences in gray level intensities.

$$\text{Strength} = \frac{\sum\limits_{i=1}^{N_g} \sum\limits_{j=1}^{N_g} \left(p_i + p_j \right)(i - j)^2}{\sum\limits_{i=1}^{N_g} s_i} \quad (4.81)$$

4.3.2.5 *Gray level run length matrix (GLRLM)*

The Gray level run length matrix (GLRLM) gives the size of homogeneous runs for each gray level. This matrix is computed for the 13 different directions in 3D (4 in 2D) and for each of the 11 texture indices derived from this matrix, the 3D value is the average over the 13 directions in 3D (4 in 2D). Fig. 4.5 represents the GLRLM matrix.

The properties of the texture features are as follows:

N_r = Number of discrete run lengths in the image
N_p = Number of voxels in the image

$$N_r(\theta) = \sum\limits_{i=1}^{N_g} \sum\limits_{j=1}^{N_r} P(i,j|\theta) 1 \leq N_r(\theta) \geq N_p \; ; \text{denotes number of runs in the image along angle } \theta$$

$P(i,j|\theta)$ is the run length matrix for an arbitrary direction

$p(i,j|\theta)$ is the normalized runlength matrix

Then,

Short Run Emphasis (SRE): It represents the distribution of short run lengths. The greater value is the indication of shorter run lengths and more fine textural textures.

$$SRE = \frac{\sum_{i=1}^{N_g} \sum_{j=1}^{N_r} \frac{P(i,j|\theta)}{j^2}}{N_r(\theta)} \tag{4.82}$$

Long Run Emphasis (LRE): It represents the distribution of long run lengths. The greater value is the indication of longer run lengths and more coarse structural textures.

$$LRE = \frac{\sum_{i=1}^{N_g} \sum_{j=1}^{N_r} P(i,j|\theta)j^2}{N_r(\theta)} \tag{4.83}$$

High Gray-Level Run Emphasis (HGLRE): It represents the similarity of gray-level intensity values in the image. The lower GLN value correlates with a greater similarity in intensity values.

$$HGLRE = \frac{\sum_{i=1}^{N_g} \sum_{j=1}^{N_r} \frac{P(i,j|\theta)}{i^2}}{N_r(\theta)} \tag{4.84}$$

Low Gray-Level Run Emphasis (LGLRE): It represents the similarity of gray-level intensity values in the image. Lower GLNN value correlates with a greater similarity in intensity values. This is the normalized version of the GLN formula.

$$LGLRE = \frac{\sum_{i=1}^{N_g} \sum_{j=1}^{N_r} P(i,j|\theta)i^2}{N_r(\theta)} \tag{4.85}$$

Short Run Low Gray-Level Emphasis (SRLGE): It represents the similarity of run lengths throughout the image. The lower value is the indication of more homogeneity among run lengths in the image.

$$SRLGE = \frac{\sum_{i=1}^{N_g} \sum_{j=1}^{N_r} \frac{P(i,j|\theta)}{i^2 j^2}}{N_r(\theta)} \tag{4.86}$$

Short Run High Gray-Level Emphasis (SRHGE): It quantifies the joint distribution of shorter run lengths with higher gray-level values.

$$SRHGE = \frac{\sum_{i=1}^{N_g} \sum_{j=1}^{N_r} \frac{P(i,j|\theta)i^2}{j^2}}{N_r(\theta)} \tag{4.87}$$

Short Run Low Gray-Level Emphasis (SRLGLE): It represents the distribution of low gray-level values, with a higher value indicating a greater concentration of low gray-level values in the image.

$$SRLGLE = \frac{\sum_{i=1}^{N_g} \sum_{j=1}^{N_r} \frac{P(i,j|\theta)}{i^2 j^2}}{N_r(\theta)} \tag{4.88}$$

Short Run High Gray-Level Emphasis (SRHGLE): It represents the joint distribution of long run lengths with higher gray-level values.

$$\text{SRHGLE} = \frac{\sum\limits_{i=1}^{N_g}\sum\limits_{j=1}^{N_r}\frac{P(i,j|\theta)i^2}{j^2}}{N_r(\theta)} \tag{4.89}$$

Gray-Level Non-uniformity (GLNU): It the similarity of gray-level intensity values in the image. Lower GLN value correlates with a greater similarity in intensity values.

$$\text{GLNU} = \frac{\sum\limits_{i=1}^{N_g}\sum\limits_{j=1}^{N_r}P(i,j|\theta)^2}{N_r(\theta)} \tag{4.90}$$

Run Length Non-uniformity (RLNU): It measures the similarity of run lengths throughout the image, with a lower value indicating more homogeneity among run lengths in the image.

$$\text{RLNU} = \frac{\sum\limits_{i=1}^{N_g}\left(\sum\limits_{j=1}^{N_r}P(i,j|\theta)\right)^2}{N_r(\theta)} \tag{4.91}$$

Run Percentage (RPC): It represents the coarseness of the texture by taking the ratio of a number of runs and the number of voxels in the ROI.

$$\text{RPC} = \frac{N_r(\theta)}{N_p} \tag{4.92}$$

Gray Level Dependence Matrix (GLDM):

A Gray Level Dependence Matrix (GLDM) quantifies gray level dependencies in an image. A gray level dependency is defined as the number of connected voxels within the distance δ that are dependent on the centre voxel. A neighbouring voxel with gray level j is considered dependent on the centre voxel with gray level.

Small Dependence Emphasis (SDE): It is the measurement of the distribution of small dependencies. The greater value indicates smaller dependence and less homogeneous textures.

$$\text{SDE} = \frac{\sum\limits_{i=1}^{N_g}\sum\limits_{j=1}^{N_d}\frac{P(i,j)}{i^2}}{N_z} \tag{4.93}$$

Large Dependence Emphasis (LDE): It is the measurement of the distribution of large dependencies. Greater value indicates larger dependence and more homogeneous textures.

$$\text{LDE} = \frac{\sum\limits_{i=1}^{N_g}\sum\limits_{j=1}^{N_d}P(i,j)j^2}{N_z} \tag{4.94}$$

Gray Level Non-Uniformity (GLN): It measures the similarity of gray-level intensity values in the image. The lower GLN value correlates with a greater similarity in intensity values.

$$\text{GLN} = \frac{\sum_{i=1}^{N_g}\left(\sum_{j=1}^{N_g}\right)^2}{N_z} \tag{4.95}$$

Dependence Non-Uniformity (DN): It measures the similarity of dependence throughout the image. Lower value indicates more homogeneity among dependencies in the image.

$$\text{DN} = \frac{\sum_{i=1}^{N_d}\left(\sum_{j=1}^{N_g}\right)^2}{N_z} \tag{4.96}$$

Dependence Non-Uniformity Normalized (DNN): Measures the similarity of dependence throughout the image, with a lower value indicating more homogeneity among dependencies in the image.

$$\text{DNN} = \frac{\sum_{i=1}^{N_d}\left(\sum_{j=1}^{N_g}\right)^2}{N_z^2} \tag{4.97}$$

Gray Level Variance (GLV): Measures the variance in gray level in the image.

$$\text{GLV} = \sum_{i=1}^{N_g}\sum_{j=1}^{N_d} p(i,j)(i-\mu)^2 \tag{4.98}$$

where $\mu = \sum_{i=1}^{N_g}\sum_{j=1}^{N_d} ip(i,j)$

Dependence Variance (DV): Measures the variance in dependence size in the image

$$\text{DV} = \sum_{i=1}^{N_g}\sum_{j=1}^{N_d} p(i,j)(j-\mu)^2 \tag{4.99}$$

where $\mu = \sum_{i=1}^{N_g}\sum_{j=1}^{N_d} ip(i,j)$

Low Gray Level Emphasis (LGLE): It quantifies the distribution of low gray-level values. The higher value mimics a greater concentration of low gray-level values of the image.

$$\text{LGLE} = \frac{\sum_{i=1}^{N_g}\sum_{j=1}^{N_d} \frac{p(i,j)}{i^2}}{N_z} \tag{4.100}$$

High Gray Level Emphasis (HGLE): It represents the distribution of the higher gray-level values, with a higher value indicating a greater concentration of high gray-level values in the image and vice-versa.

$$HGLE = \frac{\sum_{i=1}^{N_g} \sum_{j=1}^{N_d} P(i,j) i^2}{N_z} \tag{4.101}$$

Small Dependence Low Gray Level Emphasis (SDLGLE): It presents the joint distribution of small dependence with lower gray-level values.

$$SDLGE = \frac{\sum_{i=1}^{N_g} \sum_{j=1}^{N_d} \frac{P(i,j)}{i^2 j^2}}{N_z} \tag{4.102}$$

Large Dependence Low Gray Level Emphasis (LDLGLE): It quantifies the joint distribution of large dependence with lower gray-level values.

$$LDLGLE = \frac{\sum_{i=1}^{N_g} \sum_{j=1}^{N_d} \frac{P(i,j) j^2}{i^2}}{N_z} \tag{4.103}$$

Large Dependence High Gray Level Emphasis (LDHGLE): It is the measurement of the joint distribution of large dependence with higher gray-level values.

$$LDHGLE = \frac{\sum_{i=1}^{N_g} \sum_{j=1}^{N_d} P(i,j) i^2}{N_z} \tag{4.104}$$

4.4 Object recognition

Object recognition in the context of pulmonary nodule detection refers to the automated process of identifying, localizing, and classifying nodules within medical images. It involves techniques such as localization, segmentation, feature extraction, and classification to accurately detect and analyze pulmonary nodules. Object recognition algorithms aid in early detection, classification, and standardization of the nodule detection process, improving efficiency and patient outcomes.

4.4.1 Feature selection

This section briefs several feature selection algorithms. In feature selection, it has been observed that combinations of n number of good features can't give you an optimal result.

4.4.1.1 Maximum relevance and minimum redundancy (MrMr)

MrMr feature selection methodology selects those features who have shared more mutual information. Let's consider two variables x and y, the mutual information of these variables are dependent on their probability density functions $p(x)$, $p(y)$ and $p(x,y)$.

$$I(x;y) = \iint p(x,y)\log\,\log\frac{p(x,y)}{p(x)p(y)}dxdy \qquad (4.105)$$

where $I(x;y)$ denotes the mutual information.

MrMR Techniques select those features which have the largest dependency on the target class.

In order to quantify the mutual information among several variables, the measurements of dependency among several variables becomes a necessary step. The maximum dependency can be calculated as

$$\max D(S,c) = I(\{x_i, i=1,\ldots.., m\};c). \qquad (4.106)$$

When the value of m is 1, it gives the optimum set of features. When $m > 1$, a incremental search scheme is applied to find out the optimum feature values. In this regard, the mth feature can be selected as follows:

$$I(S_m,c) = \iint p(S_m,c)\log\,\log\frac{p(S_m,c)}{p(S_m)p(c)}dS_mdc$$

$$= \iint p(S_{m-1},x_m,c)\log\,\log\frac{p(S_{m-1},x_m,c)}{p(S_{m-1},x_m)p(c)}dS_{m-1}dc \qquad (4.107)$$

Due to absence of sufficient number of samples and the formation of high dimensional covariance matrix often computation of Max-Dependency is become harder. Another disadvantage of mRMR technique is its computation speed. Though, in medical image analysis, the execution time is not an important constrains but the performance of the model is under consideration.

The mean value of all mutual information is calculated as

$$\max D(S,c), D = \frac{1}{|S|}\sum_{x_i \in S} I(x_i c) \qquad (4.108)$$

The selected features by this algorithm may have high redundancy value which eventually decreases the performance of the model. This can be alleviated if one of the features is removed from the selected feature set. Now, the question is that which feature is removed from the feature set. In response to this context, calculation of minimal redundancy can help to determine the optimum feature set. The following equation calculates the minimal redundancy value

$$\min R(S), R = \frac{1}{|S|^2}\sum_{x_i,x_j \in S} I(x_i,x_j) \qquad (4.109)$$

After combining the above-mentioned criterion, we obtained the minimal-redundancy-maximal-relevance value and it can be calculated as

$$\max \Phi(D, R), \Phi = D - R \tag{4.110}$$

In fact, in incremental feature selection method, when we select the mth feature, it can be quantified as

$$\left[I(x_j; c) - \frac{1}{m-1} \sum_{x_i \in S_{m-1}} I(x_j; x_i) \right] \tag{4.111}$$

Selecting the Candidate Feature set.

4.4.1.2 *Binary Particle Swarm Optimization*

The concept of PSO was inspired by how fish and birds behave in groups. It is a stochastic-based metaheuristic that looks for the best answer by examining global minima. We chose BPSO over PSO since our extracted feature vector is discrete in nature. The main difference between BPSO and PSO, which operates under the same general idea, is that BPSO limits the position's value to either 0 or 1, i.e., the updated position = 1 implies that it is a selected feature or vice-versa. Each individual feature has been treated as a particle in the PSO-based feature selection technique, and the extracted feature vector is referred to as a swarm. Each particle is given a speed and location value, which the algorithm uses to find the best feature subset. The particles have altered their speeds and placements in each iteration while taking into account the pbest, the local best solution. This procedure is repeated until the gbest, or global best solution, is discovered. In order to get the greatest results, these local and global best solutions have updated their value using their own memory and knowledge. The fitness value of the objective function of the metaheuristics has been used to measure the effectiveness of an EC-based feature selection method. We took into account the precision of the object identification technology in this investigation because precision is unaffected by the imbalanced class problem. Eq. (4.112) defines the objective function.

$$\text{Objective function} = \frac{\text{TP}}{\text{TP} + \text{FP}} \tag{4.112}$$

where

TP = True Positive findings
FP = False Positive findings

Now, in algorithmic implementation, let's consider N number of particles or features are moving through D-dimensional space.

Each of the particles then changes its position using its velocity as described in Equation ~\ref{eqn:velocity}.

$$v_{\text{pd}}^{\text{new}} = \omega v_{\text{pd}}^{\text{old}} + c_1 \text{rand}_1 \left(\text{pbest}_{\text{pd}} - x_{\text{pd}}^{\text{old}} \right) + c_2 \text{rand}_2 \left(\text{gbest}_{\text{pd}} - x_{\text{pd}}^{\text{old}} \right) \tag{4.113}$$

$$S\left(v_{\text{pd}}^{\text{new}} \right) = \frac{1}{1 + e^{-v_{\text{pd}}^{\text{new}}}} \tag{4.114}$$

$$X_i^{t+1} = X_i^t + v_i^{t+1} \qquad (4.115)$$

where X_i^{t+1} and v_i^{t+1} are the positions and velocity at time t and Wt is the inertia weight can be defined as follows:

$$W^t = W_{\max} \times \frac{W_{\max} - W_{\min}}{t_{\max}} \times t \qquad (4.116)$$

If $v_{pd}^{new} \notin (V_{\min}, V_{\max})$ then

$$v_{pd}^{new} = \max\left(\left(V_{\max}, v_{pd}^{new}\right), V_{\min}\right) \qquad (4.117)$$

$$x_{pd}^{new} = \left\{ 1 \text{ if}(\text{rand} < S\left(v_{pd}^{new}\right) \ 0 \quad \text{otherwise} \right.$$

where

$c_1, c_2 = $ constant, $V_{\max} = $ maximum Velocity of the particle, $V_{\min} = $ minimum Velocity of the particle, $x_{pd}^{new} = $ new position, rand, rand$_1$, rand$_2 = 3$ random numbers between $(0.0 - 1.0)$
$x_{pd}^{new} = 1$ indicates the particles are selected for next iterations otherwise the features are irrelevant for this problem.

Until the fitness function reaches its maximum number of iterations, the entire procedure is carried out iteratively. As the maximum error rate permitted in the medical system is 5%, we have set the targeted fitness value here to 0.95.

4.4.2   Imbalance class handling

According to the medical literature, the non-nodules lesions are out numbers the nodules. Then, to implement a precise nodule detection methodology, researchers should focus on selecting an appropriate imbalanced learning methodology. In literature, there exist several imbalanced learning methodologies namely oversampling, under sampling, synthetic data generation, data augmentation, implementation of loss functions, ensemble learning that can easily cope with the imbalanced class problem and improve the efficacy and efficiency of the model.

In binary class problem, it has been observed that the samples of two classes are present in a disproportionate ratio. The class label which has the majority of the sample is termed as majority class and the other class is known as minority class. Under sampling is a methodology that removes samples from the majority class and make the dataset a balanced one. Among different under sampling techniques Random Under sampling (RUS) randomly selected the majority class samples from the training set and executes the operations until the dataset becomes a balanced dataset. This technique may be well-suited for extensive amount training data, however, due to randomly deletion of the teat data, there exist probability of losing some important information (Fig. 4.7).

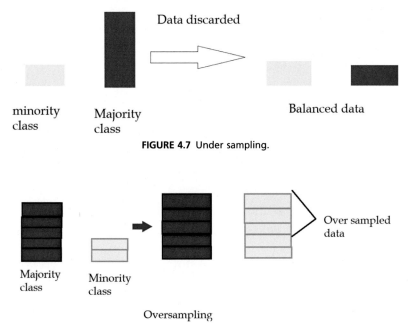

Data discarded

minority class

Majority class

Balanced data

FIGURE 4.7 Under sampling.

Majority class

Minority class

Over sampled data

Oversampling

FIGURE 4.8 Oversampling technique.

Synthetic data generation is one of the sub-categories of oversampling methodology that can alleviate the shortcomings of under sampling methodologies. In this technique, synthetic data of the majority class is generated and the entire training data becomes a balanced one. Synthetic Minority Over-Sampling Technique (SMOTE), borderline SMOTE and ADASYN are some methodologies that can generate synthetic data. In the context of nodule detection methodology, the selected features of nodule class are belonged from minority class sample (Fig. 4.8).

SMOTE is an algorithm that includes synthetic data points to the actual data points to obeying the principle of data augmentation. SMOTE can be viewed as an improved form of oversampling or as a particular data augmentation procedure. With SMOTE, you avoid producing duplicate data points and instead produce synthetic data points that are marginally different from the original data points.

The total number of oversampling observations, *N*, is first established. The binary class distribution is often chosen to be 1:1. But, if necessary, that may be turned down. The iteration then begins by first picking a random member of minority class. The KNN is applied for that instance. Finally, *N* is picked from among these *K* instances to interpolate fresh synthetic instances. To do that, the distance between the feature vector and its neighbours is determined using any distance metric. The preceding feature vector is now multiplied by this difference plus any random value within the range of [0, 1]. Actually, this procedure resembles the data point being slightly moved in the direction of a neighbour.

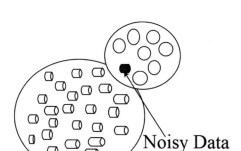

FIGURE 4.9 Noisy samples.

SMOTE efficiently cope with the imbalanced class problem, however it is biased towards noisy data generation which can be overcome by integrating under sampling with SMOTE (Fig. 4.9).

The major disadvantage of SMOTE is that it does not give emphasis on the characteristics of neighbours. Consequently, there exists probability of creating noisy synthetic samples in the training data. A combination of SMOTE with any under sampling technique can overcome this problem. Another way to solving this problem is to adaptively generate the synthetic data. Adaptive Synthetic Data Generation (ADASYN) is another synthetic data generation algorithm whose motivation is to reduce biasness and generate the data adaptively in training phase. The algorithm relies on density distribution of the training dataset, and it adaptively generates optimal number of test samples to make the training data a balanced one.

Input:

Minority class samples

k (the number of nearest neighbours to consider for synthetic sample generation)

Output:

Synthetic samples

Algorithm:

Initialize an empty set to store synthetic samples.

Calculate the number of synthetic samples to be generated, typically based on a predefined ratio or target class distribution.

For each minority class sample:

a. Find k nearest neighbours from the minority class samples (using Euclidean distance or other distance metrics).
b. Randomly select one of the k nearest neighbours.
c. Calculate the difference between the selected neighbour and the current minority sample.
d. Multiply the difference by a random number between 0 and 1.
e. Add the multiplied difference to the current minority sample, creating a synthetic sample.
f. Append the synthetic sample to the set of synthetic samples.

Return the set of synthetic samples.

ADASYN:

ADASYN (Adaptive Synthetic Sampling) is an algorithm designed to address the class imbalance problem in supervised learning, particularly in the presence of highly imbalanced datasets. It is an extension of the SMOTE (Synthetic Minority Over-sampling Technique) algorithm. ADASYN focusses on generating synthetic samples for the minority class that are more challenging to classify correctly, thereby adapting the synthetic sample generation to the specific dataset.

The key idea behind ADASYN is to introduce a level of adaptability in the synthetic sample generation process based on the difficulty of classifying minority class examples. Here's a brief overview of the ADASYN algorithm:

Input:

Minority class samples

Majority class samples

k (the number of nearest neighbours to consider for synthetic sample generation)

Output:

Synthetic samples

Algorithm:

Initialize an empty set to store synthetic samples.

Calculate the number of synthetic samples to be generated, typically based on a predefined ratio or target class distribution.

For each minority class sample

a. Compute the density distribution of minority class samples based on their distance to the k nearest neighbours.
b. Calculate the relative ratio of the density distribution of the minority class to the density distribution of the majority class.
c. Compute the imbalance ratio to measure the imbalance level between the two classes.
d. For each minority class sample, determine the number of synthetic samples to generate by multiplying the predefined ratio by the imbalance ratio.
e. Generate synthetic samples for each minority class sample by interpolating between the sample and its k nearest neighbours, similar to the SMOTE algorithm.
f. Adjust the synthetic samples based on the density distribution of the minority class to emphasize more challenging or difficult-to-classify samples.
g. Append the synthetic samples to the set of synthetic samples.

Return the set of synthetic samples.

By adapting the synthetic sample generation based on the difficulty of classifying minority class examples, ADASYN aims to provide more targeted and effective over-sampling. This helps in improving the classification performance of the minority class while maintaining the balance between the classes.

ADASYN can be a valuable tool when dealing with highly imbalanced datasets, particularly in scenarios where the minority class examples are spread across different regions of the feature space. By generating synthetic samples that specifically address these challenging regions, ADASYN helps to alleviate the impact of class imbalance and enhances the learning process for classifiers.

Cost-Sensitive Learning:

Traditional learning algorithms frequently struggle with imbalanced datasets in which one class is overrepresented. In real-world circumstances, however, the penalty for misclassifying different classes might vary substantially, making precise classification even more important. This is where cost-sensitive learning appears as a powerful strategy for addressing the unbalanced data problem while considering classification failures. Cost-sensitive learning allows models to prioritize accurate minority class prediction while accounting for the potential consequences of misclassifications.

Cost-sensitive learning is a method of assigning various misclassification costs to distinct classes in order to represent the real-world repercussions of prediction failures. The model can be taught to optimize its performance by adding these costs into the learning process. This method recognizes that not all errors have the same consequences, and it attempts to align the model's decision-making process with the desired results and consequences.

In many domains, imbalanced data exists, with one class greatly outnumbering the other(s). This mismatch presents difficulties since models tend to prioritize accuracy on the dominant class while neglecting the minority class, which might have serious consequences. This problem is addressed by cost-sensitive learning, which adjusts the classification threshold and takes into account the relative importance of different sorts of errors. This helps the model to strike a compromise between overall accuracy and the costs of misclassification.

This mismatch presents difficulties since models tend to prioritize accuracy on the dominant class while neglecting the minority class, which might have serious consequences. This problem is addressed by cost-sensitive learning, which adjusts the classification threshold and takes into account the relative importance of different sorts of errors. This helps the model to strike a compromise between overall accuracy and the costs of misclassification.

Misclassification costs must be assigned as part of the cost-sensitive learning process. These costs are calculated by carefully weighing the consequences and repercussions of misclassifying each class. The cost of misclassifying class A is denoted as Cost(A), and the cost of misclassifying class B is denoted as Cost(B). During training, the misclassification costs are integrated into the model's loss function, yielding the modified loss equation:

$$Loss = Loss(A) * Cost(A) + Loss(B) * Cost(B)$$

where Loss(A) represents class A's loss and Loss(B) represents class B's loss. The model is guided to minimize the overall cost of misclassifications by integrating the misclassification costs in the loss function, accounting for the various repercussions of errors.

In order to address the issues raised by unbalanced data, cost-sensitive learning can be combined with sampling strategies. Oversampling the minority population or undersampling the dominant population can help rebalance the dataset, resulting in a more representative training set. By exposing the model to a balanced representation of the data, it ensures that the learning process is not biased towards the majority class and takes the minority class into account, lowering the chance of overlooking crucial occurrences.

When evaluating the performance of cost-sensitive learning models, evaluation criteria must account for the seriousness of misclassifications. Traditional metrics like accuracy may not fully capture genuine performance, particularly when the cost of errors is uneven. Weighted accuracy, recall, F1 score, or other customized measures that account for the costs of misclassifications, on the other hand, can provide a more comprehensive assessment. These metrics assess the model's capacity to deliver the expected outcomes while taking into account the relative importance of various classes.

4.4.3   Supervised learning methodology

Supervised learning methodology plays a crucial role in the context of pulmonary nodule detection, aiding in the accurate identification and classification of nodules within medical images. This methodology leverages labelled data to train models that can make predictions and assist in the diagnosis of lung cancer or other pulmonary diseases.

In the field of pulmonary nodule detection, supervised learning begins with a carefully curated dataset of medical images, such as chest X-rays or CT scans, where each image is annotated with the presence or absence of nodules and their corresponding characteristics. These annotations serve as the ground truth or target values for training the supervised learning model.

Various supervised learning algorithms can be employed for pulmonary nodule detection, including convolutional neural networks (CNNs), support vector machines (SVMs), or ensemble methods like random forests. These algorithms are designed to learn and extract meaningful features from the input medical images and correlate them with the presence or absence of nodules.

During the training phase, the model is fed with the labelled medical images and their corresponding annotations. The model iteratively learns the patterns and relationships between the image features and the nodule classes by adjusting its internal parameters based on the discrepancies between its predicted outputs and the true labels. The model's optimization is typically guided by minimizing a predefined loss function, such as binary cross-entropy or mean squared error.

Once the model is trained, it can be utilized for nodule detection on unseen medical images. The trained model takes an input image and predicts the likelihood of nodules being present. It can also provide additional information such as nodule segmentation, size estimation, or nodule malignancy classification.

The performance evaluation of the trained model is critical to assess its accuracy and reliability. This evaluation is done using a separate set of labelled medical images, known as the test set, that were not seen during the training phase. The model's predictions are compared against the true annotations, and various evaluation metrics, such as sensitivity, specificity, accuracy, and area under the receiver operating characteristic (ROC) curve, are calculated to assess its performance.

Supervised learning methodology in pulmonary nodule detection offers significant advantages. It enables automated and efficient analysis of medical images, assisting radiologists in detecting and diagnosing nodules accurately. By learning from labelled data, supervised learning models can identify subtle and complex nodule patterns that may be challenging for human observers.

However, the success of supervised learning in pulmonary nodule detection relies heavily on the quality and diversity of the labelled training data. Obtaining accurately annotated medical images can be a laborious and time-consuming process, requiring the expertise of trained professionals. Additionally, the performance of the supervised learning model can be affected by imbalanced datasets, class overlaps, or the presence of noisy or ambiguous annotations.

Despite these challenges, supervised learning methodology has proven to be a valuable tool in the field of pulmonary nodule detection. Its ability to learn from labelled data and make accurate predictions contributes to early detection and diagnosis of lung cancer, improving patient outcomes. As advancements in data collection, annotation, and algorithm development continue, supervised learning techniques will continue to evolve and play a crucial role in the fight against pulmonary diseases.

4.4.3.1   KNN

K nearest neighbourhood classifier is a nonparametric-based and easily implementable supervised learning methodology that is capable of classifying binary class data with higher accuracy. In nodule detection methodology, researchers have data from two classes: nodule and non-nodule. When new test data is obtained, it is required to decide whether this data belongs to the nodule class or not. This algorithm finds the similarity of the test sample with nodule and non-nodule class. Here, Euclidean distance measurement is helped to determine that the test data is similar to which kth neighbour.

Pseudo Code of K-NN Algorithm

1. The test dataset has been loaded.
2. Kth neighbour has been calculated. K is always an integer value.
3. The following steps have been performed for each of the data points:
   a. Calculate the distance using either the Euclidean, Manhattan, or Hamming methods between each row of training data and the test data. Euclidean is the approach that is most frequently used to compute distance.
   b. The distance values are sorted in ascending order.
   c. Top k rows have been selected from the sorted array.
   d. Based on the most common class of these rows, it will assign a class to the test data.

Support Vector Machine (SVM):

SVM is another supervised learning methodology whose aim is to classify the data based on a boundary. In SVM this is known as a hyperplane. Here, each of the data

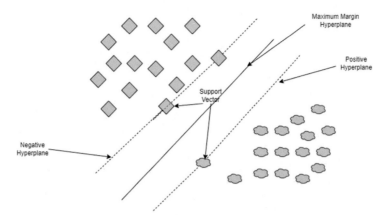

FIGURE 4.10 Support vector machine.

points is known as a vector, and extreme data points are known as a support vector (Fig. 4.10).

The Equation of a hyperplane of 2D is:

$$\beta_0 + \beta_1 X_1 + \beta_2 X_2 + \dots + \beta_n X_n \tag{4.118}$$

where X is the number of extracted features of a particular problem. In a binary class problem, the value of the hyperplane of one class will be > 0 and for another class it will be < 0.

SVM is grouped into two categories namely Linear SVM and Non-linear SVM. Linearly separable data can easily be classified using Linear SVM, i.e., a single straight line can distinguish the test data. When a dataset cannot be identified using a straight line, it is said to be non-linear, and the classification algorithm utilized is known as a non-linear SVM classifier. When the training dataset is linearly separable the soft margin classifier is used otherwise hard margin classifier plays the pivotal role. When the data are not linearly separable, the data have to transformed, i.e., the test data is mapped into higher dimensional space for linearly separable of data. In most of the real-life applications, this transformation increases the computational cost of the prediction model which can be overcome by kernel tricks. Here, instead of transforming the data into higher dimensional space a pairwise similarity has been calculated. In pairwise similarity comparisons via kernel methods, the data set X is represented by an $n \times n$ kernel matrix, where the entries $I j$ are selected by the kernel function: $k\ (xi, xj)$. Each of the kernel function has some unique mathematical property.

The lower dimension data are working as the input parameters of the kernel function and a dot product of the higher dimension vector is obtained as an output. Radial Basis Function (RBF) is most widely used kernel function used in SVM. The following equation defines the function

$$K\left(X, X'\right) = e^{-\gamma \left\| X - X' \right\|^2} \tag{4.119}$$

$\left\|X - X'\right\|^2$ is the squared Euclidean distance between two vectors.

$$\gamma = \frac{1}{\text{number of features} \times \sigma^2} \tag{4.120}$$

Artificial Neural Network (ANN):

ANN is a supervised learning methodology whose working principle is motivated by the activities of biological neurons. The architecture of ANN consists of one input layer, one output layer, and several hidden layers. Nodes of one layer are connected to the other nodes of the next layers. A specific node runs a nonlinear activation function on the weighted sum of its inputs. This is the node's output, which later serves as the input for a different node in the following layer. This process is carried out for each node, and the ultimate output—the signal flowing from left to right—is determined. Learning the weights connected to each edge in this deep neural network requires training.

The weighted sum of the non-linear function is calculated as follows:

$$z = f(x.w) = f\left(b + \sum_{i=1}^{n} x_i w_i\right) \tag{4.121}$$

where n is the number of features, b is the bias.

In a feed-forward neural network, the algorithm considered the mult.

4.5 State of the art lung nodule detection methodology designed using feature engineering methodology

The study by Sui et al. [4] emphasized not only balancing the dataset but also removing the noisy and duplicate attributes. In this regard, they have combined RUS and SMOTE. Prior to implementing the sampling algorithms, the authors have created the nodule and non-nodule lesions in the form of volumetric data. Finally, this balanced dataset has been classified using a support vector machine.

A CAD system for automated detection of pulmonary nodules has been discussed in [5]. In order to obtain a highly accurate nodule detection methodology, the authors have considered region growing and type-II fuzzy image enhancement methodology as a preprocessing step and modified spatial kernelised fuzzy c-means algorithm as a segmentation technique. The Gray-Level First-order statistics-based texture features and geometric features help to construct ensemble methodology using Multi-Layer Perceptron, k-nearest neighbourhood (k-NN) and SVM for detection of the pulmonary nodule. Cao et al. [6] have invented an ensemble-based hybrid probabilistic sampling technique to handle the imbalance class problem in pulmonary nodule CAD methodology. Prior to implementing the hybrid sampling technique, the authors have segmented the region of interest (ROI) by applying dot enhancement filter and 3D constrained region-growing technique followed by a feature extraction procedure to extract intensity-based, shape-based, and gradient feature from each of the segmented lesion. The nodule detection methodology developed by Saien et al. [7] aims to reduce false-positive detection rate by means of segmentation using a sparse eld level set, feature extraction using shape-based, texture-based feature descriptors and imbalance class handling and classification using RUSBoost classier.

References

[1] Netto SM, Silva AC, Nunes RA, Gattass M. Automatic segmentation of lung nodules with growing neural gas and support vector machine. Computers in Biology and Medicine November 1, 2012; 42(11):1110−21.

[2] Chawla NV, Bowyer KW, Hall LO, Kegelmeyer WP. SMOTE: synthetic minority over-sampling technique. Journal of Artificial Intelligence Research June 1, 2002;16:321−57.

[3] Wang S, Li Z, Chao W, Cao Q. Applying adaptive over-sampling technique based on data density and cost-sensitive SVM to imbalanced learning. In: The 2012 international joint conference on neural networks (IJCNN). IEEE; June 10, 2012. p. 1−8.

[4] He H, Bai Y, Garcia EA, Li S. ADASYN: adaptive synthetic sampling approach for imbalanced learning. In: 2008 IEEE international joint conference on neural networks (IEEE world congress on computational intelligence). Ieee; June 1, 2008. p. 1322−8.

[5] Farahani FV, Ahmadi A, Zarandi MH. Hybrid intelligent approach for diagnosis of the lung nodule from CT images using spatial kernelized fuzzy c-means and ensemble learning. Mathematics and Computers in Simulation July 1, 2018;149:48−68.

[6] Cao P, Yang J, Li W, Zhao D, Zaiane O. Ensemble-based hybrid probabilistic sampling for imbalanced data learning in lung nodule CAD. Computerized Medical Imaging and Graphics April 1, 2014;38(3): 137−50.

[7] Saien S, Moghaddam HA, Fathian M. A unified methodology based on sparse field level sets and boosting algorithms for false positives reduction in lung nodules detection. International Journal of Computer Assisted Radiology and Surgery March 2018;13:397−409.

Further reading

[1] Otsu N. A threshold selection method from gray-level histograms. IEEE Transactions on Systems, Man, and Cybernetics January 1979;9(1):62−6.

[2] Kapur JN, Sahoo PK, Wong AK. A new method for gray-level picture thresholding using the entropy of the histogram. Computer Vision, Graphics, and Image Processing March 1, 1985;29(3):273−85.

[3] Stember JN. The normal mode analysis shape detection method for automated shape determination of lung nodules. Journal of Digital Imaging April 2015;28:224−30.

[4] Niehaus R, Stan Raicu D, Furst J, Armato S. Toward understanding the size dependence of shape features for predicting spiculation in lung nodules for computer-aided diagnosis. Journal of Digital Imaging December 2015;28:704−17.

[5] Saien S, Pilevar AH, Moghaddam HA. Refinement of lung nodule candidates based on local geometric shape analysis and Laplacian of Gaussian kernels. Computers in Biology and Medicine November 1, 2014;54:188−98.

[6] Cao P, Liu X, Yang J, Zhao D, Li W, Huang M, et al. A multi-kernel based framework for heterogeneous feature selection and over-sampling for computer-aided detection of pulmonary nodules. Pattern Recognition April 1, 2017;64:327−46.

[7] Suresh S, Lal S. An efficient cuckoo search algorithm based multilevel thresholding for segmentation of satellite images using different objective functions. Expert Systems with Applications October 1, 2016;58:184−209.

[8] Chang CC, Lin CJ. LIBSVM: a library for support vector machines. ACM Transactions on Intelligent Systems and Technology (TIST) May 6, 2011;2(3):1−27.

[9] Suykens JA, Vandewalle J. Least squares support vector machine classifiers. Neural Processing Letters June 1999;9:293–300.

[10] Lawrence J. Introduction to neural networks. California Scientific Software; January 2, 1993.

[11] Vieira SM, Mendonça LF, Farinha GJ, Sousa JM. Modified binary PSO for feature selection using SVM applied to mortality prediction of septic patients. Applied Soft Computing August 1, 2013; 13(8):3494–504.

[12] Haralick RM, Shanmugam K, Dinstein IH. Textural features for image classification. IEEE Transactions on Systems, Man, and Cybernetics November 1973;(6):610–21.

[13] Bhandari AK, Kumar A, Singh GK. Modified artificial bee colony based computationally efficient multilevel thresholding for satellite image segmentation using Kapur's, Otsu and Tsallis functions. Expert Systems with Applications February 15, 2015;42(3):1573–601.

[14] Raja NS, Rajinikanth V, Latha K. Otsu based optimal multilevel image thresholding using firefly algorithm. Modelling and Simulation in Engineering January 1, 2014;2014:37.

[15] Ouadfel S, Taleb-Ahmed A. Social spiders optimization and flower pollination algorithm for multilevel image thresholding: a performance study. Expert Systems with Applications August 15, 2016;55:566–84.

[16] Sarkar S, Das S, Chaudhuri SS. Hyper-spectral image segmentation using Rényi entropy based multi-level thresholding aided with differential evolution. Expert Systems with Applications May 15, 2016;50:120–9.

[17] Gao H, Xu W, Sun J, Tang Y. Multilevel thresholding for image segmentation through an improved quantum-behaved particle swarm algorithm. IEEE Transactions on Instrumentation and Measurement October 13, 2009;59(4):934–46.

[18] Gong J, Liu JY, Wang LJ, Zheng B, Nie SD. Computer-aided detection of pulmonary nodules using dynamic self-adaptive template matching and a FLDA classifier. Physica Medica December 1, 2016; 32(12):1502–9.

[19] ur Rehman MZ, Javaid M, Shah SI, Gilani SO, Jamil M, Butt SI. An appraisal of nodules detection techniques for lung cancer in CT images. Biomedical Signal Processing and Control March 1, 2018; 41:140–51.

[20] de Carvalho Filho AO, de Sampaio WB, Silva AC, de Paiva AC, Nunes RA, Gattass M. Automatic detection of solitary lung nodules using quality threshold clustering, genetic algorithm and diversity index. Artificial Intelligence in Medicine March 1, 2014;60(3):165–77.

[21] Mukherjee J, Kar M, Chakrabarti A, Das S. A soft-computing based approach towards automatic detection of pulmonary nodule. Biocybernetics and Biomedical Engineering July 1, 2020;40(3): 1036–51.

[22] Mukherjee J, Poddar T, Kar M, Ganguli B, Chakrabarti A, Das S. An automated classification methodology of sub-centimeter pulmonary structures in computed tomography images. Computers & Electrical Engineering June 1, 2020;84:106629.

[23] Wang B, Qi G, Tang S, Zhang L, Deng L, Zhang Y. Automated pulmonary nodule detection: high sensitivity with few candidates. In: International conference on medical image computing and computer-assisted intervention. Cham: Springer International Publishing; September 16, 2018. p. 759–67.

[24] John J, Mini MG. Multilevel thresholding based segmentation and feature extraction for pulmonary nodule detection. Procedia Technology January 1, 2016;24:957–63.

[25] Bergtholdt M, Wiemker R, Klinder T. Pulmonary nodule detection using a cascaded SVM classifier. In: Medical Imaging 2016: Computer-Aided Diagnosis. 9785. SPIE; March 24, 2016. p. 268–78.

[26] Zhou T, Lu H, Zhang J, Shi H. Pulmonary nodule detection model based on SVM and CT image feature-level fusion with rough sets. BioMed Research International September 18, 2016:2016.

Application of convolution neural networks for automated detection of pulmonary nodules

5.1 Introduction

Chapter 4 discussed several challenges and feature learning-based methodologies for detection of pulmonary nodules from CT scan images. These techniques do, however, have some drawbacks. Methods for feature engineering are created using predetermined guidelines and certain assumptions. They might not generalize well to diverse image sources, i.e., if the CT scanning machine's manufacturing differs, it might not behave properly. The effectiveness of feature engineering-based models frequently depends greatly on the calibre and applicability of the selected features, making them less adaptive to changes in the data or potential new problems. Furthermore, intricate patterns, textures and relationships that are difficult for handcrafted features to capture can be seen in pulmonary nodules. The intricate nuances of nodule properties may not be adequately captured by feature engineering methods, which frequently rely on straightforward statistical measures or pre-defined descriptors. It could be challenging for feature engineering-based techniques to recognize subtle or nuanced features that are essential for accurate nodule recognition as a result. Additionally, these methods frequently need a lot of effort and expertise when creating and extracting characteristics. When working with large datasets or analyzing a lot of medical photos, this can be a disadvantage. The feature engineering approach may not scale well and may become problematic or wasteful when automated and efficient analysis is required. These methods are typically susceptible to data noise and fluctuation as well. The effectiveness of these methods can be affected by differences in picture acquisition procedures, discrepancies in image quality, or the presence of artefacts. Handcrafted features could not be strong enough to handle these fluctuations, resulting in lower pulmonary nodule identification accuracy and dependability.

The manual feature selection, limited generalization, difficulty in capturing complex patterns, scalability and susceptibility to variability and noise of feature engineering-based techniques may be limitations when compared to deep learning-based systems. These drawbacks serve to highlight the benefits of deep learning models, which can use feature engineering techniques to automatically extract pertinent features from raw data and fix problems.

5.2 Introduction to convolutional neural network

A computational model known as a 'neural network' is one that is based on the composition and operation of biological neural networks, such as the brain. It is an effective method of machine learning made up of layers of interconnected neurons or nodes. Each neuron receives input, calculates a weighted sum and then passes the final value through an activation function to produce output. To find patterns and correlations in the data, the weights — the connections between neurons — are modified throughout training. CNN's general architecture is shown in Fig. 5.1.

On the basis of incoming data, neural networks are capable of learning complicated patterns and producing predictions or classifications. They are exceptional in processes like image recognition, natural language processing and time series analysis. Different designs are possible for feed-forward neural networks, convolutional neural networks (CNNs), recurrent neural networks (RNNs) and other types of neural networks. Each sort has unique qualities and is most suitable for particular uses.

An optimization algorithm-based weight adjustment process is used to train a neural network, which entails feeding it a labelled dataset and then iteratively enhancing its performance. Forward propagation is used to pass the inputs through the network and compute the outputs, while backpropagation is used to alter the weights based on the differences between the expected and actual outputs. The neural network may learn the underlying patterns as a result of this repetitive training process, and generalize this learning to make predictions on fresh, unexpected data.

One image recognition and processing task where a convolutional neural network (CNN) excels is image identification. Considering that CNNs are built to automatically learn and extract characteristics from input images, they are particularly well suited for tasks like object recognition, image classification and image segmentation.

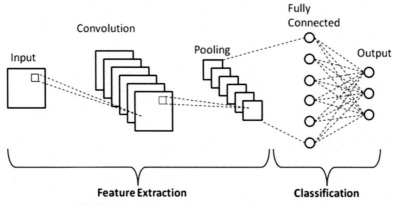

FIGURE 5.1 Architecture of convolutional neural network.

The capacity of a CNN to capitalize on spatial relationships and local patterns found in images is one of its key features. Convolutional layers, specialized layers, are used by CNNs to apply kernels or filters to the input image. These filters move across the image and execute convolution operations to extract pertinent properties. The dot product of the filter and a small portion of the input image is used in the convolution procedure. Using this method across the image, a feature map that displays the existence of specific features at distinct spatial positions is created.

Pooling layers, which are used in CNNs in addition to convolutional layers, are used to shrink the spatial dimensions of feature maps while retaining the most crucial information. This decreases computational complexity while making it simpler to extract the most important traits. On the basis of the gathered features, fully linked layers are usually added at the network's end to perform classification or regression tasks.

Convolutional, pooling and fully connected layers are alternated in a CNN's peculiar design, which enables it to automatically produce hierarchical representations of pictures. Layers that are closer to the input learn low-level components like edges and textures, whereas deeper layers learn more intricate and abstract properties. Because of their ability to recognize both local and global relationships in input data through hierarchical learning, CNNs excel at picture analysis tasks.

Mathematically, the operation in a convolutional layer can be represented by the equation:

$$y[i,j] = f\left(\sum_{(k,l) \in S} w[k,l] \times x[i+k, j+l] + b \right) \tag{5.1}$$

where y[i, j] represents the output at spatial position (i, j), f is the activation function, w is the weight of the convolutional filter, x is the input image, S represents the spatial extent of the filter, and b is the bias term. This equation captures the essence of the convolution operation, where the filter is applied to overlapping regions of the input image, weighted by the filter weights, and summed to produce the output feature map.

The two most popular activation functions are the sigmoid function and the rectified linear unit (ReLU) function. While the ReLU function returns the input directly if it is positive and 0 otherwise, the sigmoid function maps inputs to outputs between 0 and 1. This section continues by describing various activation functions that were looked into to increase object detecting precision.

Multiple layers of neurons with nonlinear activation functions are stacked in neural networks to learn intricate connections between input and output data. Using an optimization strategy like gradient descent, the network alters its weights and biases during training to reduce the discrepancy between its predictions and the actual output.

In general, neural networks are an effective tool for addressing a range of machine learning problems, from image identification to natural language processing to predictive analytics.

5.2.1   Different types of activation functions

Sigmoid function:

The sigmoid function is a smooth curve that maps inputs to outputs between 0 and 1. It is given by the following equation:

$$\text{sigmoid}(x) = 1 \,/\, (1 + \exp(-x)) \tag{5.2}$$

Here x is the input to the neuron, and $\exp(-x)$ is the exponential function of $-x$. The sigmoid function is often used in binary classification problems, where the output of the neuron represents the probability that the input belongs to one of the two classes.

One drawback of the sigmoid function is that its gradient can be very small for large or small values of x, which can slow down the learning process.

ReLU function:

The ReLU (rectified linear unit) function is a piecewise linear function that returns the input directly if it's positive, and 0 otherwise. It is given by the following equation:

$$\text{ReLU}(x) = \max(0, x) \tag{5.3}$$

ReLU is a well-liked function for neural networks because it is simple to compute and does not have the gradient vanishing issue that the sigmoid function has. The effectiveness of the network may be compromised by 'dead' neurons, which have zero output for all inputs.

Tanh function:

The tanh (hyperbolic tangent) function is similar to the sigmoid function, but maps inputs to outputs between -1 and 1. It is given by the following equation:

$$\tanh(x) = \frac{(e^x - e^{-x})}{(e^x + e^{-x})} \tag{5.4}$$

The tanh function is frequently employed in binary classification issues, much like the sigmoid function. It can also be applied to regression issues in which the neuron's output stands in for a continuous variable.

Softmax function:

The softmax function is a generalization of the sigmoid function that maps inputs to a probability distribution over multiple class. It is given by the following equation:

$$\text{softmax}(x_i) = \frac{e^{x_i}}{\sum e^{x_j}} \tag{5.5}$$

Here x_i is the input to the i-th neuron, and sum($\exp(x\_j)$) is the sum of the exponential values of all the inputs. The output of the softmax function represents the probability that the input belongs to each of the classes.

The softmax function is often used in multi-class classification problems, where the output of the network represents the predicted class of the input.

5.2.2   Pulmonary structure segmentation

Due to a variety of reasons, lung structural segmentation is critical prior to the detection of pulmonary nodules. First and foremost, appropriate lung region localization and lung boundary segmentation enable focussed nodule identification algorithms to be applied to the lung region. This improves the accuracy of the nodule identification method and reduces false positives outside of the lung area. Furthermore, segmentation allows for the measurement of nodule volume and size, which is critical for nodule characterization and tracking disease progression. Clinicians can analyze the development of nodules over time and make educated decisions about patient management by adequately defining the pulmonary structures. Additionally, segmentation makes retrieving crucial information from the lung region easier, including shape features and texture patterns essential for nodule detection algorithms. The algorithms can distinguish the lung structures so that they may concentrate on processing the data they have been given, improving the accuracy and efficiency of the nodule identification method. Lung structure segmentation, in general, enhances diagnostic accuracy, facilitates nodule diagnosis and enables more efficient treatment planning in patients with pulmonary nodules. This section summarizes the UNet architecture's basic principles for precise segmentation of pulmonary nodules.

5.2.2.1   UNet

In 2015, Olaf Ronneberger et al. presented UNet, a convolutional neural network architecture for biomedical picture segmentation. UNet has been widely used for a variety of medical image segmentation tasks, including the segmentation of tumours, organs and other structures in medical images.

Encoder networks and decoder networks are the UNet architecture's two primary elements. The pooling layers and a series of convolutional layers that gradually diminish the spatial resolution of the input distinguish the encoder network from a typical convolutional neural network. In contrast, the decoder network samples the feature maps of the encoder network and combines them with features from the necessary layers of the encoder network to create a segmentation map. Fig. 5.2 depicts the architecture of UNet for pulmonary nodule segmentation.

The usage of skip connections, which combine the up sampled feature maps from the decoder network with the feature maps from the encoder network, is the main innovation of UNet. As a result, the decoder network can utilize both the high-level and low-level information from the input image to enhance the segmentation map.

The architecture of UNet can be represented mathematically as follows:

Let X be the input image with size H x W x C, where H is the height, W is the width, and C is the number of channels.

The encoder network can be represented as a series of convolutional and pooling layers. The decoder network can be represented as a series of up-convolutional and concatenation layers. The output of the decoder network is a segmentation map of the same size as the input image.

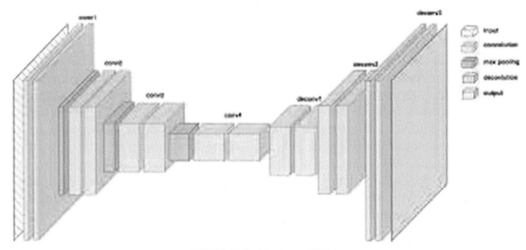

FIGURE 5.2 Architecture of UNet.

Zhou et al. [1] proposed a 3D UNet and contextual convolutional neural network (CNN) to automatically segment and detect lung nodule from CT images. This methodology consists of three stages namely lung segmentation, nodule detection or segmentation and false-positive reduction. Morphological approaches have been employed in the lung segmentation stage to segment pulmonary parenchyma from raw CT images. 3D UNet is used to extract suspicious nodules from preprocessed CT images in order to segment lung nodules. Generative Adversarial Network (GAN) has been applied to boost model training in order to improve model accuracy. An online sampling technique to supplement data and 3D contextual CNN with inception blocks employed to evaluate whether the volume is a cancerous nodule or not. The experimental results show that the proposed approach may efficiently detect the malignant nodule in CT scans. In order to increase nodule segmentation performance [2], dense feature extraction and multi-dilated context learning utilizing dilated convolutions are combined. Instead of using entire CT scan images or nodule patches, lung ROIs are derived from CT scans using k-mean clustering and morphological operators to minimize the model's search space. These ROIs are then utilized by our suggested architecture for nodule segmentation, which handles various forms of lung nodules efficiently. The dice score of 81.1% and a Jaccard score of 72.5% of the proposed methodology have been obtained by validating the model's performance with respect to LIDC-IRDI dataset.

5.3 Pulmonary nodule detection

Deep learning-based techniques have shown considerable potential in the field of lung nodule detection. The lungs contain little abnormal growths known as pulmonary nodules, which can be early indicators of lung cancer. When utilizing standard procedures to discover and describe these lesions, radiologists must usually do time-consuming and subjective manual examinations. Convolutional neural networks (CNNs) have proven to be very effective at automating this procedure.

Deep learning models can learn to recognize and classify pulmonary nodules by training CNNs on massive datasets of annotated chest CT scans. These models, which are successful at extracting attributes from pictures, can catch the intricate patterns and minute details that can be symptomatic of nodules. The ability of deep learning algorithms to learn from massive amounts of data improves its generality and robustness in recognizing nodules across varied patient groups and imaging techniques. Furthermore, as deep learning advances, researchers are constantly developing more complicated structures and tactics to increase the performance and usefulness of pulmonary nodule identification models.

Deep learning-based techniques for pulmonary nodule detection have the potential to greatly improve the precision and efficacy of early lung cancer diagnosis. These approaches can assist radiologists in screening a large number of chest CT images by automating the detection process, reducing their effort and increasing diagnostic efficacy. Deep learning algorithms can also be used to detect nodules at an earlier stage, allowing for more timely treatment and potentially better patient outcomes. To ensure the dependability and efficacy of these approaches in clinical practise, it is critical to continue enhancing and verifying them using a variety of datasets and stringent evaluation measures.

5.3.1 Types of CNN well-suited for pulmonary detection

There are several deep methodologies that are capable of differentiating pulmonary nodules from CT images.

Region proposal convolutional neural networks (R-CNN): A family of deep learning models called R-CNNs are very good at object detection tasks. They entail producing region suggestions inside a picture and identifying each suggested region as a nodule or non-nodule. R-CNNs are effective for precision detection since they are able to localize nodules correctly inside a given image.

(a) **3D Convolutional Neural Networks:** Conventional CNNs function on 2D picture slices on their own, which may miss important contextual data seen in 3D volumes. Because 3D CNNs can analyze the entire volume at once, spatial relationships and contextual cues may be effectively utilized. This method has produced encouraging outcomes for identifying and classifying lung nodules in 3D CT imaging.

(b) **Generative Adversarial Networks (GANs):** GANs consist of a generator network that produces realistic synthetic images and a discriminator network that distinguishes between real and fake images. GANs have been explored for augmenting training data, generating synthetic nodules, and improving the generalization of deep learning models for nodule detection.

(c) **Attention Mechanisms:** During the detecting phase, attention mechanisms concentrate on significant areas of an image. They enable the model to suppress unnecessary data and give salient features higher weights. Deep learning algorithms that are attention-based have the potential to increase the precision and interpretability of lung nodule identification.

The aforementioned CNN algorithms have several architectures to improve the nodule detection methodology. Rest of the chapter we will discuss several architectures of CNN.

5.3.1.1   Residual network

Kaiming He et al. created the deep convolutional neural network architecture known as ResNet (short for Residual Network) in 2015. By tackling the issue of vanishing gradients, ResNet is renowned for its ability to train incredibly deep neural networks with great accuracy.

In conventional deep neural networks, the accuracy of the network frequently reaches saturation and then rapidly declines as the number of layers rises. This is because it becomes challenging to update the weights of the lower layers during training because the gradient of the loss function with respect to those weights gets very small. The vanishing gradient problem is the name given to this issue.

Skip connections, which enable information to move directly from one layer to another, are a ResNet solution to this issue. ResNet is composed of residual blocks, each of which has a shortcut link that skips one or more layers. The convolutional layer's input and output are added to produce the residual block's output. This means that if the input to the residual block is x, and the output of the convolutional layer is f(x), then the output of the residual block is given by:

$$\text{Residual\_block\_output} = f(x) + x \tag{5.6}$$

This is referred to as the residual connection because it enables the network to learn the residual mapping, or the distinction between the convolutional layer's input and output. By giving the gradients a clear path to follow, the residual connection also aids in addressing the disappearing gradient issue.

Multiple residual blocks with various numbers of layers make up the ResNet architecture. For instance, the ResNet-50 design has 50 layers and 16 residual blocks. The final output is created by passing the output of the final residual block through a fully connected layer, then a global average pooling layer.

$$\text{ResNet\_output} = f(\text{Residual\_block\_1\_output}) + \text{Residual\_block\_1\_output}$$

$$= f(f(\text{Residual\_block\_2\_output}) + \text{Residual\_block\_2\_output}) + \text{Residual\_block\_1\_output}$$

$$= \ldots \tag{5.7}$$

$$= f(f(\ldots(f(\text{Residual\_block\_n\_output}) + \text{Residual\_block\_n\_output}) + \ldots$$
$$+ \text{Residual\_block\_2\_output}) + \text{Residual\_block\_1\_output}$$

where f is the convolutional layer, and n is the number of residual blocks in the network.

In the field of pulmonary nodule detection, ResNet (Residual Neural Network) has emerged as a powerful tool. ResNet is a deep learning architecture widely used in computer vision tasks, and it can be leveraged as the backbone network within a larger detection framework. To utilize ResNet for pulmonary nodule detection, a dataset of chest CT scans with annotations indicating the presence or location of nodules is prepared. The CT scans undergo preprocessing steps such as resizing and intensity normalization. The ResNet architecture, consisting of residual blocks, is then used as the backbone, with pretrained weights from ImageNet serving as a starting point for transfer learning. On top of the ResNet backbone, an object detection head is added to perform nodule localization and classification. The model is trained using appropriate loss functions and optimization algorithms. Evaluation metrics such as precision, recall, and F1 score are used to assess its performance. Once trained, the ResNet-based model can be used for inference on new chest CT scans, providing predictions of nodule locations and probabilities. However, it's important to consider specific implementation details and additional steps, such as data augmentation and post-processing techniques, to ensure accurate and reliable pulmonary nodule detection in presence of class imbalance.

The author of [2] uses 3D DCNNs based on a squeeze-and-excite network and a residual network (SE-ResNet) for lung nodule candidate detection and false-positive reduction. A 3D region proposal network with a UNet-like structure is specifically intended for finding pulmonary nodule candidates. A 3D SE-ResNet-based classifier is provided to accurately distinguish genuine nodules from candidates for further false-positive reduction. The 3D SE-ResNet modules improve the network's representational power by adaptively recalibrating channel-wise residual feature responses. Both models make use of 3D SE-ResNet modules to efficiently learn nodule features and increase nodule identification performance.

5.3.1.2 VGGNet

The University of Oxford's Visual Geometry Group came up with the convolutional neural network (CNN) architecture known as VGGNet, or Visual Geometry Group Network. It is renowned for being both straightforward and successful in image categorization tasks.

The process begins by acquiring a dataset of chest CT scans that have been annotated to identify the presence or absence of pulmonary nodules. These scans are pre-processed by resizing them to a consistent input size and normalizing the pixel intensities.

VGGNet, with its deep architecture consisting of multiple convolutional and pooling layers, is then utilized as a backbone network. The pretrained weights from large-scale image datasets, such as ImageNet, are often used for transfer learning. This enables the network to leverage the learnt features from the pretraining and adapt them to the specific task of pulmonary nodule detection.

To train the VGGNet-based model for nodule detection, the dataset is split into training and validation sets. The model is optimized using appropriate loss functions, such as binary cross-entropy, and optimization algorithms, such as stochastic gradient descent (SGD) or Adam. The training process aims to iteratively update the model's parameters to minimize the loss and improve the network's ability to detect nodules accurately.

Once the model is trained, it can be utilized for inference on new CT images. The VGGNet-based model analyzes the input CT scans and generates predictions regarding the presence or absence of pulmonary nodules. These predictions can be further processed to obtain bounding box coordinates and probability scores, indicating the likelihood of nodule presence.

The application of VGGNet for pulmonary nodule detection from CT images showcases the power of deep learning in medical imaging analysis. By leveraging the network's ability to learn intricate features and patterns, VGGNet contributes to the accurate and efficient detection of pulmonary nodules, aiding in early diagnosis and treatment planning for lung diseases.

A number of convolutional layers are present in the design of VGGNet, which is followed by fully linked layers. The fundamental idea behind VGGNet is to stack several smaller (3x3) convolutional filters together to create a deeper network with fewer parameters than would be possible with larger filters.

Let's denote the input image as I, and the output of the ith convolutional layer as H(i). The convolution operation in VGGNet is denoted by * and can be represented as

$$H(i) = f(W(i) * H(i-1) + b(i)) \tag{5.8}$$

where

H(i-1) is the output of the previous layer (i-1)
W(i) represents the learnable weights of the ith convolutional layer
b(i) is the bias term of the ith convolutional layer
f($\cdot$) denotes the activation function, typically the Rectified Linear Unit (ReLU) activation

In VGGNet, multiple convolutional layers are stacked together to form the network. The architecture is characterized by repeating blocks of convolutional layers followed by max pooling layers, which reduce the spatial dimensions of the feature maps. The final output of the convolutional layers is then flattened and fed into fully connected layers for classification.

The architecture of VGGNet is typically defined by the number of convolutional layers and their depths. For example, VGG16 has 16 layers, including 13 convolutional layers and three fully connected layers. VGG19 has 19 layers, including 16 convolutional layers and three fully connected layers.

The architecture of VGG16 can be summarized as follows:

Input layer (I)
Convolutional layers:
Convolutional layer with 64 filters, each of size 3x3

Convolutional layer with 64 filters, each of size 3x3
Max pooling layer
Convolutional layer with 128 filters, each of size 3x3
Convolutional layer with 128 filters, each of size 3x3
Max pooling layer
Convolutional layer with 256 filters, each of size 3x3
Convolutional layer with 256 filters, each of size 3x3
Convolutional layer with 256 filters, each of size 3x3
Max pooling layer
Convolutional layer with 512 filters, each of size 3x3
Convolutional layer with 512 filters, each of size 3x3
Convolutional layer with 512 filters, each of size 3x3
Max pooling layer
Convolutional layer with 512 filters, each of size 3x3
Convolutional layer with 512 filters, each of size 3x3
Convolutional layer with 512 filters, each of size 3x3
Max pooling layer
Fully connected layers:
Fully connected layer with 4096 units
Fully connected layer with 4096 units

Fully connected layer with the desired number of output units (e.g., for ImageNet classification, 1000 units)

It's important to note that the equations provided above are simplified representations of the VGGNet architecture.

In addition to the convolutional and fully connected layers, there are a few more elements required to implement VGGNet:

Padding: In convolutional layers, padding is frequently utilized to maintain the spatial dimensions of the feature maps. The input image or feature map must have additional rows and columns of zeros added around it. The padding in VGGNet is typically 1 pixel, which implies the input is padded with a border of zeros the size of 1 around each side of the feature map or image.

Activation function: After each convolutional and fully connected layer, VGGNet frequently employs the Rectified Linear Unit (ReLU) activation function. The ReLU function allows the network to introduce non-linearity by producing the maximum between zero and the input value.

Pooling: After every two or three convolutional layers, VGGNet adds the maximum number of pooling layers. By choosing the highest value possible within a preset window, max pooling decreases the spatial dimensions of the feature maps. The feature maps in VGGNet are commonly downsampled by a factor of 2 using a pooling window of size 2x2 with a stride of 2 (non-overlapping).

Dropout: Dropout is a regularization technique used to prevent overfitting. It randomly sets a fraction of the input units to zero during training, which helps in reducing co-adaptation between neurons. In VGGNet, dropout is typically applied after the fully connected layers.

Softmax: For classification tasks, VGGNet usually employs the softmax activation function in the last fully connected layer. Softmax converts the output values into a probability distribution over the different classes, enabling the network to assign probabilities to each class.

Padding, activation functions (ReLU), pooling, dropout and softmax are just a few of the extra components that are essential for fully implementing the VGGNet architecture and obtaining its excellent performance in image classification tasks.

5.3.1.3   You only look once version 3

YOLOv3 is a popular object detection algorithm that is widely used in computer vision applications. It is an improvement over the previous versions of YOLO, with better accuracy and faster inference times. YOLOv3 uses a single convolutional neural network (CNN) to perform object detection in real time.

The architecture of YOLOv3 consists of a backbone CNN, followed by multiple detection heads. The backbone CNN is typically a pre-trained network such as Darknet-53, which is used to extract features from the input image. These features are then passed to the detection heads, which predict the class and location of objects in the image.

The YOLOv3 algorithm predicts bounding boxes, class probabilities and confidence scores for each object in the image. The bounding box is represented as (x, y, w, h), where (x, y) are the coordinates of the centre of the box, and (w, h) are the width and height of the box. The class probabilities represent the likelihood of the object belonging to a particular class, and the confidence score represents the confidence of the algorithm in its prediction.

The final output of the YOLOv3 algorithm is a tensor of shape (N, G, G, (Bx5 + C)), where N is the batch size, G is the grid size, B is the number of bounding boxes predicted per grid cell, and C is the number of classes. The equation for the final output can be represented as

$$\text{YOLOv3\_output} = [\text{t1}, \text{t2}, \ldots, \text{tG\textasciicircum 2}] \quad \# \text{ tensor of shape } (N, G, G, (Bx5 + C))$$

where t is a vector of length (Bx5 + C), representing the predicted bounding boxes, class probabilities, and confidence scores for each grid cell.

In order to use YOLOv3 for pulmonary nodule detection, a dataset of annotated CT images is required. The images are preprocessed by resizing them to a suitable input size and normalizing the pixel values. YOLOv3 uses a convolutional neural network architecture with several convolutional layers, followed by fully connected layers. It divides the image into a grid and predicts bounding boxes, class probabilities and confidence scores for each grid cell.

The model is trained by optimizing a combination of localization loss and classification loss using techniques such as backpropagation and gradient descent. The goal is to adjust the network's parameters to accurately identify and localize pulmonary nodules in CT images. The annotated dataset is used to train the model, and the model is evaluated using metrics such as precision, recall and F1 score to assess its performance.

During inference, the trained YOLOv3 model is applied to new CT images to detect and localize pulmonary nodules. The model scans the image and predicts bounding boxes around the nodules, along with corresponding class probabilities. Post-processing steps such as non-maximum suppression may be applied to refine the detection results and remove duplicate or overlapping bounding boxes.

The application of YOLOv3 for pulmonary nodule detection offers several advantages, including real-time detection, the ability to handle multiple nodules simultaneously and the potential for integration into clinical workflows. By leveraging YOLOv3's object detection capabilities, it becomes possible to enhance the efficiency and accuracy of pulmonary nodule detection, leading to improved diagnosis and treatment of lung diseases.

Haibo et al. [3] offer a method for detecting lung nodules based on enhanced yolov3. This technique proposes using superimposed extended convolution first, and then processing the 104 * 104 feature map produced from the second residual block in darknrt-53, which is the backbone feature extraction network of yolv3, and the superimposed extended convolution. Finally, a new 52 * 52 detection feature fusion map is produced after twice down sampling and 52 * 52 detection feature map fusing to boost the network feature extraction capabilities. On the luna16 open lung CT image data set, a vast number of tests were performed. The model's average accuracy is 73.9%.

5.3.1.4 Cascaded dual pathway residual network

The Cascaded Dual Pathway Residual Network (CDPN) is a deep learning architecture designed for image super-resolution tasks. It was proposed in the paper 'Learning a Single Convolutional Super-Resolution Network for Multiple Degradations' by Zhang et al. (2018).

CDPN aims to address the challenge of handling multiple types of image degradations simultaneously, such as noise, blur and compression artefacts, in a single model. The architecture achieves this by incorporating dual pathways, where each pathway focusses on handling a specific type of degradation. The dual pathways are then fused to generate the final high-resolution output.

Here is an overview of the CDPN architecture:

Input Image: The low-resolution (degraded) input image is fed into the network.

Feature Extraction: The input image is passed through a set of convolutional layers, which perform the initial feature extraction. This helps in capturing low-level image details.

Dual Pathways:

a. Pathway 1—Direct Mapping: This pathway aims to directly map the low-resolution input image to the high-resolution output. It focusses on capturing the overall structure and details of the image.
b. Pathway 2—Residual Learning: This pathway focusses on learning the residual information required to refine the output generated by Pathway 1. It aims to handle specific degradations, such as noise, blur or compression artefacts. This pathway consists of several residual blocks, where each block contains convolutional layers followed by batch normalization and non-linear activation (e.g., ReLU).

Fusion: The output features from both pathways are fused to obtain a comprehensive representation that incorporates both the direct mapping and the residual learning information. Various fusion techniques can be used, such as concatenation followed by convolutional layers.

Reconstruction: The fused features are then processed by a set of convolutional layers, which progressively upscale the feature maps and refine the details to generate the final high-resolution output.

The CDPN architecture is trained using a combination of pixel-wise mean squared error (MSE) loss and perceptual loss, such as the content loss based on a pre-trained deep network (e.g., VGGNet). The network is optimized using gradient-based optimization methods like stochastic gradient descent (SGD) or Adam.

By incorporating dual pathways and fusion, CDPN can effectively handle multiple degradations in a single model, leading to improved performance in image super-resolution tasks compared to traditional single-pathway models. Fig. 5.5 picturises the dual-pathway neural network.

Liu et al. [4] consider the multi-view and multi-scale features of different ROIs to detect pulmonary nodules from CT images. In this methodology, a residual block-based dual-path network extract features of segmented ROIs as mentioned earlier. In addition, the author designed an improved weighted sampling strategy to select training samples based on the edge. They validate their model's performance with the annotations of four radiologists and this comparison clearly indicates the improved performance of CAD model over human interpretation.

5.3.1.5 Region proposal network

The Region Proposal Network (RPN) is a key component of the Faster R-CNN (Region-based Convolutional Neural Network) architecture, which is widely used for object detection tasks. The RPN is responsible for generating potential object proposals in an image, which are then used for subsequent object classification and bounding box regression.

The main purpose of the RPN is to propose regions in the image that are likely to contain objects of interest. It accomplishes this by sliding a small window, called an anchor, over the convolutional feature map obtained from the backbone network (such as a CNN). Anchors are predefined bounding boxes of different scales and aspect ratios that cover various spatial locations across the feature map.

For each anchor, the RPN predicts two values: the probability of the anchor containing an object (objectness score) and the adjustment to the anchor's coordinates to better fit the object's bounding box. This is done through a set of convolutional layers applied to the feature map. These layers are typically followed by two sibling fully connected layers: one for objectness classification and the other for bounding box regression.

The RPN uses a binary classification loss (e.g., logistic loss) to determine whether each anchor contains an object or not. Additionally, it calculates the regression loss (e.g., smooth L1 loss) between the predicted bounding box adjustments and the ground truth bounding box coordinates for positive anchors (anchors with high objectness scores). The loss is computed only for a subset of anchors known as anchor targets, which are selected based on their overlap with ground truth objects.

After the RPN generates the object proposals, they are further processed by non-maximum suppression (NMS) to eliminate redundant proposals and select the most promising ones based on their objectness scores. These final proposals are then fed into the subsequent stages of the Faster R-CNN pipeline for object classification and precise bounding box regression.

The RPN is trained end-to-end with the rest of the Faster R-CNN network. During training, the RPN loss is combined with the losses from the object classification and bounding box regression stages, forming a multi-task loss. This joint optimization enables the RPN to learn to propose accurate object regions while being guided by the downstream tasks.

The Region Proposal Network significantly improves the efficiency and accuracy of object detection systems by generating region proposals that effectively reduce the search space for object detection. By focussing on likely object locations, the RPN allows subsequent stages of the Faster R-CNN pipeline to perform object classification and localization with greater precision and computational efficiency.

The architecture of the Region Proposal Network (RPN) consists of several convolutional layers followed by fully connected layers. Let's denote the input feature map as F, and the output of the RPN as P, representing the objectness probability and bounding box regression adjustments for each anchor. Figs. 5.6 and 5.7 describe the architecture of RPN.

Here is the general architecture of the RPN:

Input feature map (F): The feature map is obtained from the backbone network, such as a CNN, that processes the input image.

Convolutional layers: The feature map F is passed through a series of convolutional layers to extract higher-level features. The convolutional layers typically have a small kernel size (e.g., 3x3) to capture local patterns.

Anchor generation: Anchors are generated by sliding a set of predefined bounding boxes of different scales and aspect ratios over the feature map. Let's denote the set of anchors as A.

Objectness classification branch:

a. Convolutional layers: The feature map obtained from the previous step is fed into a set of convolutional layers. These layers are responsible for predicting the objectness probability for each anchor.

b. Objectness score (S): The output of the convolutional layers is passed through a sibling fully connected layer that produces a scalar value representing the objectness score for each anchor. The objectness score indicates the probability of an anchor containing an object of interest.

Bounding box regression branch:

a. Convolutional layers: Similar to the objectness classification branch, the feature map is further processed by convolutional layers.

b. Bounding box adjustments (B): The output of the convolutional layers is passed through a sibling fully connected layer that outputs four values for each anchor, representing the adjustments to the anchor's coordinates. These adjustments refine the anchor to better fit the ground truth bounding box of the object.

The equations for the RPN can be summarized as follows:

Objectness score (S) for each anchor:

$$S = \sigma(W\_cls * \varphi(F)) \tag{5.9}$$

where

$\varphi(F)$ represents the feature map obtained from the convolutional layers,
W_cls denotes the weights of the fully connected layer for objectness classification,
$\sigma(\cdot)$ is the sigmoid activation function that maps the output to the range [0, 1].

Bounding box adjustments (B) for each anchor:

$$B = W\_reg * \varphi(F) \tag{5.10}$$

where

W_reg denotes the weights of the fully connected layer for bounding box regression.

During training, the RPN is optimized using two types of loss functions:

Objectness classification loss: The binary cross-entropy loss is typically used to measure the discrepancy between the predicted objectness scores (S) and the ground truth labels for each anchor.

Bounding box regression loss: The smooth L1 loss is commonly employed to calculate the difference between the predicted bounding box adjustments (B) and the ground truth bounding box coordinates for positive anchors.

The RPN is trained end-to-end along with the rest of the object detection pipeline, allowing it to learn to generate accurate object proposals that effectively reduce the search space for subsequent object classification and localization stages.

Li et al. [2] integrated auto-encoder decoder technique with region proposal network to improve the performance of nodule detection methodology. They have considered dynamically scaled cross entropy loss function to overcome the imbalanced class problem associated with pulmonary nodule detection methodology. In later stage, squeeze-and-excitation structure is considered to learn effective image features which helps to retain the inter-dependency information of different feature maps in nodule detection stage.

5.3.1.6 Feature Pyramid Network

The Feature Pyramid Network (FPN) is a convolutional neural network architecture designed to address the problem of scale variance in object detection and segmentation tasks. FPN aims to improve the accuracy of object detection and segmentation by incorporating features from multiple scales and resolutions.

The key idea behind FPN is to build a feature pyramid that combines features from different levels of the convolutional network, allowing the network to capture both high-level semantic information and fine-grained details at multiple scales. FPN achieves this by introducing a top-down pathway and lateral connections within the network.

Here is the architecture of the Feature Pyramid Network:

Backbone network: The input image is processed by a backbone network, such as a convolutional neural network (e.g., ResNet, VGGNet), which extracts feature maps at different levels with varying spatial resolutions. Let's denote the feature maps from the backbone network as C_3, C_4, C_5, where C_i represents the feature map at the ith level.

Top-down pathway: FPN starts by upsampling the feature map C_5 to match the resolution of the feature map C_4. This is done through upsampling or interpolation. The upsampled C_5 is then added element-wise to the feature map C_4, forming the first level of the FPN pyramid. Let's denote this level as P_4.

Lateral connections: To ensure seamless information flow across different levels, FPN introduces lateral connections. These connections are achieved by applying 1x1 convolutional layers to the lower-resolution feature maps (C_3, C_4) to reduce their channel dimensions and match the channel dimensions of the upsampled feature maps (C_5, P_4). The resulting feature maps from the lateral connections are denoted as P_3 and P_4, respectively.

Further levels: FPN can be extended to include more levels by repeatedly applying the top-down pathway and lateral connections. The next level, denoted as P_5, is generated by upsampling the feature map C_4 and adding it to the feature map P_4. This process can be continued by upsampling the lower-resolution feature maps (C_3, C_4) and adding them to the higher-resolution feature maps (P_3, P_4), generating additional levels of the pyramid (P_3, P_4, P_5, etc.).

The resulting feature pyramid P includes feature maps at different scales, where each level corresponds to a specific spatial resolution. These feature maps capture both high-level semantic information (from the top-down pathway) and fine-grained details (from the lateral connections), enabling the network to make accurate predictions at different scales.

The equations for the Feature Pyramid Network can be summarized as follows:

Upsampling:

$$U\_i = UpSample(C\_i) \tag{5.11}$$

where UpSample($\cdot$) represents the operation to upsample or interpolate the feature map C_i to match the resolution of the corresponding higher-level feature map.

Lateral connections:

$$L\_i = 1x1Conv(C\_i) \tag{5.12}$$

where 1x1Conv($\cdot$) denotes the 1x1 convolutional layer applied to reduce the channel dimensions of the feature map C_i.

Feature pyramid level:

$$P\_i = L\_i + U\_i \tag{5.13}$$

where P_i represents the feature map at the ith level of the feature pyramid, obtained by element-wise addition of the upsampled feature map U_i and the lateral connection L_i.

The Feature Pyramid Network architecture allows for multi-scale feature representation, facilitating accurate object detection and segmentation at various scales. By incorporating features from different levels of the network, FPN enhances the network's ability to handle objects of different sizes and provides a more comprehensive understanding of the visual scene.

5.3.1.7 *Transfer learning*

Transfer learning is a technique widely used in deep learning for tasks with limited training data or computational resources. In the context of pulmonary nodule detection, transfer learning involves leveraging pre-trained models on large-scale image datasets and adapting them to perform nodule detection tasks. Transfer learning is implemented in the context of pulmonary nodule detection for several reasons. Firstly, pulmonary nodules are relatively rare and diverse, making it challenging to collect a large labelled dataset solely for nodule detection. By utilizing transfer learning, models can benefit from pre-trained networks that have learnt general image features from large-scale datasets, such as ImageNet. This approach allows the model to leverage the knowledge gained from a diverse range of images and generalize well to the task of nodule detection. Secondly, transfer learning helps overcome the limitations of limited annotated data in the medical field. Training deep learning models from scratch requires a substantial amount of labelled data, which may not be readily available for pulmonary nodule detection. Transfer learning enables the model to start with pre-trained weights, significantly reducing the number of training samples required and effectively utilizing the available labelled data. Furthermore, transfer learning helps in accelerating the training process. Pre-trained models have already learnt lower-level features, such as edges and textures, which are essential for nodule detection. By fine-tuning these pre-trained models on specific nodule detection datasets, the model can converge faster, allowing for quicker development and deployment of reliable pulmonary nodule detection systems. Overall, transfer learning in pulmonary nodule detection addresses the challenges of limited labelled data, enables better generalization and accelerates the model development process, leading to improved accuracy and efficiency in detecting pulmonary nodules, which is crucial for early diagnosis and treatment of lung diseases.

Here's an explanation of how transfer learning can be applied to pulmonary nodule detection:

Pre-trained Model Selection: Choose a pre-trained model that has been trained on a large-scale image dataset, such as ImageNet. Models like VGGNet, ResNet or InceptionNet are commonly used due to their strong performance on a variety of image recognition tasks.

Model Adaptation: The pre-trained model is adapted for the specific task of pulmonary nodule detection. The adaptation involves modifying the last layers of the pre-trained model to suit the target task. Typically, the fully connected layers at the end of the network are replaced or fine-tuned, while the lower layers are kept frozen or fine-tuned with a smaller learning rate.

Dataset Preparation: Gather a dataset of lung CT scans labelled with nodule annotations. This dataset should include both positive (nodules) and negative (non-nodules) samples. The dataset is split into training, validation and testing sets.

Transfer Learning Process:

a. Initialization: Load the pre-trained model weights and architecture.
b. Modification: Replace or fine-tune the last layers of the pre-trained model for nodule detection. The modified layers are typically designed to output the probability of a region being a nodule or to regress the bounding box coordinates of the nodules.
c. Training: Train the modified model using the labelled lung CT scan dataset. The training process involves minimizing a loss function, such as binary cross-entropy or mean squared error, between the predicted nodule detection and the ground truth annotations.
d. Evaluation: Evaluate the trained model on the validation set to monitor its performance, adjust hyperparameters, and prevent overfitting.
e. Testing: Finally, assess the model's performance on the independent testing set to measure its ability to accurately detect nodules.

The main advantages of transfer learning in pulmonary nodule detection are that it allows leveraging the learnt representations from large-scale datasets, which capture general image features, and it reduces the need for training from scratch on a limited dataset. This approach helps in achieving better generalization and improving the detection performance, even with a smaller annotated dataset for the specific task of nodule detection.

It's important to note that the success of transfer learning depends on the similarity between the source task (pre-training) and the target task (nodule detection), as well as the availability of a sufficient amount of labelled data for fine-tuning and adapting the model.

Inception Module:

The InceptionNet architecture employs multiple inception modules in its network. Each inception module performs parallel convolutions of different filter sizes and concatenates their outputs, allowing the network to capture both local and global features at different scales. The architecture of the inception module can be represented as

In the above diagram Fig. 5.8, the input of the inception module is fed into three different convolutional operations: 1x1 convolution, 3x3 convolution, and 5x5 convolution. The 1x1 convolution reduces the dimensionality of the input, while the 3x3 and 5x5 convolutions capture local features. The outputs of these operations are concatenated along the channel dimension, forming the output of the inception module. Another detailed architecture is framed in Fig. 5.9.

Stem:

The stem is the initial part of the network responsible for capturing low-level features from the input image. In InceptionNet, the stem consists of a series of convolutional and pooling layers to process the input image.

Inception Blocks:

InceptionNet employs several repeated blocks of inception modules, which progressively capture more complex and abstract features. These blocks are stacked on top of each other to form the main body of the network. The specific arrangement and number of inception modules can vary depending on the version of InceptionNet.

Auxiliary Classifiers:

To address the issue of vanishing gradients during training, InceptionNet includes auxiliary classifiers at intermediate layers of the network. These auxiliary classifiers are small branches that consist of average pooling, convolutional layers and fully connected layers. They are trained to classify the inputs into different classes. The outputs of these auxiliary classifiers are used as additional supervision during training to improve gradient flow and regularize the network.

Final Classification Layer:

At the end of the network, there is a global average pooling layer followed by a fully connected layer with softmax activation. This final classification layer maps the features extracted from the previous layers to the predicted class probabilities.

The overall architecture of InceptionNet can vary depending on the version (e.g., InceptionV1, InceptionV2, InceptionV3, etc.). The number and arrangement of inception modules, as well as the specific parameters, can differ. However, the key idea of the inception modules and the overall concept of capturing features at multiple scales remain consistent across versions.

The InceptionNet architecture has played a significant role in advancing deep learning for computer vision tasks, showcasing the effectiveness of the inception modules in improving both accuracy and efficiency.

5.3.2 Addressing imbalance class problem in CNN

Imbalanced class problems are common in medical image analysis, including pulmonary nodule detection. In such cases, the number of positive samples (nodules) is much smaller than the number of negative samples (non-nodules), which can lead to biased model performance.

5.3.2.1 Generative adversarial network

A generative adversarial network or GAN is a technique of generative modelling which is used to generate new data sets based on training data sets. The property of these newly generated data set is very similar to the training data sets. This network consists of two parts namely discriminator and generator. In this architecture, objectives of generator are to generate several test data which helps to cope with imbalanced class problem. However, these data may be noisy data which directly affects the performance of the model. On the other hand, discriminator distinguishes these abnormal data from training data set and helps to improve the performance of the model.

5.3.2.1.1 Different loss functions considered in GAN

One loss function for generator training and the other for discriminator training are both possible for GANs. How do two loss functions combine to represent a measure of separation between probability distributions?

The generator and discriminator losses in the loss schemes we'll examine here are derived from the same measure of separation between probability distributions. The term that represents the distribution of the fictitious data is the sole term in the distance measure that the generator can modify in either of these two approaches. Therefore, we eliminate the other term, which represents the distribution of the actual data, during generator training.

The GAN architecture has considered the Minimax Loss and Wasserstein Loss function to implement the system. Minimax loss function is defined as

$$E_x[\log (D(x))] + E_z[\log \log (1 - D(G(Z)))]$$

where $D(x)$ is the discriminator's estimate of the probability that real data instance x is real.

E_x is the expected value over all real data instances.
$G(z)$ is the generator's output when given noise z.
$D(G(z))$ is the discriminator's estimate of the probability that a fake instance is real.
E_z is the expected value over all random inputs to the generator (in effect, the expected value over all generated fake instances $G(z)$).

It can be challenging and have numerous difficulties to optimize the networks of the generator and discriminator for the GAN. First off, the minimax game framework's rivalry between the generator and the discriminator can have a significant impact on how the GAN is trained and is relatively unstable [5]. In other words, producing high-quality sample synthesis requires a good generator—discriminator equilibrium. However, a good equilibrium cannot always be guaranteed by the gradient descent used to train the networks.

For instance, the gradient of the generator may disappear quickly if a discriminator in the training process has a strong potential for differentiation. As a result, the generator's optimization might not be able to proceed to approximate the target domain's true distribution. It is stated that if the discriminator is purposefully made weaker, a superior generator can be trained. In such a situation, it might necessitate numerous iterations of trial and error, making the entire training process challenging and unstable. Second, there is a phenomenon in GAN known as 'mode collapse' when the generator frequently generates samples with little variation. When the generator is forced to synthesize comparable samples at the same local minimum of the cost function, the mode collapse results. In this context, the generated samples do not adequately reflect the entire distribution of the target domain, making it difficult to solve the issue of data imbalance.

The Wasserstein GAN (WGAN) is a brand-new GAN designed to reduce the normal GAN's training complexity and prevent the potential mode collapse issue. Wasserstein loss function is considered here. Fig. 5.4 depicts an overview of the WGAN's process structure for synthesis of sample data. The goal functions of the discriminator between the WGAN and the typical GAN are different when compared to Fig. 5.3. As opposed to

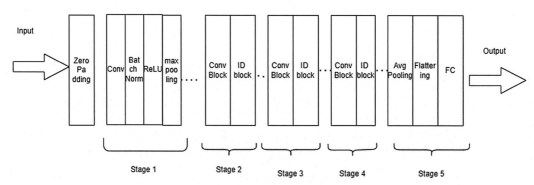

FIGURE 5.3 ResNet architecture.

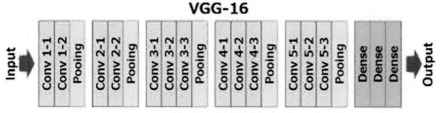

FIGURE 5.4 Architecture of VGG16.

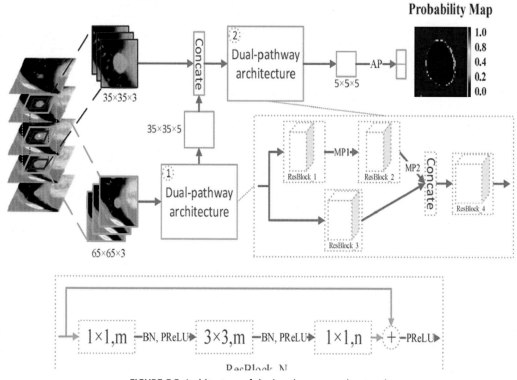

FIGURE 5.5 Architecture of dual pathway neural network.

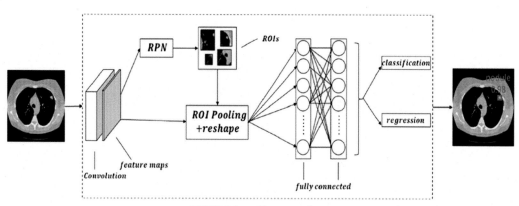

FIGURE 5.6 Architecture of RPN.

the WGAN's discriminator, which represents the Earth Mover (EM) distance between genuine and synthetic distributions, the standard GAN's discriminator's objective function is determined by the binary categorization of true and synthetic samples. In order to achieve this, learning the WGAN's discriminator is conceptualized as a regression task rather than a classification task.

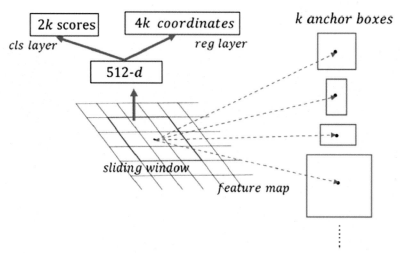

FIGURE 5.7 Building block of RPN.

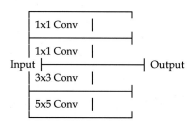

FIGURE 5.8 "InceptionNet."

The asymmetry issue of the Kullback–Leibler divergence that could cause mode collapse as well as the discontinuous problem of the loss function with Jensen–Shannon divergence that may lead to subpar synthetic results can both be avoided by incorporating the Earth Mover (EM) distance for the measurement of the two comparing distributions in the WGAN. The gradient for the loss function may be reliably provided by the EM distance, making it easier to get higher-quality synthesis results.

Let

$$W(P_r, P_s) = \inf \delta \in \prod(P_r, P_s) E_{(x,y) \in \delta} \|x - y\|$$

Here, x and y represent the real and synthetic samples.

$\prod(P_r, P_s)$ are the all-disjoint sets of the distribution

Infimum calculation of the above equation is an impracticable option. Hence the equation can be written as

$$E_{x \sim P_r}[D(x)] - E_{y \sim P_s}[D(y)]$$

where D refers to the discriminator's neural network.

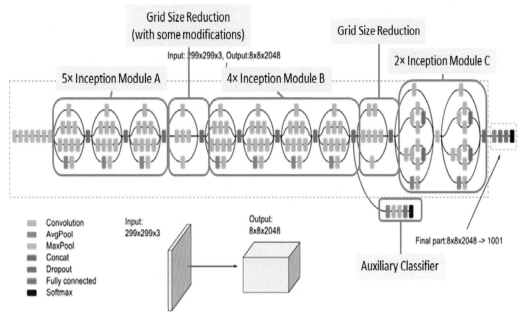

FIGURE 5.9 Architecture of Inception V3.

Then, using the discriminator D's optimization, which is motivated by maximization of the term ExPr [D(x)] EyPs [D(y)] [26], the EM distance can be roughly found. The goal of the generator network, G, is to create samples from a distribution Ps that closely resembles the real data distribution Pr.

$$E_{x \sim P_r}[D(x)] - E_{y \sim P_s}[D(y)]$$

With reference to Eqs. (5.1)−(5.3), finding the maximum in Eq. (5.3) roughly transformed the solving of the infinity in Eq. (5.1). The maximum in Eq. (5.3) can indicate the EM separation between Pr and Ps. Additionally, we want to modify Ps to be as near to Pr as possible.

Adjusting the synaptic weights of the generator G, which is identical to min G W(Pr, Ps), will reveal this.

Consequently, the full WGAN training process can be described as

$$E_{x \sim P_r}[D(x)] - E_{y \sim P_s}[D(y)]$$

Both the discriminator's and the generator's networks could be CNNs.

In particular, an image sample (either real or artificial) with size of 6464 pixels serves as the discriminator's input layer. The discriminator's subsequent layers consist of convolutional layers connected by batch normalization and leaky rectified linear units (LReLU). Batch normalization can permit gradient flow into deeper layers while stabilizing the leaning process. To prevent sample oscillation and model instability, it is not advised to use batch normalization for the input layer of the discriminator and the output layer of the generator.

he InceptionNet architecture, also known as GoogLeNet, is a deep convolutional neural network (CNN) that was designed to achieve high accuracy while minimizing computational complexity. It introduced the concept of 'inception modules', which consist of multiple parallel convolutional operations of different sizes within the same layer.

Wasserstein generative adversarial network (WGAN) is an edge cutting technology to address the imbalanced class problem of pulmonary nodule detection. The aforementioned technology is an oversampling technique that generates synthetic data, considering the distribution of the minority class sample. In this approach, the regions of potential nodule candidates have been cropped into 64× 64 pixels. The above-mentioned procedure has been performed by considering the Hounsfield Unit whose range is [-1400,200].

The experimental results establish that WGAN based oversampling technique outperforms the data augmentation methodology which is more widely used imbalance class handling methodology in image-based classification methodology.

5.3.2.2   Cascaded neural network

A cascaded neural network for pulmonary nodule detection aims to identify and classify nodules in medical images, specifically in lung CT scans. The network consists of multiple stages that progressively refine the detection and classification of nodules. Here's an overview of the architecture and equations for each stage (Fig. 5.10).

Stage 1: Nodule Candidate Generation

The first stage focusses on generating potential nodule candidates in the input lung CT scan. It typically utilizes a 3D convolutional neural network (CNN) to scan the entire volume and predict the likelihood of each voxel being part of a nodule. The equation for this stage can be represented as

$$Output\_1 = CNN\_1(Input\_CT\_Scan)$$

Stage 2: Nodule Candidate Refinement

The output of the first stage provides a set of nodule candidates. However, these candidates may include false positives or miss some true nodules. The second stage aims to refine the candidate set by using a more detailed analysis. It can employ another 3D CNN or a region-based approach to classify and refine the nodule candidates. The equation for this stage can be represented as

$$Output\_2 = CNN\_2(Nodule\_Candidates)$$

During inference, the cascaded neural network processes an input lung CT scan through each stage sequentially, gradually refining the nodule candidates.

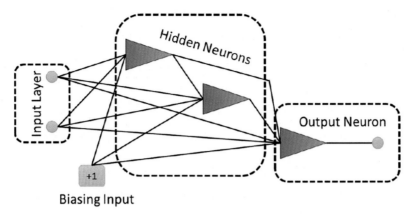

FIGURE 5.10 Cascaded neural network.

It's important to note that the architecture and equations provided here are general and simplified representations of a cascaded neural network for pulmonary nodule detection. In practice, the specific architecture, network depth and training methodology can vary, and more advanced techniques, such as feature fusion, attention mechanisms or multi-scale analysis, may also be incorporated to enhance performance.

Sakamoto and Nakano applied cascaded neural networks with selective filters to reduce the false-positive detection rate of lung nodule CAD. In this methodology, the cascaded neural networks have been considered for two purposes namely transformed the skewed dataset to a balance one and worked as a selective filter to find out potential nodule candidates. Another study by Sakamoto et al. considered a multi-stage neural network with single-sided classifier to deal with the detection of false-positive cases in skewed dataset. The multi-stage neural network represents ensemble of different neural networks and each of the stages have some unique working principle to solve different problems of classifications. As a consequence, the accuracy of the nodule detection in presence of skewed dataset has been increased.

5.3.2.3 RetinaNet

RetinaNet is a one-stage object detection model that addresses class imbalance during training by using a focal loss function. To focus learning on challenging negative examples, focal loss modifies the cross-entropy loss. RetinaNet is a single, integrated network made up of two task-specific subnetworks plus a backbone network. The backbone, which is an off-the-self convolutional network, computes a convolutional feature map over the whole input image. On the output of the backbone, the first subnet applies convolutional object classification, and the second subnet applies convolutional bounding box regression. The authors' straightforward architecture for the two subnetworks is intended primarily for dense, one-stage detection (Fig. 5.11).

RetinaNet architecture consists of four major components namely,

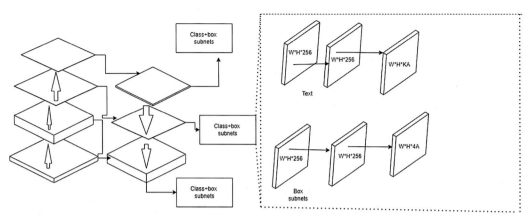

FIGURE 5.11 RetinaNet architecture.

Bottom-up pathway: The backbone network (such as ResNet) produces the feature maps at various sizes without depending upon the size of the images.

Top-down pathway and lateral connections: The lateral connections combine the top-down layers and the bottom-up layers with the same spatial size, whereas the top-down pathway upsamples the spatially coarser feature maps from higher pyramid levels.

Classification subnetwork: According to each anchor box and object class, it forecasts the likelihood that an object will be found at each spatial point.

Regression subnetwork: For each ground-truth item, it regresses the offset for the bounding boxes from the anchor boxes.

The introduction of Focal Loss (FL), an improvement over Cross-Entropy Loss (CE), addresses the class imbalance issue with single-stage object detection models. The high foreground-background class imbalance problem in single stage models is caused by extensive sampling of anchor boxes (potential object placements) [1]. At each pyramid layer in RetinaNet, thousands of anchor boxes may be present. The great majority of them will be background class, and only a small number will be allocated to a ground-truth object. Despite having small loss values individually, these simple examples of high probability detections can overwhelm the model. The value of correcting misclassified examples is increased by focal loss, which lessens the loss contribution from simple examples.

In this case, two-stage cascade and sampling heuristics are used to address the class imbalance. The proposal step quickly reduces the number of potential object locations to a small number (e.g., 1-2k), filtering away the majority of background samples (e.g., Selective Search, EdgeBoxes, DeepMask, RPN). To keep the foreground and background in a tolerable balance, sampling algorithms like a set foreground-to-background ratio or online hard example mining (OHEM) are used in the second classification step.

5.3.3 Implementation of loss functions

Apart from the focal loss function, there exist several lost functions that can easily cope with imbalanced class problems for detecting pulmonary nodules. Loss function is a mathematical interpretation that quantifies the best suited for evaluating the relationship between the test dataset and the prediction model.

One approach to handling imbalanced class problems is to use a loss function that weighs the positive and negative samples differently. One commonly used loss function for imbalanced class problems is the weighted cross-entropy loss function, which assigns a higher weight to the positive samples to increase their influence on the model training.

Imbalanced class problems are common in medical image analysis, including pulmonary nodule detection. In such cases, the number of positive samples (nodules) is much smaller than the number of negative samples (non-nodules), which can lead to biased model performance.

One approach to handling imbalanced class problems is to use a loss function that weighs the positive and negative samples differently. One commonly used loss function for imbalanced class problems is the weighted cross-entropy loss function, which assigns a higher weight to the positive samples to increase their influence on the model training.

5.3.3.1 *Weighted cross-entropy loss function*
The weighted cross-entropy loss function can be defined as follows:

$$L(w) = -[w * y * \log(p) + (1 - w) * (1 - y) * \log(1 - p)]$$

where w is the weight assigned to the positive samples, y is the ground truth label (0 for negative, 1 for positive), p is the predicted probability of the positive class, and log is the natural logarithm.

The weight w can be calculated as

w = (total samples)/(2 * number of positive samples)
where (total samples) is the total number of samples in the dataset and (number of positive samples) is the number of positive samples.

The weighted cross-entropy loss function penalizes the model more for misclassifying positive samples than negative samples, which helps to balance the influence of positive and negative samples on the model training. This can lead to improved performance in detecting pulmonary nodules in CT images, especially in cases where the positive class is underrepresented.

5.3.3.2 *Binary cross entropy loss function*
Binary Cross Entropy (BCE) loss function is a commonly used loss function for binary classification tasks in machine learning, including medical image analysis. It measures the dissimilarity between the predicted probability and the ground truth binary label.

The BCE loss function is defined as follows:

$$BCE(p, y) = -(y * \log(p) + (1 - y) * \log(1 - p))$$

where p is the predicted probability, y is the ground truth binary label, and log is the natural logarithm.

The BCE loss function measures the difference between the predicted probability and the ground truth label for each sample in the dataset. It penalizes the model more for misclassifying samples that should be positive than for misclassifying samples that should be negative. The loss function is minimized by adjusting the model parameters during training.

$$L(y, \hat{y}) = -\frac{1}{n} \sum_{i=1}^{n} \{y_i \log \log \hat{y}_i + (1 - y_i)\log(1 - \hat{y})\}$$

Here n is the number of samples, y_i is the true label of a sample, and $\hat{y}$ is its prediction probability.

5.3.3.3   Dice loss function

The Dice loss function is a commonly used loss function for semantic segmentation tasks, including medical image analysis. It is a similarity-based loss function that measures the overlap between the predicted segmentation map and the ground truth segmentation map. The Dice coefficient ranges from 0 to 1, with 1 indicating a perfect overlap between the predicted and ground truth segmentation maps.

The Dice loss function is defined as follows:

Dice(p, y) =
1 − (2 * Σi = 1 to n Σj = 1 to m pij) / (Σi = 1 to n Σj = 1 to m pi + Σi = 1 to n Σj = 1 to m yi)

where p is the predicted segmentation map, y is the ground truth segmentation map, n is the number of classes, m is the number of pixels in each class, pij is the intersection between predicted and ground truth for class i and pixel j, pi is the total number of pixels in class i, and yi is the total number of pixels labelled as class i in the ground truth.

The Dice loss function measures the similarity between the predicted and ground truth segmentation maps by taking into account both the true-positive and false-positive rates. It penalizes the model more for misclassifying pixels that should be positive than for misclassifying pixels that should be negative.

$$DL = 1 - \frac{\sum_{n=1}^{N} p_n r_n + \varepsilon}{\sum_{n=1}^{N} p_n + r_n + \varepsilon} - \frac{\sum_{n=1}^{N} (1 - p_n)(1 - r_n) + \varepsilon}{\sum_{n=1}^{N} 2 - p_n - r_n + \varepsilon}$$

5.3.3.3.1   Generalized dice loss function

The Generalized Dice Loss (GDL) function is a commonly used loss function for semantic segmentation tasks, including medical image analysis. GDL is particularly useful when dealing with imbalanced datasets, where certain classes may have a much smaller representation than others.

The GDL function is defined as follows:

$$GDL(p,y) = 1 - 2 * (\Sigma i = 1 \text{ to } n \text{ wi} * \Sigma j = 1 \text{ to } m \text{ pij}) / (\Sigma i = 1 \text{ to } n \text{ wi}$$
$$* (\Sigma j = 1 \text{ to } m \text{ pi} + \Sigma j = 1 \text{ to } m \text{ yj}))$$

where p is the predicted segmentation map, y is the ground truth segmentation map, n is the number of classes, m is the number of pixels in each class, pij is the intersection between predicted and ground truth for class i and pixel j, pi is the total number of pixels in class i, yj is the total number of pixels labelled as class j in the ground truth, and wi is the weight for class i.

The weight for each class i can be calculated as follows:

$$wi = 1 / (\Sigma j = 1 \text{ to } m \text{ yij})^\wedge 2$$

where yij is the number of pixels labelled as class i in the ground truth for pixel j.

The GDL function takes into account the class imbalance by weighting each class according to its frequency in the ground truth. The function penalizes the model more for misclassifying rare classes than for misclassifying common classes. This can lead to improved performance, especially in cases where certain classes are underrepresented.

Cost Sensitive Loss Function:

Cost-sensitive loss functions are commonly used in machine learning for imbalanced classification problems, where the cost of misclassifying samples in the minority class is much higher than misclassifying samples in the majority class. In medical imaging, this can occur when the positive class (disease) is rare compared to the negative class (no disease). The cost-sensitive loss function can be defined as follows:

$$L(p,y) = - \Sigma i = 1 \text{ to } n \ (\alpha i * yi * \log(pi) + \beta i * (1 - yi) * \log(1 - pi))$$

where p is the predicted probability, y is the ground truth label, n is the number of classes, αi is the weight for positive samples in class i, βi is the weight for negative samples in class i, and log is the natural logarithm.

The weight for positive samples αi can be calculated as follows:

$$\alpha i = (\text{total samples} - \text{positive samples}) / (\text{total samples} - 2 * \text{positive samples})$$

where (total samples) is the total number of samples in the dataset and (positive samples) is the number of positive samples.

The weight for negative samples βi can be calculated as follows:

$$\beta i = \text{positive samples} / (\text{total samples} - 2 * \text{positive samples})$$

The cost-sensitive loss function weights the positive samples more heavily than the negative samples to reduce the false-negative rate. This is accomplished by giving a higher weight to the positive samples in the loss function. The weights are calculated based on the class balance in the training dataset.

5.3.3.3.2 Data augmentation

Data augmentation is required to reduce the occurrence of class imbalance as well as to fill the dataset with more examples. Along with increasing the sample size, data augmentation also causes the examined dataset to be translated, viewed from different angles, size invariant, and artificially diverse, enhancing the model's capacity for generalization. All of the extracted patches and the original 2D slices of CT images were subjected to augmentation for the 2D networks, respectively. In the case of the 3D CNN, the same augmentation parameters were used to process each volume as a single entity. In an iterated training process, models were trained starting with the initial number of samples (no augmentation), and then augmenting the data up to the highest number of samples possible without compromising convergence or generalization. This resulted in the optimal number of the augmented samples from both classes.

5.3.4 Ensemble methods

Ensemble methods can be effectively applied to overcome the class imbalance problem in CNN architecture for pulmonary nodule detection. Ensemble methods involve training multiple models with different subsets of the data and combining their predictions to improve overall performance. In the context of pulmonary nodule detection, ensemble methods can help address the challenge of imbalanced classes by ensuring that the minority class receives adequate attention during training.

To implement an ensemble approach, multiple CNN models are trained using different balanced subsets of the dataset. Each model learns to detect pulmonary nodules based on its subset of data. During inference, the predictions from all the models are combined, often through voting or averaging, to obtain the final ensemble prediction. This ensemble prediction tends to be more robust and accurate, as it leverages the diverse perspectives captured by the individual models.

Ensemble methods help alleviate the bias towards the majority class by ensuring that the models are exposed to a balanced representation of both classes. This allows the models to learn more effectively from the minority class, enhancing their ability to detect pulmonary nodules accurately. By aggregating the predictions from multiple models, ensemble methods can mitigate the impact of class imbalance and improve the overall detection performance.

Additionally, ensemble methods provide a form of model regularization, reducing the risk of overfitting. Each model in the ensemble has its own set of learnt features and biases, which helps to capture different aspects of the data. The ensemble combines these diverse perspectives, leading to more robust and generalized predictions.

5.3.5 Anomaly detection

Anomaly detection techniques can be applied to overcome the class imbalance problem in CNN architecture for pulmonary nodule detection. Anomaly detection treats the minority class, representing pulmonary nodules, as a rare event or anomaly. By considering the minority class as distinct from the majority class, anomaly detection approaches aim to identify and classify instances that deviate from the normal patterns.

In the context of pulmonary nodule detection, anomaly detection methods can be utilized to identify nodules that may be underrepresented in the dataset. These methods, such as Autoencoder-based CNNs or Siamese CNNs or One-class CNNs, learn a representation of the normal class (non-nodule samples) and classify instances based on their deviation from this representation. By focussing on detecting anomalies or rare events, these techniques can effectively handle imbalanced classes and improve the detection of pulmonary nodules.

During training, the anomaly detection model learns to capture the characteristics of the normal class by using a representative set of non-nodule samples. The model then estimates the boundaries or decision boundaries of normalcy. During inference, input CT images are evaluated based on their similarity to the normal class. If an input image is considered to deviate significantly from the normal patterns, it is classified as an anomaly, indicating the presence of a pulmonary nodule (Fig. 5.11).

By leveraging anomaly detection in CNN architectures for pulmonary nodule detection, the focus shifts from class imbalance to detecting abnormal patterns associated with nodules. This approach allows for more accurate identification and localization of nodules, even in cases where the class distribution is highly imbalanced. Anomaly detection provides a valuable alternative to address class imbalance by treating the minority class as a distinct anomaly, enabling more effective detection of pulmonary nodules.

5.3.5.1   One-class CNNs

One-class CNNs are a valuable approach in the context of pulmonary nodule detection, where the objective is to model the normal class and detect anomalies that deviate significantly from the learnt representation. In this scenario, a one-class CNN is trained using only normal CT images, without the presence of pulmonary nodules. This allows the model to learn the characteristic features and patterns associated with the normal lung structure.

The training process involves optimizing the one-class loss function, which aims to separate the normal class from potential anomalies. One commonly used equation for the one-class loss function is the margin-based loss:

$$\text{Loss} = \max\left(0, \text{margin} - ||f(x) - c||^{\wedge}2\right)$$

where

$f(x)$ represents the feature representation of the input image x obtained from the CNN,
c is the centre of the normal class features,
margin is a predefined margin that determines the separation between the normal class and anomalies.

During training, the one-class CNN adjusts its weights to minimize the loss, ensuring that the feature representations of the normal instances lie within the margin. This allows the model to define a boundary that encloses the normal patterns while separating them from potential anomalies.

During inference, an input CT image is passed through the trained one-class CNN. The model calculates the distance between the input image's feature representation and the centre of the normal class. If the distance exceeds the margin, the input image is classified as an anomaly, indicating the presence of a pulmonary nodule.

The use of one-class CNNs for pulmonary nodule detection allows for effective anomaly detection, even in scenarios with imbalanced classes. By focussing solely on the normal class and learning its representation, the model can better identify and classify instances that deviate significantly from the normal lung structure, helping to improve the accuracy and reliability of pulmonary nodule detection systems.

The architecture of a one-class CNN for pulmonary nodule detection typically follows a similar structure to traditional CNN architectures but with some modifications to cater to the one-class setting. Fig. 5.12 picturises the architecture of one-class CNN.

Input Layer: The network takes as input CT images of a fixed size, typically represented as a 3D array of pixel values.

Convolutional Layers: Several convolutional layers are used to extract hierarchical features from the input images. Each convolutional layer consists of multiple filters that perform convolutions across the input volume, capturing different patterns and features

FIGURE 5.12 Architecture of one class CNN.

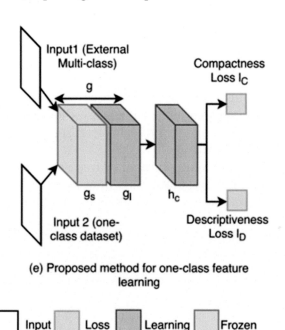

Input1 (External Multi-class)

Compactness Loss l_C

g

g_s g_l h_c

Input 2 (one-class dataset)

Descriptiveness Loss l_D

(e) Proposed method for one-class feature learning

☐ Input ▨ Loss ▨ Learning ▨ Frozen

at various spatial scales. Activation functions such as ReLU (Rectified Linear Unit) are commonly applied after each convolution operation to introduce non-linearity.

Pooling Layers: Pooling layers are inserted after some of the convolutional layers to down sample the feature maps and reduce spatial dimensions. Max pooling is commonly used, where the maximum value within a pooling region is retained, effectively summarizing the most salient features in that region.

Fully Connected Layers: The output of the convolutional layers is flattened and connected to one or more fully connected layers. These layers serve as classifiers, learning to map the high-level features extracted by the convolutional layers to the desired output. Activation functions like ReLU are typically used in the fully connected layers as well.

Output Layer: The final layer of the network produces the output prediction. In the case of one-class CNNs for pulmonary nodule detection, the output is a single value indicating the probability or confidence that the input image belongs to the normal class. This can be achieved using a sigmoid activation function, which squashes the output into the range of [0, 1].

The weights of the one-class CNN are trained using normal CT images, without the presence of pulmonary nodules. The objective is to optimize the model's ability to distinguish normal lung structures from potential anomalies. During training, the network adjusts its weights to minimize the one-class loss function, as described in the previous response, allowing the model to define a boundary that separates normal patterns from anomalies.

It's important to note that the specific architecture details, such as the number of layers, filter sizes, and the presence of additional techniques like dropout or batch normalization, can vary depending on the specific implementation and dataset requirements. These choices are typically made through experimentation and optimization to achieve the best performance for the pulmonary nodule detection task.

5.3.6   Auto encoder and decoder

Auto encoder:

Autoencoders are not specifically designed to address the imbalanced class problem directly. However, they can be used as part of a broader approach to tackle class imbalance by learning meaningful representations of the data and potentially improving the performance of subsequent classifiers.

Here's a high-level explanation of how autoencoders can be utilized within a framework to address class imbalance:

Pre-processing: First, the dataset is pre-processed by balancing the class distribution. This can be done using techniques such as oversampling the minority class, under sampling the majority class, or using more advanced methods like SMOTE (Synthetic Minority Over-sampling Technique).

Autoencoder Training: The balanced dataset is then used to train an autoencoder. An autoencoder is a type of neural network that is trained to reconstruct its input. It consists of an encoder network that maps the input data to a lower-dimensional latent space representation and a decoder network that reconstructs the original input from the latent space representation (Fig. 5.13).

Latent Space Representation: The trained encoder part of the autoencoder is used to obtain the latent space representations of the original data, which capture the essential features and patterns of the input samples. These latent space representations are expected to be more informative and less influenced by the class imbalance.

Classifier Training: The latent space representations obtained from the autoencoder are then used as the input to train a classifier, such as a logistic regression model or a support vector machine (SVM). This classifier can leverage the more balanced and informative representations to make more accurate predictions on the imbalanced dataset.

The equations involved in training an autoencoder typically include

Encoder: The encoder maps the input data x to a lower-dimensional latent representation z.

$$z = f\_enc(x)$$

Decoder: The decoder reconstructs the original input data x from the latent representation z.

$$\hat{x} = f\_dec(z)$$

Reconstruction loss: The autoencoder is trained by minimizing the reconstruction loss, which measures the discrepancy between the original input x and its reconstruction $\hat{x}$.

$$L\_rec = loss(x, \hat{x})$$

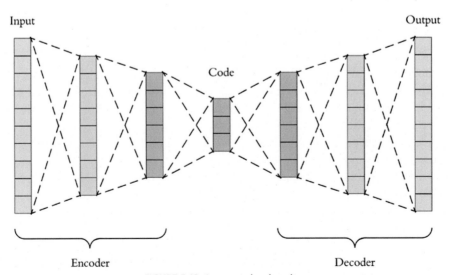

FIGURE 5.13 Autoencoder decoder.

Training objective: The overall training objective is to minimize the reconstruction loss, typically using optimization methods such as stochastic gradient descent (SGD) or Adam.

$$\min L\_rec$$

Remember that while autoencoders can aid in learning meaningful representations and mitigating the effects of class imbalance, they are just one component of a broader approach. Additional techniques such as resampling, cost-sensitive learning or ensemble methods may also be employed to address the imbalanced class problem effectively.

Susan et al. proposed a class-weighted convolutional autoencoder technique to cope with the imbalanced class problems in the pulmonary nodule detection problem. The photos are from the Lung Image Database Consortium image collection (LIDC-IDRI), which includes lung Computed Tomography (CT) scans. The annotated CT scans are separated into picture patches marked 'nodule' or 'non-nodule' images. Understandably, the number of samples with nodules is significantly lower than that of non-nodules. A class-weight equal to the ratio of total population to class population is introduced to solve the class-imbalance problem and eliminate bias in decision-making. During the training phase, the class-weights are multiplied by the loss-function associated with each class to compute the aggregate loss function. At the output stage, the training module consists of a feature-extractor that is the encoder part of a convolutional autoencoder (CAE) pre-trained on the lung nodule dataset and a classifier composed of randomly initialized fully connected layers. Experiments show that our class-weighted technique outperforms the state-of-the-art for the imbalanced dataset.

In summary, the deep learning-based strategies have emerged as effective approaches for detecting lung nodules, especially in the presence of class imbalance. These approaches make use of neural network capabilities to automatically learn useful features from raw input data, eliminating the need for manual feature engineering. In particular, Convolutional Neural Networks (CNNs) have shown amazing ability in extracting complicated patterns and properties from medical images.

Deep learning algorithms can be trained on large-scale datasets to detect pulmonary nodules, capturing the complex and subtle properties of both benign and malignant nodules. The models can learn discriminative representations automatically, optimizing their performance to categorize nodules accurately while allowing for class imbalance. Furthermore, approaches like data augmentation, transfer learning and ensembling can help the model detect pulmonary nodules more correctly and generalize effectively to fresh data. To reduce overfitting and increase generalization performance, careful model construction, regularization approaches and hyperparameter adjustment are required. Finally, deep learning model interpretability remains an issue. Understanding their logic and communicating the model's predictions to medical practitioners is critical for fostering trust and promoting adoption in clinical settings. Deep learning models are being studied to develop strategies for analyzing and explaining them in the context of lung nodule identification.

References

[1] Zhao C, Han J, Jia Y, Gou F. Lung nodule detection via 3D U-Net and contextual convolutional neural network. In: 2018 international conference on networking and network applications (NaNA). IEEE; October 12, 2018. p. 356−61.

[2] Li Y, Fan Y. DeepSEED: 3D squeeze-and-excitation encoder-decoder convolutional neural networks for pulmonary nodule detection. In: 2020 IEEE 17th international symposium on biomedical imaging (ISBI). IEEE; April 3, 2020. p. 1866−9.

[3] Haibo L, Shanli T, Shuang S, Haoran L. An improved yolov3 algorithm for pulmonary nodule detection. In: 2021 IEEE 4th advanced information management, communicates, electronic and automation control conference (IMCEC). Vol. 4. IEEE; June 18, 2021. p. 1068−72.

[4] Wang B, Qi G, Tang S, Zhang L, Deng L, Zhang Y. Automated pulmonary nodule detection: high sensitivity with few candidates. In: Medical image computing and computer assisted intervention−MICCAI 2018: 21st international conference, Granada, Spain, September 16-20, 2018, proceedings, part II. Cham: Springer International Publishing; September 2018. p. 759−67.

[5] Shi H, Lu J, Zhou Q. A novel data augmentation method using style-based GAN for robust pulmonary nodule segmentation. In: 2020 Chinese control and decision conference (CCDC). IEEE; August 22, 2020. p. 2486−91.

6

A fully automated methodology for localization of pulmonary nodules

6.1 Introduction

Due to its importance in the precise location and characterization of nodules inside the lungs, pulmonary nodule localization plays a crucial role in the context of pulmonary nodule detection. Each of the lobes that make up the lungs has distinct anatomical traits and physical properties. Right upper lobe (RUL), right middle lobe (RML), and right lower lobe (RLL) are the three lobes that make up the right lung. Left upper lobe (LUL) and left lower lobe (LLL) are the two lobes that make up the left lung. The boundary surfaces of the lung's lobes are indicated by two oblique fissures and one horizontal fissure that separate these lobes. The RML and RLL are distinguished from one another by the horizontal fissure, which also divides the RUL and RML in the right lung from one another, and the LUL and LLL from one another in the left lung. Any of these lobes can have a pulmonary nodule. Accurate localization and characterization of pulmonary nodules inside the lung are aided by identifying the precise lobe in which they are situated. For the purposes of future evaluation and treatment planning, this information is essential. The size and shape of pulmonary nodules might vary, as was already mentioned. Healthcare experts can evaluate the nodule's size and shape in relation to the lobe's size by determining the lobe in which it is placed. The results of this investigation add to our understanding of the nodule's importance and propensity for malignancy. Monitoring the evolution of pulmonary nodules over time is also crucial for controlling lung health. Clinicians can track the growth or regression of nodules inside a given lobe and evaluate their progression by associating them with particular lobes. Determining the best course of action, such as additional imaging or intervention, is made easier with the use of this information. Additionally, knowing the lobe position aids in surgical planning and identifying the amount of resection in situations where intervention, such as surgical resection, is necessary for lung nodules. It guarantees that the targeted lobe is precisely recognized and dealt with during the operation, enhancing the accuracy and efficacy of the therapy. Additionally, standardized, transparent documentation is needed for correct reporting and communication of pulmonary nodules. The inclusion of the lobe information in the radiological report aids in communicating to referring physicians and other healthcare professionals the exact location of the nodule, facilitating thorough patient care and follow-up.

Application of Artificial Intelligence in Early Detection of Lung Cancer. https://doi.org/10.1016/B978-0-323-95245-3.00006-8

Chapter 3 of this book reveals that the pulmonary nodules of the right upper lobe have a higher probability of becoming cancerous. Manual detection of pulmonary fissures has grown more difficult as a result of extensive image slices and the inferior images produced by low-dose computed tomography (LDCT) images. This calls for computer-assisted pulmonary fissure and lobe recognition from CT images. The intensity values of these pulmonary fissures are greater than those of the voxels that make up the lung parenchyma.

Contrarily, it contains fewer voxels than the lung parenchyma. Consequently, resolving the imbalanced class problem presents a significant hurdle for the computerized pulmonary fissures identification methods. However, a thick-slice CT scan adds a new obstacle to detection. Another noteworthy aspect is that motion artefacts and partial volume effects may cause the CT scanner to produce low-contrast and blurry fissure pictures. The aforementioned fact leads to the conclusion that LDCT and thick sliced images are unable to localize pulmonary nodules with any degree of accuracy. The completeness of pulmonary fissures is another intriguing characteristic of automated fissures. If there are patches of parenchymal fusion between the lobes and the cleft that do not extend to the hilum, the fissures are incomplete. When the fissures are fully developed, the lobes are only held together at the hilum by the bronchi and pulmonary arteries. Parenchymal fusion of varied degrees is also found along the floor in situations of incomplete cracks. There could not even be any fissures in some instances. These cracks appear as a thin-like curvature in two-dimensional image slices. This chapter will go through a number of approaches that can aid researchers in overcoming the aforementioned difficulties.

The rest of the chapter is organized as follows:

In Section 6.1, we discuss several methodologies that can be helpful to quantify the completeness of pulmonary fissures. The later section of this chapter describes the automated complete fissure detection, automated detection of incomplete fissures and pulmonary lobe segmentation and localization of pulmonary nodules.

6.2 Fissure completeness measurement

The degree of intactness and complete separation of the pulmonary fissures is referred to as pulmonary fissure completeness. Fissures, which are slender, connective tissue-based structures that resemble sheets and split the lungs into lobes. The oblique fissure, which divides the upper and lower lobes of the left lung, and the horizontal fissure, which divides the middle and upper lobes of the right lung, are the two main fissures in the lungs.

The integrity and completeness of the fissures should be assessed because it may have an impact on surgical planning and lung illnesses. Each lobe can function independently and maintain its structural integrity when the lobes are properly isolated by a complete and undamaged fissure. There may be aberrant connection or overlap between lobes when a fissure is absent or partial, which can have an impact on how illnesses, such as infections or tumours, are distributed within the lungs. Furthermore, under-standing the fissure's completeness is important for surgical procedures since it in-fluences how feasible and effective lung resections and other interventions are. An accurate segmentation of the pulmonary lobe is needed to determine fissure completeness. Accurate lobe segmentation of thoracic CT image slices is increasingly difficult due to the anatomy and the dense volume of image slices. In this context, improving accuracy might be possible with the use of an interactive pulmonary lobe segmentation methodology. We attempt to briefly discuss several fissure completeness in this section.

A thin plane surface representation methodology is needed in the aforementioned lobe segmentation methodology. It is necessary to represent the border form and then classify the fissures afterwards before employing this representation. In a word, TPS interpolating surfaces are gently curved surfaces that pass through a group of points. The source of the TPS formula is

$$f(x,y) = a_0 + a_1 + a_2 + \sum_{j=1}^{N} \omega_j U(r)$$

where N = selected coordinate points,

$$a_0, a_1, a_2 = \text{coefficient vector}$$

$$\omega_1, \omega_2, \cdots, \omega_j = \text{weight vector}$$

$$U(r) = \text{radial basis function}$$

(x, y) are the coordinate positions.

In this instance, the coefficient vector and weight vector assist in choosing N selected surface locations. To detect sites along each of the three borders of interest, the algo-rithm considers each point in the axial plane and iterates over voxels in the caudal-cranial direction until it identifies a transition from one lung lobe label to another. Depending on the particular transition, these voxels identify different lobe boundaries. Any such transition is the single line separating the lower lobe from the upper lobe in the left lung. A transition from the lower to the middle or higher lobe is referred to as the boundary corresponding to the right oblique fissure in the right lung. A transition from the centre to the top lobe designates the border that connects to the right horizontal fissure. Using the point sets for those borders, create comparable TPS surface repre-sentations for each of the three boundaries. In reality, every fourth point in both the x and y directions in our investigations is taken into account by the TPS surfaces as a regular subsample of the detected boundary points. As a result, further interpolation procedures are sped up.

The three lobe boundary surfaces' total surface areas are using TPS surface repre-sentations for each of the three surfaces. TPS interpolation has been utilized to calculate the z value for each of the border voxels based on the voxel's (x, y) position and the

z values for four adjacent locations. Four triangles with different 3D orientations are defined by these coordinates. Heron's formula is applied to quantify boundary surface area where area is estimated intercepted by the voxel by computing the area of each triangle using and adding the results. This is repeated for each of the three boundaries of interest's detected boundary voxels.

The solid arc (from A to C) symbolizes a fissure, and the solid arc combined with the shaded arc segment (from A to E) depicts the totality of a border between adjacent lobes in this simplified 2D schematic. The level of completeness is 50% when using the voxel (or in this example, pixel) counting approach ($\times 1$ and $\times 2$ relating to fissure; $\times 1$, $\times 2$, $\times 3$, and $\times 4$ corresponding to lobe boundary). The level of fissure completeness in this example, however, is obviously underestimated by this. The arc length from A to C certainly accounts for more than 50% of the arc length from A to E, hence this clearly understates the level of fissure completeness in this example. The dashed line segments connecting A and B are piecewise linear line segments (surface patches) that approximate nonlinear arcs (surfaces), akin to the triangle mesh surface approximating method mentioned above. (To prevent clutter, we did not draw approximation line segments for the other arc segments.)

In order to perform lobe boundary area estimation particle sampling is implemented to represent the fissure direction.

6.2.1   Particle sampling

By creating and modifying particles, particle sampling can be used to estimate the distribution of pulmonary lobes in a given dataset of lung CT scans. Here is a summary of the potential applications of particle sampling.

Initialization of a particle: Create a collection of particles that represent each potential pulmonary lobe found in the lung CT images. The positions and orientations of the particles within the lung volume can be used to depict them.

Particle Weighting: Give each particle a weight based on how closely it resembles the pulmonary lobes shown in the lung CT scans. By contrasting the traits or qualities of the particles (such as shape, intensity or texture) with the comparable features shown in the lung CT scans, this weighting can be carried out.

Resampling: Choose heavier particles to produce the following batch of particles. A particle's weight has an impact on its selection probability. In order to simulate the survival of fitter particles, this technique duplicates heavier particles and destroys lighter particles.

Particle Update: Update the selected particles by perturbing their positions and orientations. This step introduces variability and allows the particles to explore different configurations within the lung volume.

Repeat Steps 2–4: Iterate the process by repeating steps 2–4 multiple times to refine the particle distribution and improve the approximation of the pulmonary lobe distribution.

The equation used in particle sampling for pulmonary lobe assessment can be summarized as follows:

Particle Initialization:

Initialize a set of particles:

$$P = \{p\_1, p\_2, \ldots, p\_N\}$$

Particle Weighting:

Compute the weight for each particle based on its fitness or similarity to the observed pulmonary lobes:

$$w\_i = \text{Weight}(p\_i)$$

Resampling:

Generate a new set of particles by selecting particles from the current set with probabilities proportional to their weights:

$$P' = \text{Resample}(P, w)$$

Particle Update:

Update the selected particles by perturbing their positions and orientations:

$$P' = \text{Update}\left(P'\right)$$

Repeat Steps 2–4 for a specified number of iterations.

The distribution of the particle positions and orientations gradually converges to a distribution that resembles the distribution of pulmonary lobes in the lung CT scans by iteratively updating the particle positions and orientations based on their weights and resampling the particles. When examining and evaluating the features and spatial organization of pulmonary lobes in medical imaging data, this technique can be helpful.

Because the surfaces between lung lobes exhibit higher radio-opacity than the lobes themselves, the fissure can be distinguished as a ridge surface, defined as the locations of points where the gradient of the image is orthogonal to the minor eigenvector of the Hessian. The particles sampling technique uses a potential energy that depends on the distance between neighbouring particles and the third eigenvalue of the Hessian, which is designated as the image feature strength term in each case, to relocate points. Upon convergence, the system obtains a dense and uniform feature sampling in physical space. Although we have previously deployed particles sampling directly on the CT image, particles can also be deployed on alternative ridge-surface representations that capture fissure detections, such as probability and binary detection pictures. In the case of probability or binary detection images, smoothing (Gaussian blurring) is required prior to the actual operation of sampling the particles.

The particle system picks up on all locally planar structures, including fissures, supernumerary (accessory) fissures, and non-fissure (noise) structures. Noise particles must be removed and the fissure detections must be categorized according to the fissures they most likely represent before a given fissure's completeness can be assessed.

Despite the fact that accessory fissures are common, clinical praxis typically gives them little consideration. Then, each researcher should complete a task involving many classes, with the classes being given the names right oblique fissure, left oblique and right horizontal fissure. The classifier considers two factors when ranking the ith particle: i, the particle's orientation with respect to the normal vector of the lobe boundary, and di, the particle's shortest path to the lobe boundary. The likelihood that a particle is a fissure particle increases with the minor eigenvector's general parallelism to the local surface normal and proximity to the fit surface. In order to reduce variance and maintain a good separation between the means of the two classes (noise particles and fissure particles), the two-dimensional feature vector composed of the distance to the lobe surface and the angle of the particle with respect to the surface normal is then projected onto a one-dimensional subspace.

In the case of the right lung, where we must distinguish between the horizontal and oblique fissures, the distance and angle vectors are computed with respect to both lobe boundaries (the boundary separating the right middle lobe from the upper lobe and the boundary separating the lower lobe from the other two lobes). If both one-dimensional projections are over the discriminant threshold, the class assignment (oblique or horizontal) is determined by which projection is furthest above the threshold. In a previous study, we talked about a stage of fitting the shape model that fed data to the Fisher linear discriminant classifier.

The lobe borders are accurately quantified by the aforementioned algorithms. However, a casting ray approach is used to identify the voxels on lobe boundaries that belong to the fissures. If the ray intersects the pertinent fissure mesh, we add the estimated surface area of the voxel to the total fissure surface area. It is common to anticipate a little difference between the positions of the lobe borders, which were established using the segmentation input, and the locations of the fissure surfaces, which were established using the fissure detection inputs. A user-specified tolerance is provided to allow for discovered fissure locations to be slightly above or below the lobe border. The fraction of fissure completeness is then determined by dividing the total fissure surface area by the corresponding total lobe boundary surface area.

6.2.2   Fissure completeness assessment using deep learning-based algorithm

Each image's voxel size has been resampled to a 1 mm^3 isotropic size. Each image is split into two smaller ones that show the images that, when viewed through the lung mask, are localized to the left and right lungs, respectively. This reduces input size and aids in memory maintenance during training by eliminating material that the network does not require to fulfil its function. The CT image is further processed to eliminate intensities outside of the $(-1024, 200)$ HU range after scaling the intensities between $(-1,1)$. Through this procedure, the system's inputs are more consistent, and the effects of different HU calibrations between scans are lessened.

To quantify and localize fissure integrity, a single U-Net structured network examines three images and produces a fissure completeness/incompleteness segmentation. The inputs are convolved with a series of convolutional kernels in four phases of encoding to produce features with progressively lower resolution/higher order that describe the input data.

In order to construct a full-resolution output image and identify areas of completeness and incompleteness along the fissure, the decoding half of the network mirrors the encoding, or contracting path, and up-samples the inputs received from the contracting path in latent space. The input and output images from IntegrityNet have the same size and have three spatial dimensions in common. The number of input channels, which equals the number of feature maps in the input, and the number of output channels, | YY|, which equals the number of classes possible in the output segmentation (i.e., the output is one-hot encoded), are used to describe the number of channels in each image.

Three additional algorithms are done to the network output to get the final fissure integrity images. First, false positives must be removed from the network forecast. To do this, the non-fissure class (BGRD) classification is simply applied to all voxels outside of the segmented fissure.

The regions inside the BGRD fissure are then subjected to the average of the fissure's neighbours, denoted by the labels COMP or INCOMP. During this process, fake negatives are eliminated from the image. Applying a smoothing technique as the final stage will eliminate any jagged or uneven labelling. The output label is the average of all the non-BGRD neighbours, and each voxel along the fissure surface is smoothed using a neighbourhood with 26 connections.

6.2.3   Pulmonary lobe segmentation

Numerous automatic lobe segmentation techniques focussed on finding visible fissures under the presumption that the fissures were the same as those discovered using interpolation when deciding lobe segmentation. The interpolation of boundaries based on observed fissures may not be adequate to precisely pinpoint lobe borders due to the occurrence of incomplete fissures. Instead of only looking for fissures to explain partial fissures, anatomical links between lobes and nearby airways, arteries and the lung borders were utilized. A voxel wise classification challenge is what the automated lobe segmentation is. In fact, the segmentation of the pulmonary lobes is a multi-class problem with classes for the backdrop, the left upper and lower, the right upper and lower and the right middle lobe.

Cascaded Convolutional Neural Networks based on several resolutions are a technique that can be regarded as an effective segmentation algorithm. This algorithm's ability to extract both global and local pulmonary lobe information makes it beautiful. The method stated above uses U-Net as its fundamental design.

The initial RU-Net scans an input scan at a down-sampled resolution in order to coarsely segment the lobes and lobe borders. Then, these rough outputs are upsampled to a higher resolution via trilinear interpolation. The high-resolution input scan and the first RU-Net's output are concatenated and cropped into 3D patches to train the second RU-Net to precisely segment lobes and lobe boundaries.

Using a cascade of two relational U-Nets that are trained end-to-end, it is possible to learn both local specifics and scan-level context in the same optimization process. Additionally, we use the errors found in the initial RU-Net's predictions to choose the optimum sample of 3D patches for training the second stage. A 3D U-Net design with an additional non-local module and fewer convolution filters is the relational U-Net architecture (RU-Net). Three down-sampling layers, each made up of two convolutions and a max-pooling operation, are present in the RU-Net's encoding process. To offer a total of four convolution filters, two more convolutions are added to the down sampling circuit. After that, the non-local module is included before upsampling. The resolution is rebuilt using three layers, each of which includes a tri-linear interpolation before two convolutions are used to reduce the effects of the interpolation. The features are finally rearranged into two concurrent output branches, each of which corresponds to a different learning target, using a single $1 \times 1 \times 1$ convolution. For the purpose of separating the background from the five lobes, one of these branches creates 6-channel softmax probabilities. The other provides a single channel probability map with sigmoid function for predicting the lobe border. Features from $3 \times 3 \times 3$ convolutions are normalized and activated in a batch rectifier linear unit (ReLU). No dropout is employed.

The first RU-Net uses padded convolutions in contrast to the second RU-Net's real convolutions.

6.2.4   PLS Net

PLS-Net refers to the fusion of partial least squares (PLS) regression and neural networks in the context of pulmonary lobe segmentation. To take advantage of the advantages of both approaches, it includes incorporating the PLS regression principles into a neural network architecture. Here is a description of PLS-Net along with the relevant equations:

PLS Regression Equations:

PLS regression breaks down the input matrix X and the target vector y into a collection of latent variables known as the PLS components in order to identify the underlying links between the input features and the target variable. The weights are chosen by maximizing the covariance between the input characteristics and the target variable, and each component is a linear combination of the original variables.

The PLS regression equations can be represented as follows:

$$X = T * P' + E \tag{6.1}$$

$$y = U * Q' + F \tag{6.2}$$

In Eq. (6.1), X represents the input matrix, T represents the PLS scores matrix for X, P represents the loading matrix for X, and E represents the residual matrix. In Eq. (6.2), *y* represents the target vector, *U* represents the PLS scores matrix for *y*, *Q* represents the loading matrix for *y*, and *F* represents the residual vector.

Neural Network Integration:

To take advantage of the nonlinear mapping capabilities of neural networks, PLS-Net integrates PLS regression within a neural network framework. An input layer, one or more hidden layers with nonlinear activation functions, and an output layer make up the conventional neural network architecture.

The neural network layers receive the PLS scores (T and U) derived from Eqs. (6.1) and (6.2) as inputs. The inputs are transformed by the hidden layers using nonlinear activation functions, and the output layer generates the final segmentation prediction.

Training:

To take advantage of the nonlinear mapping capabilities of neural networks, PLS-Net integrates PLS regression within a neural network framework. An input layer, one or more hidden layers with nonlinear activation functions, and an output layer make up the conventional neural network architecture.

The neural network layers receive the PLS scores (T and U) derived from Eqs. (6.1) and (6.2) as inputs. The inputs are transformed by the hidden layers using nonlinear activation functions, and the output layer generates the final segmentation prediction.

By integrating PLS regression with neural networks, PLS-Net combines the ability to capture complex nonlinear relationships offered by neural networks with the interpretability and feature selection capabilities of PLS regression. This integration allows PLS-Net to effectively model the relationships between the input features and the target variable, resulting in accurate pulmonary lobe segmentation from medical imaging data.

6.2.5   RPLS Net

To take advantage of the nonlinear mapping capabilities of neural networks, PLS-Net integrates PLS regression within a neural network framework. An input layer, one or more hidden layers with nonlinear activation functions, and an output layer make up the conventional neural network architecture.

The neural network layers receive the PLS scores (T and U) derived from Eqs. (6.1) and (6.2) as inputs. The inputs are transformed by the hidden layers using nonlinear activation functions, and the output layer generates the final segmentation prediction.

Incorporating Spatial Relationships: To segment the pulmonary lobes, it is necessary to take into account how the various parts of the lungs are related spatially. The Partial Least Squares regression method, which explicitly takes into account the correlations between the input features and the target variable, forms the basis of RPLS-Net. The neural network architecture of RPLS-Net incorporates PLS regression to more efficiently gather and use spatial information, improving segmentation performance.

Nonlinear Mapping Capability: Dealing with intricate and nonlinear interactions between the input image data and the target segmentation masks is a common task in pulmonary lobe segmentation. The RPLS-Net model can recognize complex patterns and fluctuations in the data thanks to the neural network component's capacity to learn nonlinear mappings. As a result, RPLS-Net can effectively segment the complicated pulmonary lobe structures from the input images.

Performance and Efficiency: The performance and computational efficiency are balanced by RPLS-Net. PLS regression and neural networks can be integrated to effectively model and represent the data, producing precise segmentation outcomes. Additionally, the RPLS-Net's randomization stage eases the computational load by choosing only a portion of the input features, making it practical for real-time or expansive applications.

Adaptability and Generalizability: RPLS-Net may be trained and applied to a variety of imaging modalities, including computed tomography (CT) and magnetic resonance imaging (MRI), and it can adapt to diverse types of pulmonary imaging data. The model generalizes effectively across varied patient groups, imaging techniques and data gathering settings due to its capacity to capture spatial correlations and learn from a variety of inputs.

In general, RPLS-Net provides a promising method for segmenting the pulmonary lobes, addressing issues with noise, variability, spatial linkages and nonlinear mappings. Its integration of neural networks and partial least squares regression offers a strong and effective framework for precise pulmonary lobe segmentation from medical imaging data, improving analysis, diagnosis and treatment planning in lung-related disorders.

The architecture known as RPLS-Net, or Randomized Partial Least Squares-Net, is made for reliable regression tasks. To handle complicated and noisy data, it combines the benefits of partial least squares (PLS) regression and neural networks. An overview of the equations used in the RPLS-Net architecture is given below:

PLS Regression: PLS Regression is a method for linear modelling that seeks to identify the underlying connections between the input features and the target variable. This is accomplished by breaking down the input matrix X and target vector Y into a collection of latent variables called PLS components. The weights are chosen by maximizing the covariance between the input characteristics and the target variable, and each component is a linear combination of the original variables.

Neural Network Integration:

To take advantage of the nonlinear mapping capabilities of neural networks, RPLS-Net integrates PLS regression within a neural network framework. An input layer, one or more hidden layers with nonlinear activation functions, and an output layer make up the conventional design.

Randomization: To increase the model's robustness, the RPLS-Net incorporates a randomization step. At each training iteration, a subset of the input features is chosen at random. Outliers and noise in the data are lessened by this randomization.

Training:

By reducing a loss function that gauges the difference between projected outputs and the actual data, the RPLS-Net is trained. Depending on the particular regression job, this loss function may change. Absolute difference loss or mean squared error (MSE) are frequent options.

The following equations can be used to represent the overall RPLS-Net architecture: PLS Regression Equations:

$$X = TP' + E \tag{6.3}$$

$$y = UQ' + F \tag{6.4}$$

In Eq. (6.3), X represents the input matrix, T represents the PLS scores, P represents the loading vectors, and E represents the residual matrix. In Eq. (6.4), y represents the target variable, U represents the PLS scores for the target variable, Q represents the loading vectors for the target variable, and F represents the residual for the target variable.

Neural Network Integration:

The PLS scores (T and U) obtained from Eqs. (6.3) and (6.4) are used as input to the neural network layers. The hidden layers apply nonlinear activation functions to transform the inputs, and the output layer produces the final prediction.

Randomization:

At each training iteration, a random subset of the input features is selected, and the PLS regression and neural network components are applied only to the selected features. This randomization helps to improve the robustness of the model against outliers and noise.

Training:

The model parameters, including the weights and biases of the neural network layers, are optimized using gradient-based optimization algorithms. The loss function is minimized to improve the accuracy of the predictions.

Depending on the specifics of the regression task and the features of the dataset, the implementation details and modifications of the RPLS-Net architecture may change. A general framework for comprehending the integration of PLS regression and neural networks inside the RPLS-Net architecture is provided by the equations presented below.

Partial Randomized Least Squares-Net, or PRLS-Net, has a number of advantages over the conventional PLS-Net, which blends neural networks and partial least squares regression. The following are some of PRLS-Net's main benefits:

Improved Robustness: PRLS-Net introduces a randomization step during training, where a subset of input features is randomly selected for each iteration. This randomization helps enhance the robustness of the model by reducing the influence of outliers and noise in the data. As a result, PRLS-Net is better equipped to handle noisy or complex datasets, making it more reliable in real-world scenarios. Increased Generalization: The randomization in PRLS-Net promotes better generalization of the model across different datasets and variations within the data. By randomly selecting input features, PRLS-Net can capture more diverse information and learn to generalize well beyond the specific training dataset. This allows the model to perform effectively on unseen data and different patient populations, improving its practical applicability.

Computational Efficiency: PRLS-Net offers computational advantages compared to PLS-Net. By randomly selecting a subset of input features, PRLS-Net reduces the computational burden during both training and inference. The reduced feature space leads to faster model convergence and lower memory requirements, making PRLS-Net more efficient, particularly in large-scale or real-time applications.

Scalability: The randomization step in PRLS-Net makes it inherently scalable. As the dataset size increases, PRLS-Net can handle larger amounts of data more efficiently by randomly sampling a subset of features for each iteration. This scalability allows PRLS-Net to be applied to big data scenarios or situations where computational resources are limited.

Enhanced Interpretability: PRLS-Net retains the interpretability advantage of PLS-Net. The Partial Least Squares component in PRLS-Net enables the identification of important features and their relationships with the target variable. This interpretability helps in understanding the underlying factors driving the model's predictions, aiding in decision-making and generating insights in complex applications such as medical imaging analysis.

Overall, PRLS-Net builds upon the strengths of PLS-Net and further enhances its robustness, generalization capability, computational efficiency, scalability and interpretability. These advantages make PRLS-Net a compelling choice for various regression tasks, including those in the medical field, where reliable and interpretable models are crucial.

6.2.6 Dense V network

Pulmonary lobe segmentation using Dense V Network refers to the application of the Dense V-Net architecture for segmenting the pulmonary lobes from medical imaging data, such as computed tomography (CT) scans. The Dense V-Net is a variant of the U-Net architecture that incorporates dense connections between convolutional layers to enhance information flow and improve segmentation performance. Here's an explanation of how Dense V Network can be utilized for pulmonary lobe segmentation:

Dense V-Network:

The Dense V Network plays a significant role in the context of pulmonary lobe segmentation from medical imaging data, such as CT scans. Here are some key reasons why the Dense V Network is important in this field:

Accurate Segmentation: Pulmonary lobe segmentation requires precise delineation of the boundaries between different lobes in the lungs. The Dense V Network's architecture, with its dense connections and skip connections, enables the model to effectively capture both local and global contextual information. This enables more accurate and detailed segmentation of the pulmonary lobes, even in challenging cases where the boundaries are ambiguous or there are variations in lobe shapes and appearances.

Efficient Information Flow: The dense connections in the Dense V Network facilitate efficient information flow throughout the network. Each layer in the network receives direct input from all preceding layers, allowing for the propagation of information across different scales and depths of the network. This enhanced information flow helps in integrating features from different levels of abstraction, enabling the network to capture a more comprehensive representation of the pulmonary lobe structures.

Robust Feature Extraction: The Dense V Network's dense connections enable robust feature extraction by encouraging feature reuse and enhancing gradient flow. The dense connections ensure that features generated at each layer are accessible to subsequent layers, promoting feature reuse and facilitating the learning of more discriminative representations. This robust feature extraction capability helps in capturing the subtle differences in lung structures that are essential for accurate pulmonary lobe segmentation.

Precise Localization: The skip connections in the Dense V Network play a crucial role in precise localization. By connecting corresponding feature maps from the encoder and decoder paths, the skip connections enable the fusion of high-level and low-level features. This integration of multi-scale features helps in preserving spatial details and improves the network's ability to localize the boundaries of pulmonary lobes accurately.

Adaptability to Varying Lung Anatomy: The Dense V Network's architecture allows for flexibility and adaptability to varying lung anatomy across different individuals. The dense connections and skip connections enable the network to learn spatial relationships and patterns specific to each CT scan, accommodating anatomical variations in the shape, size and position of the pulmonary lobes. This adaptability is crucial in handling diverse datasets and improving the generalization capability of the network.

Overall, the Dense V Network brings significant advancements to pulmonary lobe segmentation by combining the strengths of dense connections and skip connections. It enables accurate segmentation, efficient information flow, robust feature extraction, precise localization and adaptability to varying lung anatomy. These factors contribute to improved analysis, diagnosis and treatment planning in lung-related diseases, providing valuable insights for medical professionals and researchers working in the field of pulmonary imaging.

The Dense V-Net architecture consists of an encoder–decoder structure with skip connections. The encoder part of the network employs multiple convolutional layers to extract features at different spatial resolutions. Dense connections are introduced between these convolutional layers, where each layer receives input from all preceding layers, promoting efficient information propagation.

The decoder part of the network uses transposed convolutions or upsampling operations to progressively recover the spatial resolution while maintaining the dense connections. The skip connections, which connect corresponding feature maps from the encoder and decoder paths, help in combining high-level and low-level features, enabling precise localization of the pulmonary lobes.

Training:

The Dense V Network is trained using annotated CT images, where the ground truth segmentation masks of the pulmonary lobes are provided. The network is trained to minimize a loss function that measures the dissimilarity between the predicted segmentation and the ground truth. Common loss functions for segmentation tasks include pixel-wise cross-entropy loss or Dice coefficient loss.

During training, the network learns to extract relevant features and capture the spatial relationships necessary for accurate pulmonary lobe segmentation. The weights and biases of the network are updated iteratively using gradient-based optimization algorithms, such as stochastic gradient descent (SGD) or Adam, to minimize the loss function and improve segmentation accuracy.

Inference:

Once trained, the Dense V Network can be applied to unseen CT images to segment the pulmonary lobes. The network takes the input CT scan as input and generates a segmentation map that delineates the boundaries of the different pulmonary lobes. This segmentation map can be further post-processed to refine the boundaries or extract additional quantitative measurements.

By utilizing the Dense V Network for pulmonary lobe segmentation, the architecture benefits from the dense connections, which promote information flow and enable the model to capture intricate patterns and details within the CT images. The dense connections facilitate the effective utilization of both local and global contextual information, leading to improved segmentation accuracy and robustness in handling variations in pulmonary lobe shapes and appearances.

6.3 Pulmonary fissure segmentation

Pulmonary fissure detection from CT images holds significant importance in the context of pulmonary nodule detection. Pulmonary fissures serve as crucial anatomical landmarks, separating different lobes and segments within the lungs. Since pulmonary nodules often occur near or along the pulmonary fissures, accurate detection and segmentation of these fissures are essential for localizing and assessing the spatial relationship of pulmonary nodules within the lung parenchyma. By identifying and analyzing the relationship between nodules and fissures, radiologists can gain valuable insights into nodule morphology, size and location, aiding in nodule classification, characterization, and subsequent treatment planning.

Pulmonary fissure detection provides valuable contextual information for pulmonary nodule detection. Fissures act as natural boundaries and can help in distinguishing between normal lung structures and potential nodules. Incorporating pulmonary fissure information into nodule detection algorithms can improve the specificity of the detection process, reducing false-positive rates. This integration helps in distinguishing nodules from normal anatomical structures that may mimic their appearance on CT images. By considering the absence of nodules in the vicinity of fissures, the accuracy of nodule detection algorithms can be enhanced, reducing unnecessary follow-up tests and interventions.

Pulmonary fissure detection from CT images is of paramount importance in pulmonary nodule detection. It provides valuable anatomical context, aids in reducing false-positive rates, facilitates multi-modality fusion and enables follow-up and treatment planning. Integrating pulmonary fissure information enhances the accuracy and clinical utility of pulmonary nodule assessments, empowering radiologists and clinicians to make informed decisions regarding patient care.

6.3.1 ODoS filter

Due to presence of high distinguish property between the intensity and orientation difference between fissures and its surrounding tissues, ODoS filter can overcome the shortcomings of traditional fissure segmentation methodologies. The kernel of above-mentioned filter has three different components namely left, middle and right and it has the capability to assign different colours in different lobes.

The nonlinear differentials perpendicular to the differential kernels can be defined as

$$\lambda_{\perp\,\min}^{s,\theta}{}_{\max}(x) = \frac{\max}{(u_M - u_L, u_M - u_R)}$$

A suppression operator has been introduced to suppress the tabular structure

$$\lambda_{\parallel}^{s,\theta}(x) = \sqrt{E\left(I_j^2\right) - E(I_j)^2}$$

Then the fissure line strength can be measured as

$$l_{\max}^{s,\theta}{}_{\min}(x) = \lambda_{\perp\,\min}^{s,\theta}{}_{\max}(x) - \kappa * \lambda_{\parallel}^{s,\theta}(x)$$

Here $\kappa = 0.7$.

In this model, the 2D strength measure function has been considered as

$$F_{\max}_{\min}(x) = \max\left(\left(l_{\max}^{s,\theta_i}{}_{\min}\right), 0\right)$$

where $L = 11$ and stand for the length and orientation of the stick, respectively. A cascaded strategy was subsequently developed to strengthen pulmonary fissures and decrease pathological anomalies.

Then,

$$F_o(x) = F_{\max}(x) {}^\circ F_{\min}(x)$$

here $\circ$ denotes the cascading operator. F_o represents response comes from axial, coronal and sagittal cross section.

Given that max F significantly affects $o\,F$ for pulmonary fissure enlargement, the orientation response was explained as follows:

$$\theta_{\max} = I_{\max}^{s,\theta_t}$$

Then the vector can be represented as

$$\overrightarrow{v}_{\max}(\theta_{\max}) = (\cos\,\cos\,\theta_{\max}, \sin\,\sin\,\theta_{\max})$$

On the other hand, a shape-tuned response from the fissure is obtained as

$$F^{3D} = (F_{\circ}^A + F_{\circ}^S + F_{\circ}^C) * \frac{\text{median}(F_{\circ}^A, F_{\circ}^S, F_{\circ}^C)}{\max(F_{\circ}^A, F_{\circ}^S, F_{\circ}^C)}$$

Thus, the intensity and orientation response of the filter can be combined as

$$\overrightarrow{F}(\theta_{\max}) = F^{3D} * \overrightarrow{v}_{\max}(\theta_{\max})$$

The ODoS filter has regularized the vector field.

A minimal criterion of 1 T = [13] was then chosen to prevent any cracks from being deleted as clutters.

Then,

$$\overrightarrow{F_v}(\theta_{\max}) = \begin{cases} \dfrac{\overrightarrow{F}(\theta_{\max})}{F^{3D}}, F^{3D} > T \\ 0, \text{otherwise} \end{cases}$$

In contrast to conventional approaches, consideration of an ODoS filter that highlights pulmonary fissure representation by integrating magnitude information with orientation information. This filter efficiently distinguishes between pulmonary fissures and clutters.

In order to nullify the presence of clutters, the normalized vector has been divided into eight overlapped sub-regions and denoted by $R_1, R_2, ..., R_n$.

Then,

$$\overrightarrow{F}_{vi} = \begin{cases} \overrightarrow{F_v}(\theta_{\max}), \theta_{\max} \in R_i \text{ and } |\overrightarrow{F_v}(\theta_{\max})|. > 0 \\ 0, \text{others} \end{cases}$$

In each of the subregion of 2D space, pulmonary fissures are constructed in a linear structure, whereas in 3D space it has planer structure. As a consequence, each of the fissures exhibits similar orientations. Wherein all objects in the sub-region are designated with the letters $S_1, S_2, S_3, ..., S_{m-1}$, and S_m, and the appropriate orientations are marked with the numbers $\theta_1, \theta_2, \theta_3, ..., \theta_{m-1}$, and θ_m. In 2D space, orientation of θ_i is an attribute of the set $[\theta_x, \theta_y]$. Here, $[\theta_x, \theta_y]$ is the corresponding orientations of the sub-regions R_i. Then the orientation curvature can be defined as

$$\theta_i(S) \subset [\theta_x, \theta_y]$$

In a probabilistic classification model of pulmonary fissure detection, there follows a conditionally probability distribution $P(Y|X)$, where X is the test dataset and Y is the finite set of class.

The three fissures plus a non-fissure class make up the class set Y for pulmonary fissure classification, and all voxels that are not fissures are assigned to the non-fissure class. In the lung mask, there are a very small number of fissure voxels compared to non-fissure voxels; at the imaging quality employed in this study, there is roughly one fissure voxel for every 100 non-fissure voxels.

6.3.1.1 Pulmonary fissure segmentation using FissureNet

By cascading two Seg3DNets, FissureNet employs a coarse-to-fine method (Fig. 6.1). A rough fissure region of interest (ROI) is detected using the first Seg3DNet, and a precise fissure location inside the ROI is detected using the second Seg3DNet. Pipelines for the left and right lungs are trained separately, producing Left fissure ROI, right fissure ROI, left fissure and right fissure making up four Seg3DNet classifiers.

In pulmonary fissures segmentation, consideration of a covNet can be considered as a viable solution. It is a specific type of neural network model created to find patterns in spatially associated data, including pictures and movies. A ConvNet includes numerous layers of learnt feature detectors grouped hierarchically at the highest level.

Although the feature detectors in each layer are local, the composition of layers allows the receptive field, or the spatial extent established on the input image, to expand with layer depth. With the help of this design, the network can learn global features without incurring the additional computational costs and parameter requirements of huge feature detectors. Because the feature detectors are spatially shared, a particular feature can be significant anywhere in the image. Convolutional layers are referred to as layers that have feature detectors. The feature detectors, or kernels, are learnt through optimization and are not explicitly encoded. In order to decrease the spatial resolution, convolutional layers are frequently followed by an elementwise nonlinearity and interspersed with pooling layers.

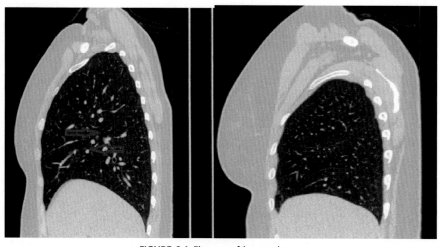

FIGURE 6.1 Fissures of human lungs.

Seg3DNet is made of an encoder that produces a high-dimensional feature representation of the picture and a decoder that extracts the features to create a segmentation. In contrast to conventional segmentation topologies, Seg3DNet uses asymmetric encoder and decoder modules. The encoder module consists of L resolution levels l_i where the activation maps in level l_i are down sampled by a factor of 2^i in comparison to the full resolution level l_0. The levels of resolution are $i = 0, 1, \ldots, L-1$. Two convolutional layers are used in each encoder level, which are followed by a max-pooling layer.

$3 \times 3 \times 3$ voxel kernels are used in all convolutional layers, and $N_i = 2i+5$ determines how many kernels are present at level l_i. Max pooling with a kernel size of $2 \times 2 \times 2$ and a stride of 2 results in the down sampling factor of 2 between levels after the second convolution layer of each level. Although pooling layers have been removed in more current ConvNet topologies, down sampling is still required to create a global receptive field on huge input volumes. The decoder network mixes representations from all scale levels to reduce the loss of precise localization data from the pooling layers.

The decoder module uses a convolutional layer with a single voxel kernel of size $3 \times 3 \times 3 \, N_i$ to compress the representation at each scale level to a single activation map.

By utilizing nearest neighbour interpolation to up-sample the lower resolution activation maps to full resolution and then convolution with filter size $2\,i + 1$, it is possible to perform a sort of deconvolution [1]. The generated activation maps are concatenated along the feature dimension to create a multi-scale representation, one from each scale level. To merge data from various scales, two more convolutional layers are applied.

Each of the $|Y|$ activation maps in the final layer of the Seg3DNet's representation has the same spatial dimensions as the input volume. It is understood that the activation map y's output at spatial point x, $fy(x)$, represents an unnormalized log probability that x belongs to the class y. The conditional probability distribution is obtained using the softmax vector nonlinearity and is represented by:

FissureNet comprises two parallel pipelines, each of which is a coarse-to-fine cascade of two Seg3DNets.

A fissure ROI is trained into the first Seg3DNet. The fissure ROI training labels are created by modifying the initial ground truth fissure segmentations. If a voxel is located within 5 mm of the associated fissure, it is considered to be part of the fissure ROI; otherwise, it is not. This single-voxel ground truth dilatation lessens the class skewness. Additionally, the network is able to concentrate on broad patterns rather than specific fissure appearance by widening the ground truth fissure.

The network is hence more resistant to minor and radiographically insufficient cracks. As expected from the process of manually drawing a single voxel curve, the fissure ROI allows for minor flaws in the training data.

To locate the specific location of the fissure, the second Seg3DNet is trained. As training labels, the initial ground truth fissure segmentations are used. Each voxel suffers from the same loss as the initial Seg3DNet [2]. The total loss, however, is a weighted average based on the likelihood that the voxel is in a fissure. ROI.

The contribution of this weighting to the exact localization of fissures while reducing the issue of class imbalance caused by the huge number of non-fissure voxels in the loss function.

6.3.2   Hessian filter

Hessian-based plateness filters are frequently used in detection of pulmonary fissures. This type of technique creates a plateness filter for fissure likelihood measurement by combining the eigenvalues of the Hessian matrix. Typically, a Gaussian filter is used first, with the proper choice of kernel scales σ, to smooth out the original CT scan. The Hessian matrix is then calculated at each voxel. Here Hessian matrix is calculated for each of the voxels. Let, $\lambda_1, \lambda_2, \lambda_3$ be the eigen values of the eigen vectors $\vec{e_1}, \vec{e_2}, \vec{e_3}$. Then the plateness likelihood function is defined as

$$P = \{0 \text{ if } \lambda_3 \geq 0 \; \max_\sigma (F_A F_B F_S), \text{ otherwise}$$

$$F_A = e^{\left(-\frac{A^2}{2\alpha^2}\right)}$$

$$F_B = e^{\left(-\frac{B^2}{2\beta^2}\right)}$$

$$F_S = 1 - e^{\left(-\frac{S^2}{2\gamma^2}\right)}$$

$A = \frac{\lambda_2}{\lambda_3}, B = \frac{\sqrt{|\lambda_1 \lambda_2|}}{|\lambda_3|}, S = \sqrt{\lambda_1^2 + \lambda_2^2 + \lambda_3^2}$, (α, β, γ) are the free parameters. The eigen vector $\vec{e_3}$ is obtained by normalizing the orientation of the pulmonary fissures.

6.3.3   DDoP filter

In CT scan images pulmonary fissures appear as anisotropic structures with an intensity greater than the lung parenchyma around them. Particularly, cracks are flat along their axial directions and very narrow in their transverse directions. In addition, there aren't many high intensity lung veins in the restricted area around the fissures. We were naturally inspired to design a filtering kernel with three parallel plates that simultaneously probes the profile of a fissure patch and its surrounding background due to the shape and appearance characteristics of fissures, specifically the anisotropic plate-like structure and the intensity differences between the fissures and surrounding parenchyma.

The derivative to the orthogonal plate is defined as

$$h_{\text{DDoP}} = \mu_{\text{Mp}} - \frac{1}{2} \left(\mu_{\text{Up}} + \mu_{\text{Dp}} \right)$$

a view of the profile of the fissure decomposing the DDoP kernel into a derivative kernel in the Z direction and an average smoothing kernel in the X–Y plane allows for the formulation of a specific definition. The definition can be expressed as

$$h_z(z) = \left\{ 0 \text{ if } |z| \geq 3S \quad -\frac{1}{2} \text{ if } S \leq |z| \leq 3S \text{ 1, otherwise} \right.$$

$$h_{xy}(x,y) = \{0 \text{ if } x^2 + y^2 \geq R^2 \text{ 1 otherwise}$$

$$h(x,y,z) = h_{xy}(x,y).h_z(z)$$

The fissure can be detected by convoluting the kernel with the image which can be defined as

$$r^*(x) = (l(x) * h_n(x))$$

$$\overrightarrow{n}(x) = \arg(l(x) * h_n(x))$$

The disadvantage of DDoP filter is that it is computationally complexed. In order to reduce the complexity of the kernel, a spherical harmonic function has been introduced. It is an orthogonal basis function which is defined on the surface of a sphere. It is formulated as

$$f(\varphi, \theta) = \sum_{l=0}^{L} \sum_{m=-l}^{l} Y_m^l(\varphi, \theta) f_m^l$$

$$Y_m^l(\varphi, \theta) = \sqrt{\frac{(l-m)!}{(l+m)!}} P_m^l(\cos(\theta)) e^{i\varphi}$$

The CT image is filtered using the suggested DDoP approach, which effectively enhances the pulmonary fissures and other plate-like structures. However, the responses of the fissures are not uniform because of the various image contexts, the high curvature fissures, and the nearby clutter, making a straightforward threshold segmentation impractical. In order to extract fissures in the filtered images, we now describe a straightforward two-stage post-processing method. First, we present an orientation partition denoising and merging algorithm to remove the non-fissure structures, which is motivated by the fact that adjacent fissure voxels typically have similar normal directions but that their adjacent interference deviates noticeably.

6.3.4 Random walk-based methodologies for pulmonary fissure segmentation

Random walk-based methodologies have been successfully applied for pulmonary fissure detection in medical image analysis. The pulmonary fissures are anatomical boundaries between lung lobes that play a crucial role in the segmentation and analysis of lung structures. Detecting and accurately delineating pulmonary fissures is important for various applications, including lung disease diagnosis, surgical planning and image-guided interventions.

Random walk-based methodologies utilize the concept of random walks on a graph to delineate the boundaries of pulmonary fissures. The algorithm starts by constructing a graph representation of the lung image, where each pixel or voxel is represented as a node, and the connectivity between nodes is defined based on the image structure. Typically, a 3D graph representation is used for volumetric lung images.

The random walk algorithm then assigns probabilities or weights to the graph edges based on the image features and similarity measures. These weights indicate the likelihood of transitioning from one pixel to its neighbouring pixels. The algorithm incorporates prior knowledge or seed points to guide the random walk process, which serves as initial boundary information for the fissures.

The random walk process iteratively propagates probabilities from the seed points to the rest of the image, gradually refining the boundary delineation of the pulmonary fissures. The probabilities propagate based on the similarity of image features and graph connectivity. Pixels or voxels with high probabilities are more likely to belong to the fissure boundaries.

The algorithm converges when the probabilities reach a stable state, indicating the final delineation of the pulmonary fissures. Post-processing techniques, such as thresholding and morphological operations, can be applied to refine the fissure segmentation and improve the accuracy.

Random walk-based methodologies offer advantages in pulmonary fissure detection, as they can effectively incorporate both local image features and global anatomical context. They can handle image noise, intensity variations and irregularities in the fissure boundaries. Additionally, the algorithm can be adapted to handle 2D or 3D image data, making it suitable for both computed tomography (CT) and magnetic resonance imaging (MRI) modalities.

Overall, random walk-based methodologies provide a robust and automated approach for pulmonary fissure detection, aiding in the accurate segmentation and analysis of lung structures for various clinical applications.

6.3.5   Random walk algorithm

The random walk algorithm is a computational technique used in image analysis and segmentation tasks, including pulmonary fissure detection. It leverages the concept of random walks on a graph to propagate probabilities and delineate boundaries between regions of interest. Here's an explanation of the random walk algorithm along with the appropriate equation:

Graph Construction: The algorithm starts by constructing a graph representation of the image. In the case of pulmonary fissure detection, a common approach is to represent the image as a 2D or 3D grid graph, where each pixel or voxel corresponds to a node in the graph. The connectivity between nodes is defined based on the spatial neighbourhood relationships in the image.

Probability Initialization: The algorithm assigns initial probabilities to the nodes in the graph based on prior knowledge or seed points. Seed points are manually or automatically selected points that lie on or near the boundaries of the regions of interest, in this case, the pulmonary fissures. These seed points serve as starting points for the random walk process.

Probability Propagation: The random walk algorithm iteratively propagates probabilities from the seed points to the rest of the graph. The probability propagation is guided by the similarity between nodes and is typically computed using a diffusion process.

The equation for probability propagation in the random walk algorithm can be represented as follows:

$$P(i) = \sum [W(i,j) * P(j)]$$

In the equation above

$P(i)$ represents the probability at node i.
$W(i, j)$ denotes the weight or similarity measure between nodes i and j.
$P(j)$ represents the probability at node j, which is being propagated to node i.

The probability at each node i is updated based on the weighted sum of the probabilities of neighbouring nodes j, multiplied by the corresponding weights $W(i, j)$. The weights capture the similarity or affinity between nodes and can be calculated using various measures, such as intensity similarity, gradient information or local image features.

Convergence and Boundary Delineation: The random walk algorithm continues propagating probabilities until a convergence criterion is met. Convergence is typically achieved when the probabilities at the nodes stabilize, indicating that the algorithm has delineated the boundaries of interest, such as the pulmonary fissures.

Post-processing steps, such as thresholding and morphological operations, can be applied to refine the segmented boundaries and improve the accuracy of the pulmonary fissure detection.

By iteratively propagating probabilities and considering the similarity between nodes, the random walk algorithm effectively delineates boundaries between different regions of interest, such as the pulmonary fissures in the case of pulmonary image analysis. The algorithm is versatile and can be adapted to different imaging modalities and segmentation tasks by appropriately defining the graph structure and similarity measures.

6.3.6   Implementation of random walk in fissure detection

To construct a graph representation of the pixels in pulmonary fissures for implementing the random walk algorithm, you can follow these steps:

Image Preprocessing: Start by preprocessing the pulmonary image to enhance the pulmonary fissure regions and remove noise or artefacts. This may involve techniques such as image denoising, contrast enhancement and image filtering.

Segmentation: Perform a preliminary segmentation of the pulmonary fissure regions using an appropriate segmentation algorithm. This step aims to separate the pulmonary fissure pixels from the background and other lung structures.

Graph Creation: Once the pulmonary fissure pixels are identified, create a graph representation where each pixel corresponds to a node in the graph. The connectivity between nodes is determined based on the spatial neighbourhood relationships between pixels.

Graph Connectivity: Define the connectivity scheme based on the desired neighbourhood relationship. For 2D images, the common choice is to consider 4-connectivity or 8-connectivity, where each pixel is connected to its immediate horizontal, vertical and diagonal neighbours. For 3D volumetric images, 6-connectivity or 26-connectivity can be used.

Edge Weight Calculation: Calculate the weights or similarity measures between the connected nodes in the graph. The edge weights capture the similarity or affinity between pixels and influence the probability propagation in the random walk algorithm. The choice of edge weight calculation depends on the specific characteristics of the pulmonary fissure and the available information in the image. It can be based on intensity similarity, gradient information, texture features or other relevant image attributes.

Seed Point Selection: Select seed points within the pulmonary fissure region as initial starting points for the random walk algorithm. These seed points serve as the sources for probability propagation and guide the random walk process.

Once the graph representation is constructed, you can apply the random walk algorithm to propagate probabilities from the seed points to the rest of the graph, gradually delineating the boundaries of the pulmonary fissures. The probabilities at each pixel/node represent the likelihood of belonging to the pulmonary fissure region.

6.3.7   IntegrityNet

IntegrityNet is a convolutional neural network (CNN) architecture specifically designed for accurate pulmonary fissure segmentation from CT images. The architecture combines innovative design choices with the power of deep learning to achieve robust and precise results. IntegrityNet incorporates various components and features, including multi-scale feature fusion, skip connections, dilated convolutions, and an appropriate loss function for training.

The architecture of IntegrityNet typically starts with a CNN backbone, such as U-Net or ResNet, which serves as the foundation. The backbone consists of multiple layers of convolutional and pooling operations that extract meaningful features from the input CT images. These features capture the image's spatial and contextual information.

Multi-scale feature fusion is an important component of IntegrityNet, enabling the network to capture both local and global context. This fusion mechanism aggregates features from multiple scales, ensuring that the network can handle variations in fissure appearance and accurately segment fissures across different image resolutions. The fusion process helps in capturing fine-grained details as well as high-level context.

Skip connections are utilized in IntegrityNet to enhance information flow and preserve spatial details. These connections enable the fusion of high-resolution features from earlier layers with lower-resolution features from deeper layers. By combining features from different levels of the network, IntegrityNet can effectively capture both fine-grained and high-level context, facilitating accurate boundary delineation of pulmonary fissures.

Dilated convolutions are employed in IntegrityNet to expand the receptive field of the network without sacrificing feature map resolution. By using dilated convolutions, the network can capture larger contextual information, which is crucial for accurately delineating the boundaries of pulmonary fissures. The dilation rate controls the size of the receptive field and allows the network to gather information from a broader area.

For training, IntegrityNet employs an appropriate loss function, such as the dice coefficient or cross-entropy, to measure the discrepancy between the predicted fissure segmentation and the ground truth. The network is trained using annotated CT image data, and through backpropagation and gradient-based optimization algorithms, the model learns to optimize the loss function and improve the accuracy of fissure segmentation.

The architectural choices and components of IntegrityNet, including multi-scale feature fusion, skip connections, dilated convolutions, and the appropriate loss function, work together to provide a robust and accurate pulmonary fissure segmentation solution. The integration of deep learning techniques in IntegrityNet showcases the potential for advanced image analysis and interpretation in lung-related applications, supporting radiologists and clinicians in their diagnostic and treatment decision-making processes.

3D patch-based CNN:

The 3D patch-based convolutional neural network (CNN) is an effective methodology for pulmonary fissure segmentation from 3D CT images. This approach takes advantage of the inherent three-dimensional structure of CT scans to accurately delineate the complex pulmonary fissures. The process begins by extracting small three-dimensional patches from the CT volume, each containing a region of interest, including the pulmonary fissure area. These patches are then fed into the CNN architecture, which consists of convolutional, pooling, and fully connected layers. The convolutional layers extract meaningful features, capturing spatial information and local structures relevant to the pulmonary fissures. The pooling layers reduce dimensionality, and the fully connected layers perform classification or segmentation based on the learnt features. During training, each patch is labelled with the corresponding ground truth segmentation mask, allowing the network to learn the mapping between the input patches and the segmentation masks. The network is optimized using a suitable loss function, such as the dice coefficient or cross-entropy, to minimize the discrepancy between the predicted and ground truth segmentations. Once trained, the network can be applied patch-wise to unseen CT volumes, generating a probability map or segmentation mask indicating the likelihood of the pulmonary fissure presence at each voxel. Post-processing steps can be employed to refine the segmentation results, ensuring accurate delineation of the pulmonary fissures. Overall, the 3D patch-based CNN approach offers a powerful and efficient solution for pulmonary fissure segmentation, aiding in the precise analysis and interpretation of CT images in lung-related applications.

The patch size in a 3D patch-based convolutional neural network (CNN) has a significant impact on the performance of the model for pulmonary fissure segmentation. The choice of patch size affects both the representation capability of the network and the computational complexity of the training and inference processes. Here are some considerations regarding the effect of patch size:

Contextual Information: Larger patch sizes capture more contextual information about the surrounding regions of the pulmonary fissures. This increased context can be beneficial as it allows the network to consider a broader context when making predictions. However, extremely large patch sizes may introduce irrelevant information or noise from neighbouring structures, potentially leading to reduced accuracy.

Spatial Detail: Smaller patch sizes provide higher spatial resolution and capture finer details within the pulmonary fissure regions. This can be advantageous when dealing with small or intricate fissures, as the network can focus on local features. However, overly small patch sizes may not provide enough context for accurate segmentation, particularly when fissures span larger regions.

Training Data Requirements: The patch size affects the amount of training data needed for the network to generalize well. Larger patch sizes require more training samples to cover the diversity of pulmonary fissure variations adequately. On the other hand, smaller patch sizes may be more forgiving in terms of data availability, as they capture local features that may be consistent across different cases.

Computational Efficiency: The computational complexity of training and inference increases with larger patch sizes. Processing larger patches requires more memory and computational resources. Smaller patch sizes, on the other hand, reduce the computational burden but may require more iterations or augmentations to achieve convergence and generalize well.

In practice, the choice of patch size depends on several factors, including the size and complexity of the pulmonary fissures, the available computational resources and the size of the training dataset. It is common to experiment with different patch sizes and evaluate the performance of the model on validation data to determine the optimal balance between contextual information, spatial detail and computational efficiency.

It's important to note that there is no one-size-fits-all answer, and the optimal patch size may vary depending on the specific dataset and application. Therefore, conducting empirical studies and considering the trade-offs between context, detail and computational complexity are crucial in determining the most suitable patch size for the 3D patch-based CNN for pulmonary fissure segmentation.

Deep learning, and particularly convolutional neural networks (CNNs), has transformed medical picture processing. CNNs excel at learning hierarchical representations from huge datasets and can extract relevant features from CT scans automatically. CNNs may learn to detect and categorize pulmonary nodules with high accuracy by training them on annotated CT scans with known nodule sites. Because deep learning eliminates the requirement for explicit feature engineering, the model can learn complicated patterns and changes in nodule appearance.

A comprehensive approach for automatic nodule detection is provided by combining deep learning and filter algorithms. Deep learning models can be trained to detect possible nodules in CT images, while filter algorithms can help refine the detection by decreasing noise, enhancing nodule boundaries, and offering extra post-processing steps.

The use of deep learning and filter algorithms to detect lung nodules automatically has yielded promising results. These approaches have shown great sensitivity and specificity in differentiating nodules from non-nodule structures, allowing radiologists and physicians to make accurate and quick diagnosis. Furthermore, using these algorithms can dramatically minimize the time and effort necessary for manual nodule identification, resulting in more efficient and streamlined operations in radiology departments.

However, it is vital to highlight that deep learning and filter algorithms require robust training datasets, validation and fine-tuning to ensure generalizability and performance across varied CT image datasets. Ongoing research and developments in these techniques continue to increase the accuracy and efficiency of automated nodule detection, resulting in better patient outcomes in the early detection and treatment of lung cancer.

6.3.8   Localization of pulmonary nodule

After successfully reconstructing the lung lobes from the CT scan data, the focus shifts to identifying the presence of nodules within these segmented lobes. This involves a multi-step process. First, the segmented lung lobes are isolated, allowing each individual lobe to be analyzed separately. Following this, a nodule detection algorithm is applied to pinpoint potential nodules within the segmented lobes. The result is a list of nodule positions in the 3D space of each lobe. The critical task is associating these detected nodules with their respective lobes. This is achieved through spatial analysis, matching nodule coordinates to the boundaries of each lobe, and considering anatomical landmarks like bronchi or fissures. This association then enables the classification of each nodule into the specific lobe it resides in. By overlaying the detected nodules on the segmented lung lobes, the visualization of nodule distribution becomes readily available. Additionally, comprehensive reports are generated, detailing the presence of nodules in each lobe, along with their characteristics and any pertinent clinical information. Through rigorous validation, seamless integration into clinical workflows, and continuous feedback from medical professionals, the accuracy and utility of this approach are refined, ensuring its valuable contribution to pulmonary nodule analysis within specific lung lobes.

Pulmonary fissure detection, lobe detection and the localization of pulmonary nodules are crucial tasks in medical imaging, facilitated by advanced computer vision techniques. These processes enhance the understanding of lung anatomy and aid in the diagnosis of lung diseases.

Pulmonary fissure detection employs image processing algorithms to identify and delineate the fine membranes that separate lung lobes. This process enhances automated lung segmentation, leading to more accurate analysis of lung structure and function.

Lobe detection utilizes computer vision methods to segment lungs into distinct lobes, allowing for the assessment of lobe-specific health conditions. By analyzing texture, shape, and anatomical landmarks, these techniques provide insights into lung functionality and assist in diagnosing diseases affecting specific lobes.

The localization of pulmonary nodules, enabled by machine learning and image analysis, is crucial for early disease detection. Computer vision techniques precisely identify nodules within lung images, incorporating spatial analysis to associate them with specific lobes. This localization aids radiologists in evaluating nodule characteristics and making informed decisions about patient care.

Computer vision techniques play a pivotal role in pulmonary fissure detection, lobe detection, and pulmonary nodule localization. These methods offer precise, automated solutions that improve the accuracy of lung assessments, contribute to disease diagnosis and enhance patient outcomes in the realm of pulmonary medicine.

References

[1] Gerard SE, Patton TJ, Christensen GE, Bayouth JE, Reinhardt JM. FissureNet: a deep learning approach for pulmonary fissure detection in CT images. IEEE Transactions on Medical Imaging August 10, 2018;38(1):156−66.

[2] Badrinarayanan V, Kendall A, Cipolla R. Segnet: a deep convolutional encoder-decoder architecture for image segmentation. IEEE Transactions on Pattern Analysis and Machine Intelligence January 2, 2017;39(12):2481−95.

Further reading

[1] Ross JC, Nardelli P, Onieva J, Gerard SE, Harmouche R, Okajima Y, et al. An open-source framework for pulmonary fissure completeness assessment. Computerized Medical Imaging and Graphics July 1, 2020;83:101712.

[2] Xiao C, Stoel BC, Bakker ME, Peng Y, Stolk J, Staring M. Pulmonary fissure detection in CT images using a derivative of stick filter. IEEE Transactions on Medical Imaging January 13, 2016;35(6):1488−500.

[3] Peng Y, Xiao C. An oriented derivative of stick filter and post-processing segmentation algorithms for pulmonary fissure detection in CT images. Biomedical Signal Processing and Control May 1, 2018;43: 278−88.

[4] Peng Y, Luan P, Tu H, Li X, Zhou P. Pulmonary fissure segmentation in CT images based on ODoS filter and shape features. Multimedia Tools and Applications March 14, 2023:1−22.

[5] Peng Y, Zhong H, Xu Z, Tu H, Li X, Peng L. Pulmonary lobe segmentation in CT images based on lung anatomy knowledge. Mathematical Problems in Engineering April 19, 2021;2021:1−5.

[6] Zhao H, Stoel BC, Staring M, Bakker M, Stolk J, Zhou P, et al. A framework for pulmonary fissure segmentation in 3D CT images using a directional derivative of plate filter. Signal Processing August 1, 2020;173:107602.

[7] Anitha S, Ganesh Babu TR. An efficient method for the detection of oblique fissures from computed tomography images of lungs. Journal of Medical Systems August 2019;43:1−3.

[8] Xie W, Jacobs C, Charbonnier JP, Van Ginneken B. Relational modeling for robust and efficient pulmonary lobe segmentation in CT scans. IEEE Transactions on Medical Imaging May 15, 2020; 39(8):2664−75.

[9] van der Molen MC, Hartman JE, Vermeulen CJ, van den Berge M, Faiz A, Kerstjens HA, et al. Determinants of lung fissure completeness. American Journal of Respiratory and Critical Care Medicine October 1, 2021;204(7):807−16.

[10] Bao N, Yuan Y, Luo Q, Li Q, Zhang LB. Edge-enhancement cascaded network for lung lobe segmentation based on CT images. Frontiers in Physics March 3, 2023;11:1098756.

[11] Zhang Y, Osanlouy M, Clark AR, Kumar H, King C, Wilsher ML, et al. Pulmonary lobar segmentation from computed tomography scans based on a statistical finite element analysis of lobe shape. In: Medical imaging 2019: image processing, vol. 10949. SPIE; March 15, 2019. p. 790−9.

[12] Park J, Yun J, Kim N, Park B, Cho Y, Park HJ, et al. Fully automated lung lobe segmentation in volumetric chest CT with 3D U-Net: validation with intra-and extra-datasets. Journal of Digital Imaging February 2020;33:221−30.

[13] Tada DK, Teng P, McNitt-Gray M, Kim GH, Brown MS, Goldin J, et al. 3D patch-based CNN for fissure segmentation on CT images to quantitatively assess fissure integrity and evaluate emphysema patients for endobronchial valve treatment. In: Medical imaging 2023: computer-aided diagnosis, vol. 12465. SPIE; April 2023. p. 321−8.

[14] Gerard SE, Reinhardt JM. Pulmonary lobe segmentation using a sequence of convolutional neural networks for marginal learning. In: 2019 IEEE 16th international symposium on biomedical imaging (ISBI 2019). IEEE; April 8, 2019. p. 1207−11.

[15] Lee H, Matin T, Gleeson F, Grau V. Efficient 3D fully convolutional networks for pulmonary lobe segmentation in CT images. September 16, 2019. arXiv preprint arXiv:1909.07474.

[16] Tang H, Zhang C, Xie X. Automatic pulmonary lobe segmentation using deep learning. In: 2019 IEEE 16th international symposium on biomedical imaging (ISBI 2019). IEEE; April 8, 2019. p. 1225−8.

7

Automated risk prediction of solitary pulmonary nodules

7.1 Introduction

Previous chapters of this book deal with several ML and DL-based algorithms that can efficiently detect pulmonary nodules from CT images in the presence of an imbalance class problem. In this chapter, we've suggested an automated method for estimating the likelihood that a lung nodule would develop cancer. As already stated in Chapter 3, clinicians considered several morphological features for predicting the likelihood of malignancy of the lesions. Indeed, these morphological features have several classes. Consequently, previously discussed binary classification methodologies are not well suited for solving the multi-class classification problem. Although the presence of a multi-class classification system reduces the degree of imbalance in the test datasets, imbalance nature of the test dataset still exists. The primary objective of this book is to aware the researchers for implementing a CAD system that can be applicable in daily clinical practice. The noteworthy fact is that the AI-based methodologies are working as a black box model, i.e., it can predict the classes of the test data but are incapable of finding out the features responsible for the predicted results. Medical fraternities don't trust a black box model, they need an explanation.

7.1.1 Support vector machine

Support Vector Machine (SVM) is a popular supervised machine learning algorithm used for classification and regression analysis. SVM works by finding the hyperplane in the feature space that best separates the data into different classes. The hyperplane is chosen to maximize the margin, which is the distance between the hyperplane and the closest data points from each class.

The SVM algorithm can be formulated as an optimization problem with the following objective function:

$$\min\left(\frac{1}{2}\|w\|^2 + C\,\mathrm{sum}(x_i)\right) \tag{7.1}$$

$$\text{Subject to } y_i(w.x_i + b) \geq 1 - x_i$$

where w is the weight vector, b is the bias term, x_i is the slack variables that allow for misclassification, C is the regularization parameter that controls the trade-off between

Application of Artificial Intelligence in Early Detection of Lung Cancer. https://doi.org/10.1016/B978-0-323-95245-3.00007-X

199

maximizing the margin and minimizing the classification error, and y_i are the class labels (+1 or −1).

The term $\frac{1}{2}\|w\|^2$ represents the regularization term that penalizes large values of the weight vector w. The sum(x_i) term represents the slack variable penalty that penalizes misclassifications. The constraints $y_i(w.x_i + b) \geq 1 − x_i$ ensure that the hyperplane separates the data into different classes with a margin of at least 1.

7.1.1.1   Kernels in SVM

SVM use kernels to transform data into a higher-dimensional space, allowing for better separation of classes. Kernels play a crucial role in SVM by defining the similarity between data points and determining the decision boundary. Here are some commonly used kernel functions in SVM along with their corresponding equations:

Linear Kernel:

The linear kernel represents a linear relationship between the data points and is suitable for linearly separable datasets.

$$K(x, y) = x \cdot y \tag{7.2}$$

In this equation, '·' denotes the dot product between the feature vectors x and y.

Polynomial Kernel:

The polynomial kernel introduces non-linearity by mapping the data points into a higher-dimensional space using polynomial functions.

$$K(x, y) = (\gamma \cdot x \cdot y + r)^{\wedge} d \tag{7.3}$$

Here, γ is the coefficient controlling the influence of the dot product, r is an optional constant, and d represents the degree of the polynomial.

Radial Basis Function (RBF) Kernel:

The RBF kernel is commonly used due to its flexibility in capturing complex patterns. It transforms the data points into an infinite-dimensional space.

$$K(x, y) = \exp\left(− \gamma \|x − y\|^{\wedge}2 \right) \tag{7.4}$$

In this equation, γ controls the influence of the distance between x and y, and $\|x − y\|$ represents the Euclidean distance between the feature vectors x and y.

Sigmoid Kernel:

The sigmoid kernel introduces non-linearity using a sigmoid function and is useful for data that may not be linearly separable.

$$K(x, y) = \tanh(\gamma \cdot x \cdot y + r) \tag{7.5}$$

Here, γ is the scaling factor, and r is an optional constant.

Gaussian Kernel:

The Gaussian kernel is similar to the RBF kernel and is often used interchangeably. It transforms the data into a higher-dimensional space using a Gaussian distribution.

$$K(x, y) = \exp\left(− \gamma \|x − y\|^{\wedge}2 \right) \tag{7.6}$$

Similar to the RBF kernel, γ controls the influence of the distance between x and y, and $\|x−y\|$ represents the Euclidean distance between the feature vectors x and y.

These equations represent the mathematical definitions of some commonly used kernels in SVM. The choice of kernel depends on the nature of the data, the problem at hand, and the desired decision boundary. SVM with appropriate kernel functions can efficiently handle both linearly separable and non-linearly separable datasets.

7.1.2   Multi-class SVM

The SVM algorithm can be extended to handle multi-class classification problems using a technique called one-vs-one (OvO) or one-vs-all (OvA) classification. In OvO classification, multiple binary classifiers are trained, each one distinguishing between one pair of classes. In OvA classification, a single binary classifier is trained for each class, which distinguishes that class from the rest of the classes.

The multi-class SVM algorithm can be formulated as follows:

$$\min\left(\frac{1}{2}\|w\|^2 + C\operatorname{sum}(x_i)\right) \tag{7.7}$$

Subject to $y_i(w.x_i + b) \geq 1 - x_i$

where w is the weight vector, b is the bias term, x_i are the slack variables that allow for misclassification, C is the regularization parameter that controls the trade-off between maximizing the margin and minimizing the classification error, and y_i are the class labels (+1 or −1).

In OvO classification, if there are K classes, K(K−1)/2 binary classifiers are trained, each one distinguishing between one pair of classes. The class with the highest number of votes across all binary classifiers is assigned to the input sample (Fig. 7.1).

In OvA classification, K binary classifiers are trained, each one distinguishing between one class and the rest of the classes. The class with the highest score across all binary classifiers is assigned to the input sample.

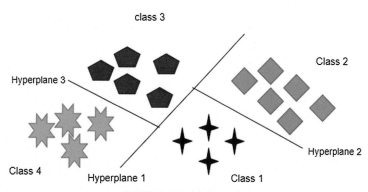

FIGURE 7.1 Multi-class SVM.

7.1.3 Ensemble learning

Ensemble learning is a machine learning technique that combines the predictions of multiple models to improve their accuracy and performance. It is based on the idea that multiple models working together can produce better results than a single model. Ensemble learning is widely used in many applications, including image recognition, speech recognition, and natural language processing.

There are several types of ensembles learning methods, including bagging, boosting and stacking. Bagging, short for bootstrap aggregating, is a technique that generates multiple models by training them on different subsets of the data. The final prediction is obtained by averaging the predictions of all the models. Boosting, on the other hand, is a technique that generates multiple models by iteratively training them on different subsets of the data. Each subsequent model is trained to correct the errors of the previous model, and the final prediction is obtained by combining the predictions of all the models. Stacking is a technique that combines the predictions of multiple models by training a meta-model on the output of the base models.

Ensemble learning has several advantages over a single model. First, it reduces the risk of overfitting, which occurs when a model is too complex and performs well on the training data but poorly on new data. Ensemble learning ensures that the models are diverse, reducing the chances of overfitting. Second, ensemble learning improves the accuracy and robustness of the model. The combination of different models reduces the impact of noise and outliers in the data, resulting in a more accurate and robust model. Finally, ensemble learning can be used with any type of machine learning algorithm, including decision trees, neural networks and support vector machines.

However, ensemble learning also has some drawbacks. First, it requires more computational resources and time to train multiple models. Second, ensemble learning can be difficult to implement, as it requires expertise in machine learning and statistics to design and train the models. Finally, ensemble learning may not always lead to improved performance, especially if the base models are not diverse enough or if the data is too noisy or biased.

7.1.3.1 Bias variance trade-off

The Bias-Variance trade-off is a fundamental concept in machine learning that refers to the trade-off between two types of errors that can occur in a model: bias and variance. Bias is the error that occurs when a model is too simple to capture the complexity of the data, while variance is the error that occurs when a model is too complex and overfits the data.

Bias refers to the error that is introduced by approximating a real-world problem with a simplified model. A high-bias model has a limited ability to represent complex relationships in the data. This often results in underfitting, where the model is unable to capture the important patterns in the data. For example, a linear regression model that is used to predict the price of a house may have a high bias if it assumes that the relationship between the price and the size of the house is linear, when in fact it may be more complex.

Variance, on the other hand, refers to the error that is introduced by modelling the noise in the training data rather than the underlying patterns. A high variance model has too much flexibility and can fit the training data too closely, resulting in overfitting. Overfitting occurs when the model becomes too complex and captures the noise in the data, rather than the underlying patterns. For example, a decision tree that is used to predict the price of a house may have high variance if it is too deep, and it captures noise and random variations in the training data.

The bias-variance trade-off states that there is a trade-off between these two types of errors, and it is important to find a balance between them. Models with high bias tend to have low variance, while models with low bias tend to have high variance. The goal of machine learning is to find a model that has low bias and low variance, which is achieved by selecting the right level of model complexity that is appropriate for the problem at hand.

The bias-variance trade-off can be illustrated using a learning curve. A learning curve plots the training and testing error of a model as a function of the amount of training data. Initially, as the model is trained on a small amount of data, the training error and testing error are both high, indicating high bias and high variance. As more data is added, the training error decreases, indicating that the model is learning more about the data. However, the testing error may initially decrease and then start to increase as the model starts to overfit the training data. The optimal point on the learning curve is the point where the testing error is minimized.

Several techniques can be used to balance the bias-variance trade-off. One approach is to use regularization, which adds a penalty term to the objective function that limits the complexity of the model. Regularization can help to reduce the variance of the model and prevent overfitting. Another approach is to use ensemble learning, which combines multiple models to reduce variance and improve the accuracy of the predictions. Ensemble learning can be used to improve the performance of models that suffer from high bias or high variance.

7.1.3.2 *Different types of voting and averaging techniques in ensemble learning*

Ensemble learning is a machine learning technique where multiple models are trained and combined to improve the predictive performance of the overall system. Voting and averaging are two common techniques used to combine the outputs of multiple models in ensemble learning.

1. Hard Voting: In hard voting, each model in the ensemble makes a prediction for a given input, and the final prediction is made by taking the majority vote of the predictions. This technique is used for classification problems, where the final output is a class label. For example, if there are five models in the ensemble, and three of them predict class A, while the other two predict class B, the final prediction will be class A.

2. Soft Voting: In soft voting, each model in the ensemble assigns a probability or confidence score to each class label for a given input. The final prediction is made by averaging these probability scores across all models and selecting the class with

the highest average probability score. Soft voting is particularly useful for problems where there is no clear majority class.

3. **Weighted Voting:** In weighted voting, each model in the ensemble is given a weight that reflects its relative importance or performance. The final prediction is made by taking a weighted average of the predictions from all models, with the weights reflecting the importance of each model.

4. **Bagging:** Bagging (Bootstrap Aggregating) is a technique where multiple models are trained on different subsets of the training data, and the final prediction is made by averaging the predictions of all models. Bagging is particularly useful for reducing the variance of the model, as each model is trained on a different subset of the data.

5. **Boosting:** Boosting is a technique where multiple weak models are trained sequentially, with each model trained to improve the performance of the previous model. In boosting, the final prediction is made by taking a weighted sum of the predictions of all models, with the weights reflecting the importance of each model.

6. **Stacking:** Stacking is a technique where the outputs of multiple models are used as inputs to a higher-level model, which makes the final prediction. In stacking, each model in the ensemble makes a prediction for a given input, and these predictions are concatenated to form a new feature vector. This feature vector is used as input to a higher-level model, which makes the final prediction. Stacking is particularly useful for combining the strengths of different types of models.

7.1.4   AdaBoost

AdaBoost (Adaptive Boosting) is an ensemble learning technique that combines multiple weak classifiers to create a strong classifier. The idea behind AdaBoost is to sequentially train weak classifiers on different weighted versions of the training data, and then combine their predictions using a weighted majority vote (Fig. 7.2).

The AdaBoost algorithm can be broken down into the following steps:

Initialize the weights for each training example to be equal ($w\_i = 1/N$, where N is the number of training examples).

For each round $t = 1, 2, \ldots, T$.

a. Train a weak classifier h_t on the training data, where each training example is weighted by w_i.

b. Compute the error of the weak classifier on the weighted training data:

$$\varepsilon_t = \sum_i w_i * \frac{y_i \neq h_t(x_i)}{\sum_i w_i} \tag{7.8}$$

where y_i is the true class label of the i-th training example, h_t(x_i) is the predicted class label of the i-th training example by the t-th weak classifier, and I( ) is the indicator function that returns 1 if the argument is true, and 0 otherwise.

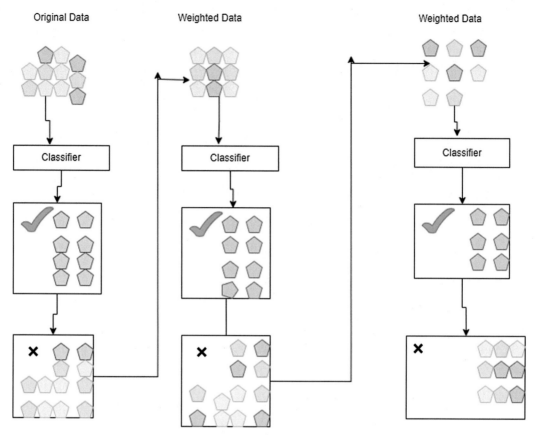

FIGURE 7.2 Adaptive boosting.

c. Compute the weight of the weak classifier in the final ensemble:

$$\alpha_t = \frac{1}{2} \times \ln\, \ln\left(\frac{(1-\varepsilon_t)}{\varepsilon_t}\right) \qquad (7.9)$$

d. Update the weights of each training example:

$$w_i \leftarrow w_i \times e^{\left(-\alpha_t \times y_i \times h_t(x_i)\right)} \qquad (7.10)$$

Normalize the weights so that they sum to 1.
1. Combine the predictions of all weak classifiers using a weighted majority vote:

$$H(x) = \text{sign}\left(\sum_t \alpha_t \times h_t(x)\right) \qquad (7.11)$$

where sign( ) is the sign function that returns +1 if the argument is positive, and −1 otherwise.

The weight of the weak classifier in the final ensemble (step 2c) is calculated using the error rate of the weak classifier (step 2b). The higher the error rate, the lower the weight of the weak classifier. If the error rate is 0.5, the weight of the weak classifier is set to 0, which means it has no contribution to the final prediction. The weight of the weak classifier is used in the weighted majority vote (step 3) to give more importance to the predictions of the better-performing weak classifiers.

7.1.5 Decision tree

A decision tree is a supervised learning algorithm that is used for classification and regression tasks. The algorithm builds a tree-like model of decisions and their possible consequences, and uses it to predict the class label or value of a new data point.

The decision tree algorithm can be broken down into the following steps:

Choose a feature to split the data into two subsets.

Calculate a splitting criterion (such as information gain or Gini impurity) for each possible split.

Choose the split with the highest splitting criterion.

Recursively apply steps 1–3 to each subset, until a stopping criterion is met (such as a maximum depth or a minimum number of samples per leaf node).

Assign a class label or value to each leaf node.

The equation for information gain can be written as:

$$IG(D, a) = H(D) - H(D|a) \tag{7.12}$$

where $IG(D, a)$ is the information gain of feature a, D is the dataset, $H(D)$ is the entropy of the dataset, and $H(D|a)$ is the conditional entropy of the dataset given feature a. The higher the information gain, the more informative the feature is for predicting the class label (Fig. 7.3).

The equation for Gini impurity can be written as follows:

$$Gini(D) = 1 - \sum_{i=1}^{c} (p_i)^2 \tag{7.13}$$

FIGURE 7.3 Decision tree.

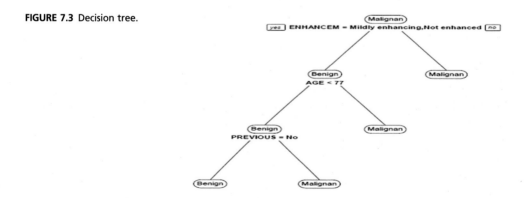

where Gini(D) is the Gini impurity of the dataset, k is the number of classes, and p_i is the proportion of examples in class k. The lower the Gini impurity, the more homogeneous the class distribution is in the dataset.

7.1.6 Random forest

Random Forest is a classifier that uses many decision trees on different subsets of the input dataset and averages the results to increase the dataset's predicted accuracy. The random forest uses the forecasts from each decision tree as opposed to just one, basing its prediction of the ultimate result on the predictions that received the most votes overall. Because the random forest combines many trees to anticipate the class of the dataset, some decision trees may predict the proper output while others may not. But when all the trees are taken into account, they accurately predict the outcome. The Gini Index, which is denoted as, determines how a decision tree is pruned.

$$\text{Gini} = 1 - \sum_{i=1}^{c} (p_i)^2 \qquad (7.14)$$

This formula calculates the Gini of each branch on a node based on the class and probability, indicating which branch is more likely to occur. In this case, p_i stands for the class's relative frequency in the dataset and c for the total number of classes.

XGBoost: Extreme Gradient Boosting, often known as XGBoost, is an ensemble algorithm that takes into account a number of weak learners in order to more accurately forecast the class of test data. The fundamental property of XGBoost is its ability to handle missing values without the need for pre-processing. In this technique, decision trees are taken into account sequentially, and a weight factor emerges as a classification factor (Fig. 7.4).

Before being fed into the decision tree that predicts results, each independent variable is assigned a weight. Before entering the second decision tree, variables that the first one mispredicted are given additional weight. Then, a strong and precise model is created by combining these various classifiers/predictors. It can be applied to the resolution of issues with regression, classification, ranking and personalized prediction.

XGBoost's implementation is exclusively reliant on the CART philosophy. Individual decision trees' prediction scores can be calculated as

$$\widehat{y}_i = \sum_{k=1}^{K} f_k(x_i), f_k \in F \qquad (7.15)$$

where K denotes the total number of trees, f is the functional space of F, F denotes all possible sets of CARTs. Then the objective function of the model is defined as

$$T(\theta) = \sum_{i}^{n} l(y_i, \widehat{y}_i) + \sum_{k=1}^{K} \Omega(f_k) \qquad (7.16)$$

In the above equation, the first term indicates the loss function and the second one is regularization parameter. Here the additive strategy is used to minimize the loss is to add

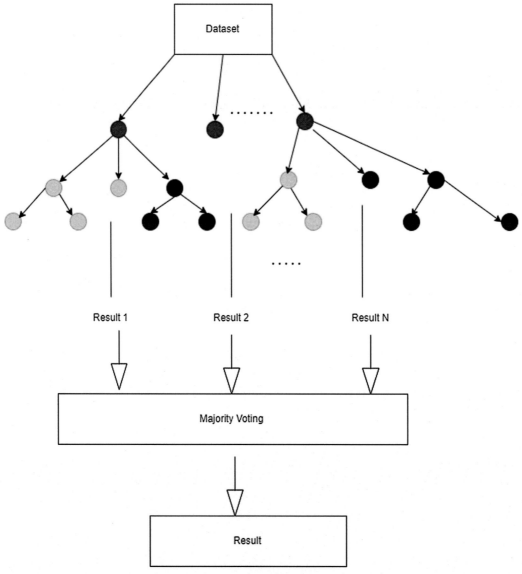

FIGURE 7.4 Random forest.

a new tree, and avoid learning the tree all at once, which makes optimization more difficult. This strategy is summarized as follows:

$$\hat{y}_i^{(0)} = 0$$

$$\hat{y}_i^{(1)} = f_1(x_i) = \hat{y}_i^{(0)} + f_i(x_i)$$

$$\hat{y}_i^{(2)} = f_i(x_i) + f_2(x_i) = \hat{y}_i^{(1)} + f_2(x_i) \tag{7.17}$$

$$\ldots\ldots$$

$$\hat{y}_i^{(t)} = \sum_{k=1}^{t} f_k(x_i) = \hat{y}_i^{(t-1)} + f_t(x_i)$$

Then the objective function can be defined as

$$T^t = \sum_{i=1}^{n} l(y_i, \hat{y}_i^{(t)}) + \sum_{i=1}^{t} \Omega(f_i)$$

$$= \sum_{i=1}^{n} l\left(y_i, \hat{y}_i^{(t-1)}\right) + f_t(x_i) + \Omega(f_t) + \text{constant} \tag{7.18}$$

Applying second-order Taylor Series Expansion, we get

$$T^t = \sum_{i=1}^{n} \left[l\left(y_i, \hat{y}_i^{(t-1)}\right) + g_i f_i(x_i) + \frac{1}{2} h_i f_t^2(x_i) \right] + \Omega(f_t) + \text{constant} \tag{7.19}$$

where $g_i = \delta_{\hat{y}_i^{(t-1)}} l\left(y_i, \hat{y}_i^{(t-1)}\right)$, $h_i = \delta_{\hat{y}_i^{(t-1)}}^2 l\left(y_i, \hat{y}_{i\,i}^{(t-1)}\right)$

Simplifying the Taylor Series Expansion and removing the constant we get,

$$T^t = \sum_{i=1}^{n} \left[g_i f_t(x_i) + \frac{1}{2} h_i f_t^2(x_i) + \Omega(f_t) \right] \tag{7.20}$$

The regularization term of the model can be defined as

$$f_t(x) = \omega_{q(x)}, \omega \in R^M, q: R^d \to \{1, 2, \ldots, M\} \tag{7.21}$$

where ω = vector score of each of the leaves of the tree (Fig. 7.5).

M is the number of leaves, and q is the function that assigns each data point to its matching leaf. The term 'regularization' is thus defined as follows:

$$\Omega(f) = \gamma M + \frac{1}{2}\lambda \sum_{j=1}^{M} \omega_j^2 \tag{7.22}$$

$$T^t \approx \sum_{i=1}^{n} \left[g_i f_t(x_i) + \frac{1}{2} h_i f_t^2(x_i) + \Omega(f_t) \right] + \gamma M + \frac{1}{2}\lambda \sum_{j=1}^{M} \omega_j^2$$

$$= \sum_{j=1}^{M} \left[\left(\sum_{i \in I_j} g_i \right) \omega_j + \frac{1}{2} \left(\sum_{i \in I_j} h_i + \lambda \right) \omega_j^2 \right] + \gamma M \tag{7.23}$$

FIGURE 7.5 XGBoost classifier.

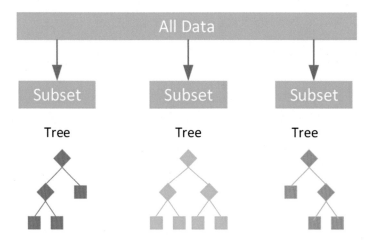

The simplified equation is as follows:

$$T^t = \sum_{j=1}^{M} \left[G_j \omega_j + \frac{1}{2}(H_j + \lambda)\omega_j^2 \right] + \gamma M \tag{7.24}$$

where $G_j = \sum_{i \in I_j} g_i$

$$H_j = \sum_{i \in I_j} h_i$$

λ = Pruning parameter which indicates the information gain for splitting. Information gain measures how accurate the tree is pruned for prediction.

$$\text{Information Gain} = \frac{1}{2}\left[\frac{G_L^2}{H_L + \lambda} + \frac{G_R^2}{H_R + \lambda} - \frac{(G_L + G_R)^2}{H_L + H_R + \lambda} \right] - \gamma \tag{7.25}$$

7.1.7   Rotation forest

Rotation forest is an ensemble learning technique that uses PCA and random rotations to create a range of base classifiers. The primary components of the original data are used to train each basis classifier, and the predictions of all basis classifiers are merged to get the final prediction.

The following steps make up the rotation forest algorithm:

- Pick k subsets of the original data at random.
- Apply PCA to each subset to make the data less dimensional and to extract the top p principal components.
- Rotate the data at random to get a new set of features for each subset.

- On each subgroup, train a base classifier (such as a decision tree or SVM). Aggregate the predictions of all base classifiers using a majority voting scheme for classification or a weighted average for regression.

The equation for PCA can be written as follows:

$$X = USV^\wedge T \qquad (7.26)$$

where X is the original data matrix, U is the matrix of eigenvectors (principal components), S is the diagonal matrix of eigenvalues, and VT is the transpose of the matrix of eigenvectors.

The equation for random rotation can be written as follows:

$$X_{rotated} = X * R \qquad (7.27)$$

where $X\_rotated$ is the rotated data matrix, X is the original data matrix, and R is a random rotation matrix that is generated for each subset.

The final prediction of the Rotation forest can be written as follows:

$$y_{final} = mode(y_1, y_2, \dots, y_k) \qquad (7.28)$$

where y_{final} is the final predicted class label, y_1, y_2, ..., y_k are the predicted class labels of the k base classifiers, and mode( ) is the function that returns the most common class label among the k predictions.

7.2 Explainable AI

The use of AI has revolutionized the field of health informatics, but it also has drawbacks that must be avoided, especially in the context of healthcare. The lack of interpretability or explicability in AI models is a major worry. Understanding how AI systems provide forecasts or suggestions for healthcare is essential since these judgements have significant ramifications. Trust, responsibility and potential biases are raised by the black box aspect of deep learning models like neural networks. The implementation of AI in healthcare contexts is hampered by this lack of openness since regulators, patients and medical professionals may be wary of using AI-based solutions without fully understanding its underlying assumptions. Additionally, when AI is applied in healthcare, ethical issues including privacy, data security, and algorithmic biases come into play.

Explainable AI (XAI) has become a crucial topic in health informatics as a means of avoiding these issues. The goal of explainable AI is to make AI models transparent and interpretable so that users can understand how decisions are made. We can increase confidence in AI-based systems by implementing XAI approaches. The model's recommendations can be evaluated and verified by doctors, patients, and regulatory agencies, thanks to the insights into decision-making that can be gained. Additionally, XAI aids in finding biases and mistakes in AI systems, enabling fairer and more precise decision-making. By giving insights into the variables impacting the model's predictions, it aids clinical decision-making and equips clinicians to make wise choices and deliver individualized patient care. Additionally, explainable AI techniques support regulatory compliance by guaranteeing accountability and transparency in AI models and upholding privacy, security and ethical standards.

Although AI has a lot of potential for health informatics, it is critical to solve the issue of interpretability. Explainable AI methods assist clinical decision-making, promote trust, expose biases and guarantee regulatory compliance. We can utilize the full potential of AI in healthcare while upholding moral standards and fostering patient-centric care by aiming for transparency and interpretability. Any bias in a model can be found once it has been understood. A healthcare strategy created for the American population, for instance, might not be suitable for Asians.

7.2.1 Global explanation

The dataset-level explanation, also known as the global explanation, presents the broad associations that the neural network has discovered. For instance, a global explanation might include dataset-level feature relevance ratings, which express how much a feature contributes to the total output. You can select the variables that are crucial for predicting the likelihood of pulmonary nodules, for instance. There are a variety of approaches available for assessing global explanations. We will talk about all of these later:

1. Partial Dependency Plot (PDP): PDP describes the overall behaviour of a model by showing the link between the marginal effects of each predictor and the response variable. It illustrates how the feature variable and the target variable are related. In such a case, a complex, monotonous, or even simple linear relationship may exist. The important characteristic, whose partial dependence is computed, is assumed not to have a significant association with the other features. If the features of the model are connected, PDP does not provide an accurate interpretation. This algorithm's drawback is that it is unable to handle very deep neural networks.
2. Individual Conditional Expectation (ICE): ICE plots demonstrate how the instance's prediction varies as a feature changes by showing one line per instance. The partial dependence plot for the average influence of a feature is a global approach because it doesn't focus on specific instances but rather an overall average. PDP equivalents for individual data instances are ICE charts.

   An ICE plot displays the relationship between the forecast and each unique instance of a characteristic, in contrast to partial dependency plots, which only display one line overall. A PDP is the average of the lines in an ICE plot. The values for a line (and one instance) can be derived by holding all other features constant, creating variations of this instance by replacing the feature's value with values from a grid, and making predictions with the black box model for these newly created instances. The result is a collection of points for a given instance that include the feature value from the grid and the accompanying predictions.

3. SHAP as Global Predictor:

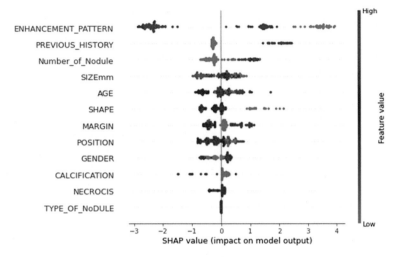

It's common practice to use SHAP (SHapley Additive exPlanations) to explain the results of machine learning models. In a game-theoretic approach called SHAP, each characteristic in a prediction is given a contribution value that indicates how much that feature contributed to the forecast. This contribution value is based on the Shapley value, a concept from cooperative game theory that allows each group member a fair portion of the overall value produced by the group.

By ranking the significance of characteristics in a dataset using the contribution values, SHAP can be utilized as a global predictor. This can be accomplished by averaging each feature's contribution value to overall dataset predictions. Features that have higher average contribution values are thought to be more significant, whilst features that have lower average contribution values are thought to be less significant.

The SHAP-generated global predictor can be applied to a number of processes, including feature selection, model optimization and data pre-processing. For instance, a feature may be a viable candidate for removal or reduction if its average contribution value is low because it does not significantly affect the model's predictions. Similarly to this, it may be worthwhile to devote more resources to gathering or developing a characteristic if its average contribution value is high.

Insights into the underlying connections between the features and the target variable can also be gained from the global predictor produced by SHAP. It may be possible to determine features that have a positive or negative impact on the target variable and to establish causal linkages between the features and the target variable by analyzing the contribution values.

Using SHAP as a global predictor has the drawback of assuming that the contribution values are unrelated to one another. In reality, however, this could not always hold true as interactions between the features could cause the contribution values to be correlated. However, subsequent research has put forth strategies to get around this issue, like using group SHAP values to take feature interactions into consideration.

Overall, SHAP has the potential to be a potent technique for developing global predictors that offer perceptions into the connections between attributes and the target variable. It is feasible to pinpoint model flaws and have a better grasp of the underlying data by utilizing SHAP to rank the relevance of features.

7.2.2   Local explanation

The significance of a single input is explained locally. Regarding this specific study issue, it can be said that the input will be the radiological and demographic characteristics of a specific patient. The patient in question's key characteristics is looked for by the local explainable model. Two well-known local explainable models are SHaply Additive exPlanations (SHAP) and Local Interpretable Model-agnostic Explanations (LIME).

7.2.2.1   LIME

A potent method in explainable artificial intelligence (XAI) is local interpretable model-agnostic explanations (LIME). LIME seeks to make sophisticated machine learning models' predictions more transparent and understandable by revealing how they make decisions. By simulating the behaviour of the model close to the instance being explained, LIME creates locally accurate explanations for specific predictions. It does this by changing the instance's features and then watching how these changes affect the model's output.

In order to approximate the behaviour of the original model, LIME builds a simpler, more understandable surrogate model by comparing the model's predictions for the original instance and the perturbed instances. Then, human-readable explanations that highlight the characteristics most responsible for the prediction are produced using this surrogate model, which is frequently a linear regression. Because LIME is model-agnostic, it may be used with a variety of machine learning methods and gives practitioners access to the black-box predictions of even the most complicated models.

Mathematically, the explanation can be defined as

$$\text{explanation}(x) = \text{argmin } g \in G\ (f, g, \pi_x) + \Omega_g \tag{7.29}$$

The model g that minimizes loss L, which assesses how closely the explanation matches the prediction of the original model f, is the explanation model for example x. Model complexity is also kept to a minimum. The family of explanations known as G includes, for instance, all potential linear regression models. The proximity measure specifies the size of the area surrounding instance x that we take into account while providing an explanation. In reality, LIME just improves the loss component. The user must choose the maximum amount of features the linear regression model may employ, for example, in order to define the complexity.

7.2.2.2 SHAP

A machine learning model's feature importance is described mathematically using the SHAP model. In the presence of multicollinearity between several features, Shapley values predicted significant features. All of the examined features have been divided up into different feature subsets $(S \subseteq F)$ using this process. F stands for the set that represents all of the features (Fig. 7.6).

A significance value is assigned to each feature, indicating the influence it will have on the model's forecast. The feature is used in the training of one model but not in the training of another. Next, the input data—where xS denotes the values of the input features in the set S—is used to compare the predictions of the two models. Since the effect of leaving out a feature depends on other model variables, the aforementioned differences are calculated for all potential subsets. The Shapley values are used as feature attributions after being calculated. They are the average of all conceivable variations, weighted.

By integrating samples from the training dataset and utilizing sampling approximations to Eq. (7.4), Shapley sampling values are made to estimate the effect of removing a variable from a model. These values can be used to explain any model. Less than 2jFj differences can now be estimated without the model needing to be retrained. Because the explanation model form of the Shapley sampling values is the same as that of the Shapley regression values, it is similarly an additive feature attribution method.

Each feature's SHAP value demonstrates how, when that feature is taken into account, the expected model prediction will change. They explain how to obtain the current output f from the expected initial value E[f(z)] if we were to have no knowledge of any features (x). There is just one ordering in this diagram. When the model is non-linear or the input features are not independent, the order in which features are added to the expectation matters. The SHAP values are obtained by averaging the i values across all possible orderings.

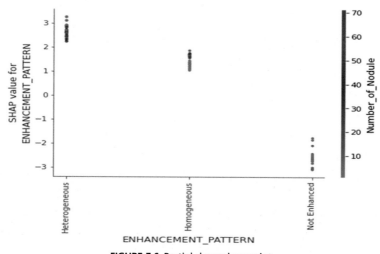

FIGURE 7.6 Partial dependency plot.

This formulation of SHAP values includes an implicit simplified input mapping, hx(z0) = zS, which includes missing values for features that are not in the collection S. Since most models cannot handle arbitrary patterns of missing input data, we approximate f(zS) with E[f(z) j zS]. This idea of SHAP values is designed to closely correlate with the Shapley regression, Shapley sampling, and quantitative input affect feature attributions and has connections to LIME, DeepLIFT, and layer-wise relevance propagation.

Accurately calculating SHAP values can be challenging. However, by merging information from already-used additive feature attribution techniques, we may estimate them. In this article, we provide two model-independent approximation methods, one of which is well-known (Shapley sampling values), and the other of which is brand-new (Kernel SHAP). We also offer four novel approximation methods (Max SHAP, Deep SHAP) that are model-type-specific. The optional assumptions of feature independence and model linearity (note that S is the set of features not in S) facilitate the computation of the anticipated values when using these methodologies.

If feature independence is assumed, it is possible to directly calculate SHAP values for predicting conditional expectations using either the Shapley sampling values methodology or, alternatively, the Quantitative Input Influence method. These methods make use of Eq. (7.8), a sampling approximation of the conventional Shapley value equations. A unique sampling estimate is used for each feature attribution. Even while it is possible to compute for a limited number of inputs, the Kernel SHAP technique, which is described next, requires fewer evaluations of the original model to obtain a similar approximation accuracy. (Notice that S is the set of features not in S.)

For Shapley regression values, h_x maps a value of 1 or a value of 0 to the original input space, where a value of 1 denotes inclusion in the model and a value of 0 denotes exclusion from the model.

7.2.3   Explainable model for CT image analysis

As previously said, the risk prediction of pulmonary nodules is based on the study of the shape, margin, and type of nodules, and these characteristics can be predicted by evaluating pulmonary nodules from CT scans. Therefore, it is impossible to describe how well some features are detected using the aforementioned methods.

7.3 Saliency maps

In visual processing, saliency refers to an image's distinctive elements (such as its pixels, resolution, etc.). These distinguishing characteristics draw attention to an image's appealing surroundings. A topographical representation of them is a saliency map.

The saliency map represents the conspicuity, or 'saliency', at each point in the visual field by a scalar variable with the intention of using the spatial distribution of saliency to guide the selection of attended locations. A combination of the feature maps serves as the bottom-up input for the saliency map, which is described as a dynamical neural network.

Saliency maps evaluate images to identify visual components. For example, coloured photographs may occasionally be converted to black and white in order to study the colours that pop out the most. Using infrared to assess temperature (red is hot, while blue is cold) and using night vision to locate sources of light (green is bright, while black is dark) are more examples.

7.4 Gradient-weighted class activation mapping

Although CNN convolution layers save all of the spatial details from the input images, fully connected convolution layers have a chance of losing part of this data. It follows that the final convolutional layers should provide the ideal mix of intricate semantics and accurate spatial information. These layers' neurons search the image for details pertaining to a specific semantic class (such as the several sorts of lung nodules).

Gradient-weighted class activation mapping (Grad-CAM) uses the gradient data that is streaming into the last convolutional layer of the CNN to assign relevance values to each neuron for a particular choice of interest. Grad-CAM's class-discriminative localization map can be expressed as

$$L_{GRAD-CAM}^{Solid} \in R^{u \times v} \tag{7.30}$$

Here solid denotes solid class of classification of pulmonary nodules based on density, u represents the height and v represents the width of class solid. The gradient score (y^{solid}) of solid class can be calculated with respect to feature map activations A^k of a convolution layer ($\frac{\partial y^{solid}}{\partial A^k}$). To determine the neuron significance weights, these gradients flowing back are global-average-pooled over the width and height dimensions which are indexed by i and j, respectively.

$$\alpha_k^{solid} = \frac{1}{Z} \sum_i \sum_j \frac{\delta y^{solid}}{\delta A_{i,j}^k} \tag{7.31}$$

where $\frac{\delta y^{solid}}{\delta A_{i,j}^k}$ is backpropagating gradients with respect to activations.

$\frac{1}{Z} \sum_i \sum_j$ is global average pooling.

A weighted combination of forward activation maps is obtained as

$$L_{Grad-CAM}^{solid} = \text{ReLU}\left(\sum_k \alpha_k^{solid} A^k\right) \tag{7.32}$$

Here, ReLU has been applied as it has the capability of forming a linear combination among different features.

When using a specific architecture where global average pooling convolutional feature maps are fed straight into softmax, CAM creates a localization map for an image classification CNN.

Let the penultimate layer create K feature maps, $A_k \in R^{u \times v}$, where each of the elements being indexed by i, j. A^k_{ij} hence refers to the feature map A^k's activation at position i, j. In order to create a score Y^{solid} for each class solid, these feature maps are then geographically pooled using Global Average Pooling (GAP) as follows:

$$Y^{\text{solid}} = \sum_k \omega_k^{\text{solid}} \frac{1}{Z} \sum_i \sum_j A^k_{i,j} \tag{7.33}$$

Global average pooled output F_k can be quantified as

$$F_k = \frac{1}{Z} \sum_i \sum_j A^k_{i,j} \tag{7.34}$$

Final Score Y^{solid} is computed by applying the CAM using the following equation

$$Y^{\text{solid}} = \sum_k \omega_k^{\text{solid}} F_k \tag{7.35}$$

The gradient of the score for class solid (Y^{solid}) with respect to the feature map F_k we get,

$$\frac{\delta Y^{\text{solid}}}{\delta F_k} = \frac{\frac{\delta Y^{\text{solid}}}{\delta A^k_{i,j}}}{\frac{\delta F_k}{\delta A^k_{i,j}}} \tag{7.36}$$

Eq. (7.36) reveals that $\frac{\delta Y^{\text{solid}}}{\delta A^k_{i,j}} = Z$ and according to Eq. (7.35) $\frac{\delta Y^{\text{solid}}}{\delta F_k} = \omega_k^{\text{solid}}$.

Hence, $\omega_k^{\text{solid}} = Z . \frac{\delta Y^{\text{solid}}}{\delta A^k_{i,j}}$

Summing up both side of Eq. (7.36), we get,

$$\sum_i \sum_j \omega_k^{\text{solid}} = \sum_i \sum_j Z . \frac{\delta Y^{\text{solid}}}{\delta A^k_{i,j}} \tag{7.37}$$

As Z and ω_k^{solid} do not depend on i and j, then we can write

$$Z . w_k^{\text{solid}} = Z . \sum_i \sum_j \frac{\delta Y^{\text{solid}}}{\delta A^k_{i,j}} \tag{7.38}$$

The equation for w_k^{solid} is the same as ck utilized by Grad-CAM, up to a proportionality constant (1/Z) that is normalized out during display. Grad-CAM is a precise generalization of CAM as a result. Using generalized CNN-based models that cascade convolutional layers with significantly more intricate interactions, we can produce visual explanations.

Model-agnostic Explanation:

In a model-agnostic explanation, the kind of neural network is unimportant; only the input and output of the network are taken into account. By changing the input, the user can analyze how the neural network's output has changed. This clarifies which regions are in charge of the output.

7.5 Evaluation metrics for explainable AI technique

Any machine learning system, including explainable AI methods, must have evaluation measures. Evaluation metrics are used to measure how well a model is working and to point out areas that could have improvement. Evaluation metrics are crucial in the context of explainable artificial intelligence systems since they allow for the evaluation of the model's explanations' level of quality.

The choice of evaluation metrics will depend on the specific application and the goals of the model. Some common evaluation metrics for explainable AI techniques include

1. Accuracy: This calculates the proportion of outcomes that were accurately predicted. Accuracy can be used in the context of explainable artificial intelligence approaches to rate the quality of the predictions made by the model and the justifications offered for those forecasts.
2. Precision and recall: These metrics are employed to assess how well the model predicts for particular classes or labels. Recall quantifies the proportion of instances that were successfully predicted out of all instances that were forecasted, whereas precision quantifies the proportion of instances that were correctly predicted out of all instances in the class.
3. F1 score: This is a combined metric that balances precision and recall. The f1 score is the harmonic mean of precision and recall, and it provides a single value that summarizes the model's performance.
4. Area under the receiver operating characteristic curve (AUC-ROC): This measures the model's ability to distinguish between positive and negative examples. The AUC-ROC is a curve that plots the true-positive rate (sensitivity) against the false-positive rate (1-specificity), and the area under the curve provides a measure of the model's performance.
5. Mean squared error (MSE) and root mean squared error (RMSE): These metrics are commonly used in regression problems to measure the distance between the predicted values and the actual values. MSE is the average of the squared differences between the predicted and actual values, while RMSE is the square root of the MSE.

Effective ways for determining the possibility of cancer in lung nodules detected on CT scans have evolved, including ensemble learning and explainable AI techniques. Predicting the malignancy of nodules accurately is essential for creating effective treatment plans and enhancing patient outcomes.

Ensemble learning is the process of combining various models or algorithms to generate predictions collectively. In the context of categorizing pulmonary nodules, ensemble learning approaches can combine the outcomes of several machine learning models, such as decision trees, support vector machines or deep learning networks. By utilizing the strengths and diversity of numerous models, ensemble learning can improve generalization, reduce bias and boost prediction performance.

Explainable AI methods aim to offer insights into the decision-making procedures of AI models, enabling doctors to grasp and appreciate the causes behind projections. In the case of pulmonary nodule classification, explainable AI techniques assist in identifying the attributes and image regions that contribute the most to the model's prediction. Establishing trust, obtaining acceptance and allowing therapeutic decision-making depends on this interpretability.

In order to predict the chance of malignancy in pulmonary nodules, ensemble learning integrates predictions from several models, each of which was trained on different nodule properties such as size, shape, texture and location. This combination makes it possible to examine nodule characteristics in more detail and improves the precision of malignancy prediction. The performance and durability of prediction models have been shown to be improved by ensemble learning techniques like gradient boosting and random forests.

Furthermore, explainable AI techniques help people understand the logic behind the prediction of nodule malignancy. By highlighting the most pertinent traits or picture regions, clinicians can gain insight into the model's conclusion and assess the therapeutic relevance of the detected features. Explainable AI encourages the growth of confidence in AI-driven forecasts, enabling better cooperation between AI models and healthcare professionals.

There are several benefits to utilizing explainable AI and ensemble learning to forecast the likelihood of cancer in lung nodules using CT scans. It increases prediction accuracy, enables a better understanding of the decision-making process, and gives clinicians relevant data to help them choose the best course of therapy. These methods hold great potential for enhancing the effectiveness and dependability of nodule categorization, which will improve patient care and result in the detection and treatment of lung cancer. Ensemble learning and explainable AI are being improved and optimized for application in therapeutic settings through ongoing research and development.

Further reading

[1] Hearst MA, Dumais ST, Osuna E, Platt J, Scholkopf B. Support vector machines. IEEE Intelligent Systems and Their Applications July 1998;13(4):18—28.

[2] Duan KB, Keerthi SS. Which is the best multiclass SVM method? an empirical study. In: Multiple classifier systems: 6th international workshop, MCS 2005, seaside, CA, USA, june 13-15, 2005. Proceedings, vol. 6. Springer Berlin Heidelberg; 2005. p. 278—85.

[3] Dietterich TG. Ensemble learning. In: The handbook of brain theory and neural networks, vol. 2; March 2002. p. 110—25.

[4] Wahba G, Lin X, Gao F, Xiang D, Klein R, Klein B. The bias-variance tradeoff and the randomized GACV. In: Advances in neural information processing systems; 1998. p. 11.

[5] Jiang W. Process consistency for adaboost. Annals of Statistics February 2004;32(1):13—29.

[6] Ho TK. The random subspace method for constructing decision forests. IEEE Transactions on Pattern Analysis and Machine Intelligence August 1998;20(8):832—44.

[7] Breiman L. Random forests. Machine Learning October 2001;45:5—32.

[8] ChenT G. XGBoost: a scalable tree boosting system. Proceedings of the 22nd ACM Sigkdd International Conference on Knowledge Discoveryand Data Mining. ACM; August 2016.

[9] Rodriguez JJ, Kuncheva LI, Alonso CJ. Rotation forest: a new classifier ensemble method. IEEE Transactions on Pattern Analysis and Machine Intelligence August 21, 2006;28(10):1619—30.

[10] Ribeiro MT, Singh S, Guestrin C. Why should I trust you?": explaining the predictions of any classifier. Proceedings of the 22nd ACM SIGKDD international conference on knowledge discovery and data mining. 2016. p. 1135—44. ArXiv160204938 Cs Stat.

[11] Sundararajan M, Najmi A. The many Shapley values for model explanation. In: International conference on machine learning. PMLR; November 21, 2020. p. 9269—78.

[12] Kuncheva LI, Rodríguez JJ. An experimental study on rotation forest ensembles. In: Multiple classifier systems: 7th international workshop, MCS 2007, Prague, Czech republic, may 23-25, 2007. Proceedings, vol. 7. Springer Berlin Heidelberg; 2007. p. 459—68.

[13] Selvaraju RR, Cogswell M, Das A, Vedantam R, Parikh D, Batra D. Grad-cam: visual explanations from deep networks via gradient-based localization. Proceedings of the IEEE international conference on computer vision. 2017. p. 618—26.

[14] Alqaraawi A, Schuessler M, Weiß P, Costanza E, Berthouze N. Evaluating saliency map explanations for convolutional neural networks: a user study. Proceedings of the 25th international conference on intelligent user interfaces. March 17, 2020. p. 275—85.

8
Summary of the book

8.1 Recap of main topics of the book

The identification and classification of nodules in medical imaging data is the goal of pulmonary nodule detection algorithms, which heavily rely on feature engineering. Here is a list of popular feature engineering methods applied in this situation:

Shape-based Features: The geometric characteristics of nodules, such as their size, volume, and form descriptors (such as sphericity and elongation), are captured by shape-based features. These characteristics help distinguish between benign and malignant nodules by revealing information about the appearance and structure of nodules.

Pixel intensity patterns found within nodules are described by intensity-based characteristics. Statistics like mean, standard deviation, skewness, and kurtosis of pixel intensities are examples of these properties. They can help distinguish between various nodule types and provide information on the texture and heterogeneity of nodules.

Features depending on texture: The spatial organization and changes in pixel brightness inside nodules are captured by texture-based features. They can be obtained using texture analysis techniques like local binary patterns (LBP), grey level run length matrices (GLRLM), and grey-level co-occurrence matrices (GLCM). Smoothness, roughness, or homogeneity are a few examples of nodule structural patterns that can be captured by texture features.

Contextual characteristics: Contextual characteristics take into account how nodules interact with the lung tissue around them. These characteristics may include things like the separation between neighbouring structures, the location of the lung boundaries or the presence of certain lung patterns. Contextual factors can help distinguish between nodules and non-nodule structures by including spatial information.

The decision to use one or more of these feature engineering strategies depends on the task's unique needs for detecting pulmonary nodules. These properties can be used for nodule recognition, segmentation and classification using a variety of methods, including support vector machines (SVM), random forests and deep learning architectures. By extracting useful information from medical pictures and increasing the precision of nodule identification and characterization, feature engineering contributes to improving the efficacy of pulmonary nodule detection approaches.

Convolutional neural networks (CNNs), in particular, are used to their full potential by deep learning-based pulmonary nodule identification methods to automatically identify and categorize nodules in medical imaging data. The following is an overview of deep learning-based methods for pulmonary nodule detection:

Application of Artificial Intelligence in Early Detection of Lung Cancer. https://doi.org/10.1016/B978-0-323-95245-3.00008-1

CNNs (convolutional neural networks): In order to detect lung nodules, CNNs are frequently employed. They are made up of many layers of fully linked, pooling, and convolutional layers. CNNs are able to recognize intricate patterns and characteristics connected to nodules because they directly learn hierarchical representations from the input images.

Region-based CNNs: Rather than processing the full image, region-based CNNs concentrate on extracting characteristics from specific potential regions. For feature extraction and classification in the CNN, these methods commonly use region proposal algorithms to produce candidate nodule sites. The efficiency of this method is increased while computation is decreased.

3D CNNs: Computed tomography (CT) scan volumetric data analysis is frequently used to identify pulmonary nodules. In order to capture spatial dependencies and contextual information in all three dimensions, 3D CNNs are made to analyze 3D volumes directly. The ability of these models to identify nodules and distinguish them from other structures has increased.

Transfer Learning: Transfer learning improves pre-trained CNN models on pulmonary nodule data using huge datasets (like ImageNet). Transfer learning allows CNN to extract pertinent characteristics related to nodule detection, even with little training data, by using the learnt representations from generic image datasets.

Ensemble Methods: To enhance overall performance, ensemble methods mix various deep learning models. In order to arrive at a final decision, various CNN designs or iterations of the same architecture are independently trained. The nodule identification system's robustness and generalizability are improved and the risk of overfitting is decreased with the aid of ensemble approaches.

Attention processes: In order to highlight informative sections in the input images that are important for nodule recognition, attention processes are used. These strategies enhance prediction precision and interpretability by helping the model concentrate on discriminative features. To improve nodule detection performance, attention techniques can be applied at several levels, such as spatial attention or channel attention.

Automating the detection and categorization of nodules in medical imaging has shown promise when using deep learning-based pulmonary nodule detection systems. They may aid radiologists in making an early lung cancer diagnosis and enhance patient outcomes. To ensure the validity and wide acceptance of these methods, issues including the requirement for sizeable annotated datasets, interpretability and generalization to different populations and imaging situations still need to be resolved.

The issues provided by imbalanced datasets, where the distribution of classes is substantially skewed, are addressed through imbalanced learning approaches in the context of deep learning. The following is a list of deep learning's imbalanced learning methodologies:

Techniques for oversampling: By increasing the number of samples from the minority class, oversampling approaches seek to balance the distribution of the classes. Synthetic Minority Over-sampling Technique (SMOTE) is a well-liked strategy that creates synthetic samples by interpolating between minority class samples from existing datasets. This lessens the disparity in class size and offers more accurate training data.

Under-sampling Techniques: In order to produce a balanced class distribution, undersampling procedures cut the number of samples in the majority class. Random Undersampling randomly chooses a portion of the majority class samples, whereas Cluster Centroids undersampling uses clustering techniques to find representative samples. Undersampling enhances the model's capacity to learn from the minority class and lessens the dominance of the majority class.

Data Augmentation: By applying changes to existing samples, data augmentation techniques artificially raise the diversity of the training data. To balance the dataset, augmentation techniques like rotation, scaling, flipping and adding noise can be employed to provide additional examples for the minority class. The model's capacity to learn discriminative features and apply them to unbalanced classes is improved by data augmentation.

In medical lung imaging, such as chest X-rays or computed tomography (CT) scans, pulmonary lobe, and fissure identification algorithms seek to recognize and segment the lobes and fissures. The following is a list of these methodologies.

8.1.1 Pulmonary lobe detection

Regional strategies: In order to identify specific lobes based on form, intensity, or connection criteria, region-based approaches first segment lung areas before using region-growing or clustering algorithms.

Morphological methods: To isolate lung regions and subsequently segment lobes based on shape, size and connection data, morphological techniques apply mathematical morphology operations.

Graph-based approaches: Graph-based approaches express the lobe detection problem as a graph partitioning problem and represent the lung as a graph. They divide the lung into lobes based on intensity and connectivity data using graph-cut algorithms or spectral clustering methods.

Convolutional neural networks (CNNs), in particular, have been used in deep learning approaches to automatically recognize lobes. CNNs can accurately segment lobes by learning distinguishing features from lung images. U-Net and Mask R-CNN architectures have demonstrated good performance in this task.

8.1.2 Fissure detection

Edge-based Approaches: Edge-based techniques concentrate on identifying the borders or sharp edges of the fissures. Based on intensity gradients, they utilize edge detection methods, such as Canny edge detection or Laplacian of Gaussian filters, to locate the fissure boundaries.

Line Tracing Approaches: By tracing along the edges of the fissures, line tracing techniques seek to extract fissure lines. To find and trace the fissures, they employ algorithms like the Hough transform or active contours.

Texture-based Approaches: Texture-based techniques take advantage of the distinctive texture patterns found in the fissure zones. They use texture analysis methods to capture the texture properties and distinguish fissures from other lung structures, such as grey-level co-occurrence matrices (GLCM) or local binary patterns (LBP).

Deep Learning Approaches: Fissure detection has also been tackled by deep learning methods. CNNs can effectively identify fissure boundaries by learning specific features from lung pictures. Fissure segmentation tasks can be customized for architectures like U-Net and Mask R-CNN.

To identify and segment pulmonary lobes and fissures in lung pictures, these strategies make use of a variety of image processing and machine learning techniques. The approach selected will rely on the precise requirements, the data at hand, and the difficulty of the work. By utilizing the strength of neural networks to automatically train discriminative characteristics for precise lobe and fissure detection, deep learning techniques, in particular, have demonstrated promising outcomes.

Class Weighting: Class weighting assigns higher weights to the minority class during training to compensate for its underrepresentation. This approach adjusts the loss function, giving more importance to correctly classifying minority class instances. By assigning higher penalties for misclassifying minority class samples, class weighting helps the model focus on learning from the imbalanced class.

Ensemble Techniques: Ensemble techniques combine multiple deep learning models to improve the overall performance on imbalanced datasets. Techniques like Bagging and Boosting train multiple models on different subsets of the data or with different weightings, respectively. Combining the predictions of these models helps mitigate the impact of imbalanced classes and improves the overall classification accuracy.

Cost-Sensitive Learning: It allots various misclassification costs to various classes. The model is incentivized to prioritize accurate predictions for the imbalanced class by assigning larger costs to misclassify the minority class. Cost-sensitive learning makes sure that the model performs at its best in light of the unique requirements and significance of each class.

Hybrid strategies integrate several methods to combat class inequality. To balance the dataset while maintaining diversity, for instance, undersampling and oversampling might be employed in combination. Hybrid methods take advantage of the advantages of many techniques to handle imbalanced datasets more effectively.

In the context of deep learning, these unbalanced learning methodologies offer methods to address the problems brought on by unbalanced datasets. These techniques let deep learning models learn from minority class samples more successfully by resolving the class imbalance, which enhances performance and yields more precise predictions on unbalanced datasets.

8.2 Summary of finding or insights

The subject of lung cancer screening has been revolutionized by the application of artificial intelligence (AI) in the early diagnosis of lung cancer using CT scans. The identification and classification of pulmonary nodules by AI algorithms have shown impressive skills via considerable study and development, improving patient outcomes and survival rates.

A significant finding is the increased accuracy attained by AI models. These algorithms use sophisticated pattern recognition techniques to identify lung cancer symptoms that may go undetected by human observers. AI algorithms can accurately identify worrisome nodules and distinguish between benign and malignant cases with high sensitivity and specificity by analyzing CT images. A considerable decrease in false positives and false negatives may result from this increased accuracy, ensuring that worrisome nodules are not missed and reducing the need for unneeded intrusive operations.

Faster detection and diagnosis are also provided by the use of AI in the early identification of lung cancer. In comparison to manual evaluation by radiologists, AI-based systems can evaluate enormous volumes of CT scans in a very short amount of time. This quickening of the process allows for quick clinical decision-making, permitting immediate interventions and therapies. The diagnostic method is further improved by AI algorithms' capacity to stratify cancer risk. AI systems assist physicians in prioritizing cases and allocating adequate resources for follow-up studies, such as biopsies to confirm the diagnosis, by evaluating the chance of malignancy for discovered nodules.

The improvement of radiologists' workflow is another important finding from AI-driven lung cancer diagnosis. For radiologists, AI algorithms are useful tools that offer a second viewpoint and support decision-making. By indicating potentially high-risk nodules for additional assessment, they can help in case triage. This increases productivity while lightening the load on radiologists, freeing them up to concentrate on more intricate interpretations and patient care.

Lung cancer screening has a bright future, thanks to the discoveries and understandings from the use of AI in the early diagnosis of lung cancer using CT scans. To improve and maximize the efficacy of AI systems, ongoing study, validation and collaboration between AI developers and healthcare experts are crucial. AI has the potential to transform lung cancer detection and contribute to better patient outcomes, having a huge impact on global healthcare with further breakthroughs.

8.3 Case studies

8.3.1 Case study 1: AI-verified detection of pulmonary nodule in a 45-year-old male

8.3.1.1 Background
A 45-year-old male patient underwent an X-ray examination for respiratory symptoms. It is suspected the presence of a pulmonary nodule. Physicians suggested a routine CT scan examination. An AI-based algorithm was used to assist in the detection of pulmonary nodules and provide accurate diagnosis.

8.3.1.2   Case details

The AI algorithm detected a suspicious nodule in the right middle lobe of the patient's lung. The nodule measured 2.2 cm in diameter. The AI findings were validated by a radiologist, confirming the presence of the nodule as a true positive.

8.3.2   Case study 2: AI-based pulmonary nodule detection for a 50-year-old female

8.3.2.1   Background

A 50-year-old female patient from India underwent an X-ray examination for respiratory symptoms. It is suspected the presence of a pulmonary nodule. Physicians suggested a routine CT scan examination. An AI-based algorithm was utilized to assist in the detection and characterization of pulmonary nodules, aiming for accurate diagnosis.

8.3.2.2   Case details

The AI algorithm identified a suspicious nodule in the left lower lobe of the patient's lung. The nodule measured 1.8 cm in diameter. The AI findings were independently reviewed by a radiologist, confirming the presence of the nodule as a true positive. Subsequent diagnostic tests, including a biopsy, confirmed the nodule to be malignant. The integration of AI-assisted detection played a crucial role in the timely diagnosis and appropriate management of the patient's condition.

8.3.3   Case study 3: AI-verified absence of pulmonary nodule in a 40-year-old female

8.3.3.1   Background

A 40-year-old female patient from India underwent a CT scan for unrelated symptoms. An AI-based algorithm was employed to assist in the detection and classification of pulmonary nodules, aiming to accurately exclude the presence of any abnormalities.

8.3.3.2   Case details

The AI algorithm analyzed the CT images and determined the absence of any suspicious nodules in the patient's lungs. The findings were further reviewed by a radiologist, who confirmed the absence of nodules as a true negative. Subsequent follow-up examinations over a period of 2 years showed no development of nodules, reaffirming the AI-assisted true negative detection.

8.3.4   Case study 4: AI-assisted exclusion of pulmonary nodule in a 55-year-old male

8.3.4.1   Background

A 55-year-old male patient from India, with a history of smoking, underwent a routine CT scan for lung cancer screening. An AI-powered system was utilized to aid in the accurate detection and characterization of pulmonary nodules.

8.3.4.2   Case details

The AI algorithm carefully analyzed the CT images and concluded the absence of any significant nodules in the patient's lungs. The AI-assisted findings were validated by a radiologist, who confirmed the absence of nodules as a true negative. Follow-up screenings conducted annually for 3 years consistently showed no evidence of nodules, reinforcing the accuracy of the AI-assisted detection.

8.3.5   Case study 5: AI-predicted likelihood of malignancy in pulmonary nodule of a 60-year-old male

8.3.5.1   Background

A 60-year-old male patient from India presented with respiratory symptoms and underwent a CT scan for evaluation. An AI-based system was implemented to predict the likelihood of malignancy in pulmonary nodules, aiming to facilitate accurate diagnosis.

8.3.5.2   Case details

The AI algorithm analyzed the CT images and predicted a low likelihood of malignancy in a nodule detected in the right middle lobe. The AI findings were validated by a radiologist, confirming the prediction as a true positive. Additional evaluations, including a PET-CT scan and a biopsy, revealed the nodule to be benign. The AI-assisted prediction provided valuable information for appropriate patient management, avoiding unnecessary invasive procedures.

8.3.6   Case study 6: AI-predicted likelihood of malignancy in pulmonary nodule of a 65-year-old female

8.3.6.1   Background

A 65-year-old female patient from India with a history of occupational exposure to pollutants underwent a CT scan for respiratory evaluation. An AI-assisted system was utilized to predict the likelihood of malignancy in pulmonary nodules, aiming for accurate diagnosis.

8.3.6.2   Case details

The AI algorithm analyzed the CT images and predicted a high likelihood of malignancy in a nodule found in the left upper lobe. The AI findings were independently reviewed by a radiologist, confirming the prediction as a true positive. Subsequent investigations, including a PET-CT scan and a biopsy, confirmed the nodule to be malignant. The integration of AI-assisted prediction facilitated early intervention and appropriate treatment planning.

8.3.7   Case study 7: AI-predicted true negative for malignancy in pulmonary nodule of a 45-year-old female

8.3.7.1   Background

A 45-year-old female patient from India underwent a CT scan for respiratory evaluation. An AI-powered system was implemented to predict the likelihood of malignancy in pulmonary nodules, aiming for accurate diagnosis.

8.3.7.2 Case details

The AI algorithm analyzed the CT images and predicted a low likelihood of malignancy in a nodule found in the left upper lobe. The AI findings were independently reviewed by a radiologist, who confirmed the prediction as a true negative. Subsequent evaluations, including follow-up CT scans and clinical assessments, consistently showed no signs of malignancy, confirming the accuracy of the AI-assisted true negative prediction.

8.3.8   Case study 8: AI-predicted true negative for malignancy in pulmonary nodule of a 65-year-old male

8.3.8.1 Background

A 65-year-old male patient from India with a history of occupational exposure to pollutants underwent a CT scan for respiratory evaluation. An AI-assisted system was utilized to predict the likelihood of malignancy in pulmonary nodules, aiming for accurate diagnosis.

8.3.8.2 Case details

The AI algorithm analyzed the CT images and predicted a low likelihood of malignancy in a nodule detected in the right lower lobe. The AI findings were reviewed by a radiologist, who confirmed the prediction as a true negative. Subsequent evaluations, including additional imaging and clinical assessments, consistently showed no signs of malignancy, confirming the accuracy of the AI-assisted true negative prediction.

8.4 Critical discussions

The success of AI in predicting the likelihood of cancers in pulmonary nodules from CT images in Indian patients is demonstrated by these case studies. Healthcare workers can increase the accuracy of lung cancer diagnosis using AI algorithms, allowing for proper management and minimizing needless intrusive procedures. It is possible to improve lung cancer screening and patient outcomes in the Indian population by integrating AI-assisted prediction into clinical practice.

The use of AI for early lung cancer detection using CT scans has sparked intense discussions and disputes among medical professionals. Critical conversations and debates include the following:

Ethics-Related Matters: Ethics issues about patient privacy, data security and potential bias in the decision-making process of the algorithm are brought up by the use of AI algorithms for lung cancer screening. To maintain patient trust and avoid any potential harm, it is essential to ensure transparency, fairness and accountability in the development and application of AI models.

Clinical Validation and Accuracy: There is a continuous discussion regarding the clinical validity and precision of AI algorithms for the identification of lung cancer. Although AI has demonstrated promising results in research investigations, more broad validation on a variety of patient demographics is required to guarantee its dependability in actual clinical settings. Large-scale clinical studies must be conducted to assess the performance of AI models against recognized gold standards.

Integration into Clinical Workflow: It is a difficult problem to incorporate AI algorithms into the current clinical process. In order to handle difficulties like interpretation time, user interface design and compatibility with current picture archiving and communication systems (PACS), it requires a seamless connection with radiologists' workflow. AI programmers, radiologists and healthcare administrators must work closely together for AI algorithms to be used in clinical practice.

Legal and Regulatory Considerations: The use of AI algorithms for lung cancer detection raises legal and regulatory considerations. There are concerns about the formation of standards and norms for AI-based diagnostic tools, the requirement for regulatory approval and liability in the event of algorithmic errors. For AI technology to be used safely and responsibly in the healthcare industry, clear laws and guidelines are required.

Cost-effectiveness and Accessibility: There is discussion surrounding the affordability and accessibility of AI-based lung cancer screening techniques. Although AI has the potential to enhance early detection and save healthcare costs in the long run, its general adoption may be hindered, particularly in environments with limited resources, by the expenses associated with its initial deployment and the requirement for specialized imaging equipment. To provide equal access to AI-enabled lung cancer screening tools, these issues must be addressed.

Collaboration with Healthcare Professionals: Collaboration and acceptance from healthcare professionals are critical for the successful implementation of AI in early lung cancer detection. Engaging radiologists, oncologists and other relevant specialists in the development, validation and deployment of AI tools fosters trust, promotes acceptance and ensures that AI complements and augments their expertise rather than replacing them.

Long-term Outcomes and Clinical Impact: Even though lung cancer early diagnosis is crucial, the ultimate objective is to enhance patient outcomes. It is crucial to assess how AI-based detection will affect survival rates, treatment results and quality of life over the course of a patient's lifetime. To determine whether AI is beneficial in lowering mortality and enhancing patient care, clinical trials and long-term studies are required.

The use of AI in the early identification of lung cancer from CT images has a lot of potential, but before it is widely adopted, there must be serious conversations and debates about the ethical, clinical, regulatory, and accessibility issues involved. To maximize the advantages of AI while minimizing any potential risks and obstacles, open communication and collaboration among stakeholders are essential.

8.5 Conclusion

The identification, localization and prognosis of malignancy in pulmonary nodules have long been difficult tasks in the realm of medical imaging. However, recent developments in deep learning and artificial intelligence (AI) have created new opportunities for precise and effective diagnosis. The importance of feature engineering and deep learning-based approaches in lung nodule detection and malignancy likelihood prediction has been discussed in this blog. We can confidently draw the conclusion that these methods are revolutionizing the field of lung cancer diagnostics after carefully examining them.

8.5.1   Feature engineering: A fundamental step

The identification and location of pulmonary nodules depend heavily on feature engineering. To extract pertinent information from CT scans, conventional image processing methods such as morphological operations, filtering and edge detection are used. These hand-crafted characteristics aid in separating nodules from healthy lung tissue. The accurate detection and localization of lung nodules have shown encouraging results when feature engineering techniques are paired with machine learning algorithms.

8.5.2   Deep learning: Unleashing the power of neural networks

There have been notable improvements in the diagnosis of pulmonary nodules and the prognosis of malignancy brought about by deep learning, notably by Convolutional Neural Networks (CNNs). Deep learning models have achieved extraordinary accuracy by utilizing CNNs' capacity to automatically learn hierarchical features from unprocessed input. Deep learning models can now be trained to distinguish between nodules and non-nodules with excellent sensitivity and specificity, thanks to the utilization of large-scale annotated datasets like the LIDC-IDRI database.

8.5.3   Localization and segmentation

Additionally, pulmonary nodules within CT scans have been successfully located and segmented using deep learning models. Bounding box regression approaches are used by localization algorithms to precisely pinpoint the area of interest containing the nodule. To precisely define the nodule's boundaries, segmentation approaches use pixel-level categorization. These developments have greatly benefited radiologists in accurately measuring and characterizing nodules, which has facilitated treatment planning and oversight.

8.5.4   Prediction of malignancy likelihood

Deep learning-based methodologies have been extremely helpful in determining whether lung nodules are likely to be cancerous. These algorithms acquire complex patterns and connections suggestive of malignancy by being trained on large datasets with annotations indicating nodule malignancy. These models' forecasts aid radiologists in risk classification by directing more research and treatment choices. The accuracy of malignancy prediction has been substantially enhanced by combining deep learning algorithms with clinical and radiological data.

The detection, localization, and likelihood of malignancy prediction of lung nodules have been transformed by the integration of feature engineering and deep learning-based approaches. These methods have demonstrated great promise for giving precise and effective diagnoses, which will ultimately result in better patient outcomes. New opportunities for lung cancer detection and treatment planning have emerged as a result of the collaboration between AI algorithms and medical knowledge. However, to assure the widespread use of these approaches and to address issues like interpretability, generalization and data bias, ongoing research, data standardization and validation studies are crucial. With continued development, the use of feature engineering and deep learning in pulmonary nodule detection has the potential to be a game-changer for the early detection and efficient treatment of lung cancer, having a favourable effect on patient care all around the world.

It is vital to recognize the flaws and restrictions of the LIDC-IDRI dataset, despite the fact that it has been frequently utilized for pulmonary nodule identification and categorization. Some of the LIDC-IDRI dataset's primary drawbacks are listed below:

Variability of Annotation: The ground truth annotations in the LIDC-IDRI dataset vary because they were annotated by several radiologists. The dataset may be inconsistent since various radiologists may view nodules differently and use different standards for labelling them. The effectiveness and generalizability of models developed using the dataset may be impacted by this heterogeneity.

Limited Diversity: The majority of the nodules in the LIDC-IDRI dataset are those that radiologists have labelled as potentially malignant. This bias in selection might not fully depict the whole range of pulmonary nodules seen in clinical practise. The lack of variety in the dataset with regard to nodule size, shape and position may restrict the model's capacity to generalize to new data.

Limited Clinical Data: The LIDC-IDRI collection primarily contains CT imaging data without a substantial amount of supplementary clinical data. Despite having basic demographic data and nodule characteristics, the dataset is deficient in specific clinical information such as patient histories, follow-up scans and treatment outcomes. The creation of models that can take into account crucial variables in predicting nodule malignancy may be hampered by this constrained clinical environment.

Class Imbalance: There are much more benign nodules than malignant ones in the LIDC-IDRI dataset, which is known to have a class imbalance problem. Due to this imbalance, machine learning models may perform poorly, producing biased results and having a worse ability to predict malignancy. Class imbalance issues must be addressed using rigorous sampling methods or specialized algorithms.

Limited Size: Despite being one of the largest publicly accessible datasets for pulmonary nodule detection, the LIDC-IDRI collection still has size restrictions. Deep learning models frequently need a lot of training data to operate at their best, especially those with complex architectures.

When using the LIDC-IDRI dataset and analyzing the findings of studies based on it, it is imperative to take these limitations into account. By combining new datasets, enhancing annotation consistency, providing a wider range of clinical data and creating methods to deal with class imbalance, researchers should work to address these shortcomings. Through such efforts, AI models for lung nodule detection and malignancy prediction may become more stable and trustworthy.

It is crucial to build an explainable model when developing an AI-based model for lung cancer early detection for various reasons:

Trust and Transparency: Explainability makes the AI model's decision-making process transparent. It enables medical professionals and patients to comprehend the reasoning behind a certain prediction or suggestion. Users can understand and verify the justification for the model's decisions, which fosters confidence and trust in the AI system.

Regulatory Compliance: In the healthcare industry, regulatory organizations frequently demand justifications for the choices AI models make. Explainable models aid in meeting these legal criteria by assuring adherence to the rules and regulations. It makes the model more responsible and gives a way to audit and confirm its decisions.

Clinical Interpretability: Explainable models make it possible for doctors to decipher and confirm the characteristics or patterns that go into making a certain prediction. Given that doctors can comprehend the reasoning behind the model's output and incorporate it with their own expertise, this interpretability aids in clinical decision-making. It facilitates communication and joint decision-making between the AI system and medical experts.

Error Detection and Bias Mitigation: Explainable models make it easier to spot biases or flaws in AI systems. Clinicians can identify instances when the model may have made false predictions because it misread certain features or relied on them. Biases can be identified and eliminated by comprehending the model's logic, ensuring fair and equitable outcomes for various patient populations.

Education and Training: Explainability encourages clinicians and other healthcare professionals to learn about and get trained in AI technology. It facilitates knowledge transmission and understanding between AI specialists and medical professionals. Clinicians can obtain knowledge of the AI model's internal workings, enabling them to offer informed feedback and aid in its development.

Ethical Considerations: Explainability fits with AI deployment's ethical standards. It upholds the ideals of accountability, fairness and transparency. Explainable models support the moral application of AI in healthcare by ensuring that decisions are not based on unobserved or biased factors.

8.6 Future directions of this research area

A fast-developing subject with multiple exciting research directions is the use of AI in the early diagnosis of lung cancer using CT scans. Future studies should focus on:

Better Nodule Recognition: Future research can concentrate on creating stronger and more precise nodule recognition algorithms in CT images. To improve the sensitivity and specificity of nodule detection, this entails investigating cutting-edge deep learning architectures, such as attention mechanisms and graph convolutional networks.

Subtype Classification: Lung cancer is a diverse disease, with distinct subtypes having varying prognoses and therapeutic outcomes. Future studies can look at AI systems that can identify distinct kinds of lung cancer from CT images, allowing for more individualized treatment planning and better patient outcomes.

Quantitative Analysis: AI can significantly contribute to the quantitative analysis of lung nodules, including the measurement of nodule size, volume and growth rate. Future research can concentrate on creating AI algorithms that can precisely and consistently measure these factors, assisting in the monitoring of diseases and the evaluation of treatment effectiveness.

Radiomics and Genomics Integration: To gain a more complete picture of lung cancer, genomic information can be combined with radiomic characteristics collected from CT images. To create prediction models for patient prognosis, treatment response and the choice of individualized therapies, future research can investigate the merging of radiomic and genetic data using AI algorithms.

Collaboration and Validation Among Multiple Centres: The creation and validation of reliable AI models can be facilitated by collaborative efforts across numerous healthcare organizations in the acquisition of different and substantial datasets. To ensure the generalizability and dependability of AI models for lung cancer diagnosis, future research can concentrate on creating partnerships and standardizing data collection techniques.

Clinical Workflow Integration: Future studies should examine the integration of AI algorithms into current healthcare workflows to help with the acceptance of AI in clinical practice. This entails creating intuitive user interfaces, achieving seamless interaction with radiology information systems and taking legal and moral issues into account.

In conclusion, improved nodule detection, subtype classification, quantitative analysis, integration of radiomics and genomics, risk assessment and prediction, multi-centre collaboration and clinical workflow integration are some of the areas of future research in the application of AI in early detection of lung cancer from CT images. The detection and treatment of lung cancer have the potential to be revolutionized by developments in these fields, improving patient outcomes and survival rates.

Index

'Note: Page numbers followed by "f" indicate figures.'

Printed in the United States
by Baker & Taylor Publisher Services